ENGLISH PRIVATE LAW

SECOND CUMULATIVE UPDATING SUPPLEMENT

ENGLISH PRIVATE LAW

SECOND CUMULATIVE UPDATING SUPPLEMENT

Edited by
PROFESSOR PETER BIRKS QC FBA
All Souls College Oxford

OXFORD
UNIVERSITY PRESS

OXFORD
UNIVERSITY PRESS

Great Clarendon Street, Oxford OX2 6DP

Oxford University Press is a department of the University of Oxford.
It furthers the University's objective of excellence in research, scholarship,
and education by publishing worldwide in

Oxford New York

Auckland Bangkok Buenos Aires Chennai
Dar es Salaam Delhi Hong Kong Istanbul Karachi Kolkata
Kuala Lumpur Madrid Melbourne Mexico City Mumbai Nairobi
São Paulo Shanghai Singapore Taipei Tokyo Toronto

Oxford is a registered trade mark of Oxford University Press
in the UK and in certain other countries

Published in the United States
by Oxford University Press Inc., New York

First published September 2004

British Library Cataloguing in Publication Data
Data available

Library of Congress Cataloging in Publication Data
Data available

Second Updating Supplement ISBN 0–19–927151–8
Main Work and Second Updating Supplement ISBN 0–19–927152–6

1 3 5 7 9 10 8 6 4 2

Typeset in Garamond by
Cambrian Typesetters, Frimley, Surrey

Printed in Great Britain
on acid-free paper by
Ashford Colour Press Limited, Gosport, Hampshire

EDITOR

Professor Peter Birks QC FBA
All Souls College Oxford

CONTRIBUTORS

Mr Neil Andrews
Clare College Cambridge

Professor John Bell FBA
University of Cambridge

Professor Michael Bridge
University College London

Mr Adrian Briggs
St Edmund Hall Oxford

Professor Andrew Burrows QC
St Hugh's College Oxford

Professor William Cornish QC FBA
Magdalene College Cambridge

Dr Stephen Cretney QC FBA
All Souls College Oxford

Mr John Davies
Brasenose College Oxford

Professor Mark Freedland FBA
St John's College Oxford

Professor Roger Kerridge
University of Bristol

Professor Ewan McKendrick
Lady Margaret Hall Oxford

Professor Charles Mitchell
King's College London

Professor Norman Palmer
University College London

Professor Francis Reynolds QC FBA
Worcester College Oxford

Professor Lionel D Smith
McGill University Montreal

Mr William Swadling
Brasenose College Oxford

Professor Sir Guenter Treitel QC FBA
All Souls College Oxford

CONTENTS—SUMMARY

VOLUME I

PREFACE

This year *Oxford English Law* took a giant step forward. In the spring, *English Public Law* was published. Between them *English Private Law* and *English Public Law* show that the common law can be presented in an orderly way and with reasonable brevity. Indifference to both has in the past tended to conceal its merits. While it is true that in certain contexts, notably in contested litigation, it is essential to see every finest detail, it is false to suppose that knowledge of the law cannot be taken to a high level other than at enormous length. It is less challenging to write a good long account than a short one. The contributors to these volumes are jurists of the highest authority. Their mastery each of their own field is the key to the reliability of their shorter versions. The intention is to keep these volumes constantly up to date. This year *English Public Law* is brand new, and *English Private Law*, which was first published four years ago, will for the moment stand renewed by this second cumulative supplement, which takes in developments up to the beginning of 2004. One or two later matters have been smuggled in at proof stage, but the official cut-off date remains 31 December 2003.

PBH Birks
April 2004

PETER BIRKS

It is with great sadness that we have to record the death, on 6th July 2004, of Professor Peter Birks, Q.C., F.B.A., General Editor of *Oxford English Law*, and Editor of *English Private Law* and of this Supplement to it. Peter Birks developed the idea for an orderly, authoritative, principled, and concise account of English law well over a decade ago. As in all his many and varied intellectual activities, he pursued his aim with determination, charm, intellectual rigour, enthusiasm, and a commitment to the highest standards of scholarship. He energized the contributors to *Oxford English Law*, and the large editorial and production team at the Oxford University Press. Throughout the project, he prompted, encouraged, and cajoled us, and constructively criticized our work. We shared his pleasure and satisfaction when first *English Private Law*, then *English Public Law*, were published to fulfil his vision. His premature death deprives the academic legal community of an outstanding and dedicated scholar, an inspiring teacher, and a courageous controversialist. Those of us who had the privilege of working with him are left to mourn a stimulating, tireless and utterly unselfish colleague, and a generous and loyal friend.

David Feldman
July 2004

TABLE OF CASES

TABLES OF LEGISLATION

Statutory Instruments

European Union

TABLE OF TREATIES AND CONVENTIONS

Note: for EC Treaty see Table of Legislation, European Union section.

1

SOURCES OF LAW

B. The Hierarchy of Norms

(2) The European Convention on Human Rights

The existing paragraph is replaced with the following:

In applying the European Convention on Human Rights in domestic law, there are several stages in reasoning. First, it is necessary to examine whether a Convention right (properly understood) is affected by domestic legislation. The clear and constant case law of the European Court of Human Rights will serve as a guide: see *R (on the application of Alconbury Developments Ltd) v Secretary of State for the Environment, Transport and the Regions* [2001] UKHL 23, [26], *per* Lord Slynn. For example, in *Alconbury Developments Ltd*, that case law established that judicial review of planning decisions did not require a rehearing of the merits of the application. It should be noted that the European Court of Human Rights takes a 'generous approach' when determining what comes within the scope of protected Convention rights: P Duffy, in University of Cambridge Centre for Public Law, *Constitutional Reform in the United Kingdom: Practice and Principles* **1.13**

(1998) 99, 100. Secondly, even if a Convention right is affected, the interference may be justified under the terms of the Convention itself. Many Convention rights are not absolute and the Convention permits interference in certain circumstances to protect other rights or to pursue a public interest goal, provided the interference is proportionate. For example, the privilege against self-incrimination has to be balanced against other Convention rights, and this may justify the requirement that the owner of a vehicle reveal the name of its driver: *Brown v Stott (Procurator Fiscal, Dunfermline)* [2001] 2 All ER 97. Thirdly, if a Convention right is affected in an apparently illegitimate way, it is necessary to examine whether the domestic legislation can be construed to be compatible with it. Here the first approach is to see whether ordinary methods of interpretation, as discussed in Main Work paras 1.42–1.51, will remove any conflict. If that is insufficient, the more radical approach of s 3(1) of the Human Rights Act 1998 (see Main Work para 1.40) will be invoked under which the domestic legislation is construed as compatible, as far as this is possible, even if the interpretation which has to be adopted to this end is linguistically strained: see *per* Lord Steyn in *R v A* [2001] UKHL 25, [44], [2001] 3 All ER 1, 17. It may be that, in order to determine either the extent or the justifiability of an interference with a Convention right, this robust approach to interpretation must be adopted: see *Poplar Housing and Regeneration Community Association v Donoghue* [2001] EWCA 595, [75], [2001] 4 All ER 604 at 624 *per* Lord Woolf CJ; see also *R v Director of Public Prosecutions, ex p Kebilene* [2000] 2 AC 326. Both the second and the third stages involve interpretation, and it may be that one judge finds no apparent interference with a Convention right, whereas another finds that there is an apparent interference, but no incompatibility between the Convention right and the legislation (properly interpreted): compare the opinions of Lord Hope and Lord Steyn in *R v A*. Finally, where it is not possible to interpret the domestic legislation in a way which is compatible with the Convention right, a competent court may make a declaration of incompatibility: eg *R (Anderson) v Secretary of State for the Home Department* [2002] UKHL 46, [2002] 4 All ER 1089. It is accepted that where a proposed compatible interpretation departs substantially from a fundamental feature of the Act, it is not a permissible interpretation, but an amendment, which only Parliament can make: Lord Nicholls of Birkenhead, *Re S (Children: Care Plan)* [2002] UKHL 10 at [41], [2002] AC 291.

Many areas of private law are likely to be affected by the Convention. For example, the liability of public authorities in tort for the exercise of their supervisory powers has been the subject of decisions of the European Court of Human Rights in *Osman v United Kingdom* Series A 1998-VIII, 3124, (2000) 29 EHRR 245 and in *Z v United Kingdom* Application 29392/95, 10 May 2001).

C. Statutes and Their Interpretation

(2) What are Judges Trying to Find Out?

(a) The 'intention of Parliament'

n48: see now also *R v Secretary of State for the Environment, Transport and the Regions, ex p Spath Holme Ltd* [2001] 2 AC 349, 397 *per* Lord Nicholls. **1.33**

Text to **n51**: this view, concerning when the permission to consult *Hansard* applies, is confirmed in *R v Secretary of State for the Environment, Transport and the Regions, ex p Spath Holme Ltd* [2001] 2 AC 349, 391, 399 and 413. Lord Hope was alone in suggesting (ibid 407–8) that *Hansard* may be consulted to clarify the meaning of the enacted text, but not the purpose of the legislation. **1.35**

(3) Where do Judges Look?

Basic rules

(ii) Identifying the appropriate context

The context of consolidating legislation may include the context in which the original legislation was enacted: see *R v Secretary of State for the Environment, Transport and the Regions, ex p Spath Holme Ltd* [2001] 2 AC 349, 388, but cf Lord Nicholls at 399. **1.46**

(4) Research to Discover the Purpose

n79: see also *R v Secretary of State for the Environment, Transport and the Regions, ex p Spath Holme Ltd* [2001] 2 AC 349. **1.50**

D. Precedent

(3) What Constitutes a Precedent?

(c) Related to an issue raised by the arguments of the parties

n121: *Rondel v Worsley* [1969] 1 AC 191 was overruled in a later case: see Supplement para 1.92. **1.75**

(5) The Rules of Precedent in Particular Courts

(b) House of Lords

When will the House of Lords overrule itself?

Clearly unjust results following from the previous decision will justify the House of Lords overruling itself. In *R v G* [2003] UKHL 50, [2003] 4 All ER 765, the definition of 'recklessness' set out in *R v Caldwell* [1982] AC 341 led to the conviction **1.90** for arson of boys of 11 and 12, who had not appreciated the likely consequences of their actions. This unfair result, combined with criticism from academics, judges and practitioners, justified overruling the previous test.

1.91 Legal certainty may sometimes justify the House of Lords refusing to overrule a previous decision which it considers to have been wrongly decided. For example, in *R v Kansal* [2001] UKHL 62, the majority of their Lordships considered *R v Lambert* [2001] UKHL 37; [2001] 3 All ER 577 to have been wrongly decided. But a majority decided not to overrule it. *R v Lambert* was a very recent and fully argued decision offering one possible interpretation of the effect of transitional provisions of the Human Rights Act 1998 on convictions entered before the Act came into force. The fact that this decision upheld a conviction was not decisive. By contrast, the Privy Council did overrule recent previous and fully argued decisions on the implications of fundamental rights for death penalty cases: *Lewis v Attorney-General for Jamaica* [2001] 2 AC 50. Lord Slynn (ibid 75) stated that legal certainty had to be balanced against the importance of saving someone's life; compare Lord Hoffmann ibid 89–90.

1.92 On the other hand, inaction by Parliament may simply indicate that it is content for the law to be changed by judicial decision. The House of Lords took this view in *Arthur J S Hall & Co (A Firm) v Simons* [2000] 3 All ER 673 in which it abolished the immunity of an advocate from being sued for the conduct of a case in court which was laid down in *Rondel v Worsley* [1969] 1 AC 191. The House of Lords considered that contemporary public policy no longer justified the immunity. In this case, because it considered that *Rondel v Worsley* was correctly decided at the time, the House of Lords did not make use of the *Practice Statement* set out in Main Work para 1.87 to justify its ruling.

(c) The Court of Appeal

(ii) Criminal Division

1.98 The Criminal Division of the Court of Appeal exercises a degree of discretion to decide whether a previous decision should be treated as a binding precedent in future or not when there are grounds for saying that the decision is wrong. (Lord Woolf CJ, *R v Simpson* [2003] EWCA Crim 1499 at [38]; [2003] 3 All ER 530 at 541). This discretion applies not only when overruling the precedent will benefit the accused, but also when it would deprive the accused of a purely technical defence.

2

FAMILY

A. The Creation of Legal Family Relationships

(1) Birth

(a) Legal parentage

The Adoption and Children Act 2002, s 111, amending the Children Act 1969, s 4, provides that the father of an illegitimate child has parental responsibility by virtue of the father's name being registered in the Register of Births under the provisions of the Births and Deaths Registration Act 1953 (as amended). **2.05**

n5: use of 'illegitimate' has been judicially disapproved: see *Re R (A Child)(Surname: Using both Parents')* [2001] EWCA Civ 1344, [2001] 2 FLR 1358. However, the need for accuracy in legal writing often makes it impossible to avoid using the term, at least if lengthy periphrasis is to be avoided: see Main Work para 2.05 as updated by this Supplement.

n12: in *Re Moynihan* [2000] 1 FLR 113, HL, it was unsuccessfully argued that the exclusion of illegitimate children from the succession to a hereditary peerage was incompatible with provisions of the European Convention on Human Rights; and in *R (on the Application of Montana) v Secretary of State for the Home Department* [2001] 1 FLR 449 the Court of Appeal rejected an application founded on the Convention for judicial review of the Secretary of State's refusal to register as a British citizen the illegitimate child of a British father and Norwegian mother.

(b) Human assisted reproduction and its implications for the determination of parentage

2.05 The following sentence needs to be added at the end of the paragraph. The Adoption and Children Act 2002 further reduces the legal consequences of illegitimacy by providing that a father who registers the birth jointly with the mother will equally have parental responsibility for the child: see above.

2.08 The legislation (in contrast to that relating to the legal adoption of children) gives a child conceived as a result of human assisted reproduction no right to information about his or her genetic parentage; and it has been argued that this denial is inconsistent with the provisions of Article 8 of the European Convention on Human Rights (respect for private and family life). However, whilst the court in *Rose and EM v Secretary of State for Health and HFEA* [2002] EWHC 1593 (Admin) [2002] UKHRR 1329 accepted that Article 8 was engaged it has not yet been determined whether or not English law is in this respect incompatible with the Convention.

n21: in *B and D v R (By her Legal Guardian)* [2002] 2 FLR 843 a man whose relationship with the mother ended before the birth of the child and who had no biological connection with the child was nonetheless held at first instance to be the child's legal father by reason of his having signed a form consenting to the course of treatment which resulted in the child's conception. But the Court of Appeal held that the necessary consent had, if it was to be effective for these purposes, to be still operative at the time when the embryo was placed in the mother, and that on the facts of the present case this was no longer true. The Court of Appeal considered that it should not be difficult for a treatment centre to make the enquiries necessary to determine the state of the parties' relationship at that time: *Re R (IVF: Paternity of Child)* [2003] EWCA Civ 182, [2003] 1 FLR 1183.

(c) Obtaining scientific evidence of parentage

2.09 The Family Law Reform Act 1987, s 23, was brought into force on 1 April 2001 by the Family Law Reform Act 1987 (Commencement No 3) Order 2001, SI 2001/777. The effect is that the court's powers now extend to directing that samples of bodily tissues and of bodily fluid other than blood be taken for the purpose of determining parentage.

The following should be added at the end of the paragraph. The court will usually consider it desirable to resolve any uncertainty about the child's parentage before seeking to determine issues about the child's upbringing: see *Leeds Teaching Hospitals NHS Trust* v *A* [2003] 1 FLR 1091.

n23: here there should be substituted a reference to the Family Law Reform Act 1969, s 21. The Child Support, Pensions and Social Security Act 2000, s 82, amends the provisions of the 1969 Act dealing with the consents required to the taking of samples from a minor aged under 16; and it is now provided that such a sample may be taken if the person who has the care and control of the minor consents or (where that person does not consent) where the court considers that it would be in the minor's best interests for the sample to be taken. It should be noted that the case of *Re T (Paternity: Ordering Blood Tests)* [2001] 2 FLR 1190 supports the proposition that it will usually be considered right that the truth about a child's parentage be established if that be possible.

(2) Adoption

The Adoption and Children Act 2002 will, when it is brought into force, make important changes to adoption law and practice. The Act will repeal all the provisions of the Adoption Act 1976 apart from those dealing with the status of adopted children (dealt with in Main Work para 2.31). The main changes in the substantive law can be summarized as follows. First, the Act provides that the child's welfare throughout his life must be the paramount consideration; and in this way erodes the distinction embodied in the earlier legislation between adoption (affecting legal status, and thus a matter in which appropriate regard should be given to the rights of the birth parents) and other procedures (for example, making custody orders) intended to settle the arrangements for a child's upbringing: cf Main Work paras 2.20 and 2.21. Secondly, the Act will allow the court to make an adoption order in favour of a couple (an expression defined by s 144(4)(b) as 'two people . . . living as parties in an enduring family relationship') whether the parties are of the same or opposite sex (compare Main Work para 2.13). Thirdly, the Act will introduce new measures (the general policy of which is to require decisions about parental consent to be taken earlier in the adoption process than is the case under the existing law) governing placement for adoption in substitution for the 'freeing for adoption' procedure described in Main Work paras 2.27 and 2.28. Fourthly, the Act will make new provision regarding access to information about adoptions (including access to the child's original birth records and other material about his birth family) in this respect greatly increasing the role of adoption agencies (such as Local Authorities). Finally, the Act will make important changes to the procedures governing adoptions with an intercountry aspect. A declared objective of the government in introducing the new legislation (which had been the subject of extended consultation) was to facilitate the adoption of children being looked after by local authorities. **2.10–2.32**

(e) The court's duty to give first consideration to the need to safeguard and promote the child's welfare

2.20 **n66**: the last sentence is to be replaced as follows. Provisions originally included in the Adoption (Intercountry Aspects) Act 1999 are incorporated in the Adoption and Children Act 2002: see Supplement paras 2.10–2.32. For details of the present practice, see D Hershman and A McFarlane, *Children: Law and Practice* H 295A.

(3) Marriage

(b) Capacity to marry

(iv) Parties not respectively male and female

2.41 It remains true, as stated in the Main Work, that English law does not accept the validity of single-sex unions; and it also remains true that the application of this rule to transsexuals who have received gender reassignment therapy has been controversial. However, in *Bellinger v Bellinger* [2003] UKHL 21, [2003] 1 FLR 1043 the House of Lords unanimously held that a person correctly classified at birth (applying the criteria laid down in *Corbett v Corbett* [1971] P 83) as a male will never be regarded as a woman for the purposes of the rules governing capacity to marry. The House of Lords also held that in the light of decisions of the European Court of Human Rights (notably that of *Goodwin v United Kingdom* (2002) 35 EHRR 18) English law was in this respect incompatible with Article 12 of the European Convention on Human Rights. The House of Lords made a declaration of incompatibility under the provisions of Human Rights Act 1998; and on 27 November 2003 the government introduced a Bill intended to provide a procedure for giving more extensive legal recognition to the consequences of change of gender reassignment than had previously been permitted. Transsexualism should, however, be distinguished from physical inter-sex where a person's biological sexual characteristics are ambiguous and not congruent at birth. In such cases it has been held (in *W v W (Physical Inter-Sex)* [2001] Fam 111) that the entry in the Register of Births is not conclusive, and that the court will determine the party's sex at the date of the marriage ceremony. In carrying out this assessment, the court will consider the party's development as well as the factors regarded as relevant in the *Corbett* case. Hence, chromosomal, gonadal, genital, psychological and hormonal factors as well as secondary sexual characteristics will all be in point. On the facts, the court held the respondent (albeit registered at birth as male) to be female at the date of the marriage, which was accordingly valid.

(d) Preliminaries to marriage

(ii) Banns, certificates and licences

2.45 Part IX of the Immigration and Asylum Act 1999 has abolished the procedure referred to in the final sentence of this paragraph whereby non-Anglican marriages could be speedily contracted by obtaining a superintendent registrar's certificate and licence. The general effect of the 1999 legislation is to require visitors to this country to reside here for three weeks before such a marriage can be solemnized.

(g) Consequence of irregularities

The following passage needs to be added at the end of the paragraph. In any event the court will (in the absence of strong and weighty evidence to the contrary) presume that a couple who have cohabited for such a length of time and in such circumstances as to have acquired the reputation of being man and wife were lawfully married; and this is so even if a particular ceremony can be shown to have been defective: see *Chief Adjudication Officer v Bath* [2000] 1 FLR 8; and *A-M v A-M (Divorce: Jurisdiction: Validity of Marriage)* [2001] 2 FLR 6, especially *per* Hughes J at 16. But there may be cases in which no attempt has been made to comply with the formal requirements imposed by English law, in which case there can be no 'marriage' not even a 'void' marriage: see *Gandhi v Patel* [2002] 1 FLR 654. **2.48**

(h) Legal consequences of marriage

References to 'a separation order' here and elsewhere in the Main Work should be replaced by references to 'a decree of judicial separation'. This is because it has been decided not to bring relevant provisions of the Family Law Act 1996 into force: see further Supplement paras 2.104–2.108 below. **2.50**

The following should be substituted for the second sentence of this paragraph. But legal discrimination against the illegitimate has in recent years been progressively removed, and the bringing into force in 2003 of the provisions of the Adoption and Children Act 2002, attributing parental responsibility to the father of an illegitimate child (provided the man's name is recorded in the Register of Births as the father) means that there are now few legal disadvantages flowing from the fact that a child's parents have never been married. See Supplement para 2.05. **2.51**

n147: the following sentence should be added to this note. Special provision is made for allowing a spouse to enter the United Kingdom with a view to settlement: see *Statement of Changes in Immigration Rules* (HC 1993–94 No 395, para 122. Details of this complex subject are given in *Halsbury's Laws of England* (4th edn 2002, reissue) para 122.

The following should be added at the end of this paragraph in the Main Work. In recent years, there has been much discussion of the extent to which the law should **2.52** move towards assimilating the rights and duties of unmarried partners to those of the married. In June 2003 the government published a Consultation Paper, *Civil Partnership Registration*, which proposed the creation of a civil registration partnership scheme under which same sex couples would be able to register their relationship and thereby attach to it many of the legal consequences traditionally associated with marriage. But it is not intended that the scheme should extend to opposite sex couples since it is considered that such couples may gain legal recognition for their relationship by marrying. Case law, sometimes influenced by the provisions of the Human Rights Act 1998, has also been influential in eroding the traditional distinctions between marriage and non-marital cohabitation and between male-female and homosexual relationships: see notably *Fitzpatrick v Sterling Housing Association Ltd* [2001] 1 AC 27 and *Mendoza v Ghaidan* [2002] EWCA Civ 1533, [2003] 1 FLR 468 (interpretation of statutory references to persons living as a 'member of the other's family' and 'as husband and wife' respectively).

B. The Termination of Legal Family Relationships

(3) Divorce and Other Matrimonial Causes

2.64 For the jurisdiction of the court, see Supplement paras 17.234ff below. In this context, the provisions of Council Regulation (EC) 1347/2000 on the Jurisdiction and the Recognition and Enforcement of Judgments in Matrimonial Matters and on Matters of Parental Responsibility for Children of Both Spouses (commonly known as 'Brussels II') are of great significance in cases with an international element since, when the regulation applies, the institution of proceedings in one jurisdiction means that any proceedings in another jurisdiction will automatically be stayed. For an illustration of the robust application of Brussels II, see *Wermuth v Wermuth (No 1)* [2002] EWHC 3049 [2003] 1 FLR 1022 and *Wermuth v Wermuth (No 2)* EWCA Civ 50 [2003] 1 FLR 1029 (where the court ceded jurisdiction to a German court and rejected a claim that an order to pay maintenance pending suit of £150,000 per annum could be regarded as a 'protective or provisional measure' and thus exempt from the normal rules).

(a) Nullity of marriage

2.66 As to whether the court may refuse to pronounce a decree of any kind on the ground that there was 'nothing like a marriage' in respect of which it could exercise jurisdiction, see *R v Bham* [1966] 1 QB 159; *A-M v A-M (Divorce: Jurisdiction: Validity of Marriage)* [2001] 2 FLR 6, 24; *Gandhi v Patel* [2002] 2 FLR 603; compare *Gereis v Yagoub* [1997] 1 FLR 854.

(i) Grounds on which a marriage is void

(5) *Parties not respectively male and female.* In *Bellinger v Bellinger* [2003] UKHL 21, [2003] 1 FLR 1043 the House of Lords accepted this view of the law. But the House of Lords held that the law was in this respect inconsistent with the provisions of Article 12 of the European Convention on Human Rights, and made a declaration of incompatibility under the Human Rights Act 1998 accordingly. It has been held that the principle that a person's biological sex is fixed for all time at birth does not apply if the case is one of physical inter-sex (as distinct from cases where one party is a transsexual): see Supplement para 2.41. **2.67**

(ii) Grounds on which a marriage is voidable

(3) *Lack of consent.* It should be mentioned that the application of the principle that only fear such as vitiates consent suffices is not always easy to apply, but that case law in the latter part of the twentieth century has shown a greater awareness of the situation of young people brought up to follow the traditional norms of their religious, cultural or ethnic group than was evident in earlier case law. In addition to *Hirani v Hirani* (1982) 4 FLR 232 reference should be made to the Scottish cases of *Mahmood v Mahmmod* 1993 SLT 589 and *Mahmud v Mahmud* 1994 SLT 599. The difficulties in this context facing such young people were highlighted by Singer J in *Re KR (Abduction: Forcible Removal by Parents)* [1999] 2 FLR 542. The Foreign and Commonwealth Office has established a dedicated forced marriage desk and helpline to provide advice and assistance. **2.68**

(iv) Effects of a nullity decree

n201: here there should be added a reference to *Rampal v Rampal* [2001] EWCA Civ 925 [2001] 2 FLR 1179 where it was held that the case law did not debar a bigamist from successfully claiming ancillary relief in any circumstances, and that on the facts of that case such a claim should be allowed to proceed.

(b) Divorce

The ground for divorce; and the 'facts' which must be proved to evidence the breakdown

In January 2001 the Lord Chancellor announced that the government did not intend to proceed with the implementation of the relevant provisions of the Family Law Act 1996 and that it proposed to invite Parliament to repeal those provisions when a suitable legislative opportunity arose. It can therefore be assumed that the process sketched out in Main Work paras 2.84–2.102 will not govern the dissolution of marriage and that the provisions of the Matrimonial Causes Act 1973 outlined at Main Work paras 2.72–2.79 will continue in force. However, the **2.72** government has not revealed its intentions in any detail and it seems that the fact that certain provisions of the 1996 Act had (as indicated at Main Work para 2.82) already been implemented will require that the proposed legislation be more than a simple repeal.

It should be noted that no petition for divorce can be presented within one year from the date of the marriage: see Matrimonial Causes Act 1973, s 3 (as substituted by the Matrimonial and Family Proceedings Act 1984). The effect of a decree absolute of divorce is as stated (in the context of a divorce order made under the Family Law Act 1996) in Main Work para 2.103, in which the words 'decree absolute of divorce' should throughout be substituted for the words 'divorce order'.

(c) Divorce under the Matrimonial Causes Act 1973

(i) The 'special procedure' and its impact on legal practice

2.75 The 'special procedure' in practice makes it difficult if not impossible for the court routinely to carry out the task imposed on it by Matrimonial Causes Act 1973, s 1(3) of inquiring into the facts; and there seems little doubt that the unscrupulous may in practice be able to obtain a decree contrary to the relevant statutory provisions (for example by making wholly groundless allegations of 'behaviour': see *Bhaiji v Chauhan, Queen's Proctor Intervening (Divorce: Marriages used for Immigration Purposes)* [2003] 2 FLR 485. But in such cases the decree may subsequently be rescinded (as in *Moynihan v Moynihan* [1997] 1 FLR 52) whilst the facts may be such as to ground a criminal prosecution for perjury.

2.76 It should not be thought, however, that defended divorce cases do not occasionally come before the courts and litigated to a conclusion: see, for example, *Hadjimilitis (Tsavliris)* v *Tsavliris* [2003] 1 FLR 81 (five days' trial of petition based on husband's 'behaviour': see Main Work para 2.73).

n208a: the text of this note should read: *Pounds v Pounds* [1994] 1 WLR 1535, 1539 *per* Waite LJ.

(ii) Resisting divorce

The Divorce (Religious Marriages) Act 2002 adds another procedure whereby the legal termination of a marriage may be postponed or prevented: a court in England and Wales may require that a Jewish marriage (or a marriage according to other prescribed religious forms) be dissolved in accordance with the appropriate religious rite before the decree *nisi* of divorce is made absolute .

(d) Divorce under the Family Law Act 1996, Part II

(ii) The ground for divorce under the Family Law Act 1996

2.84–2.103 Paragraphs 2.73–2.102 should be deleted: see Supplement para 2.72. Paragraph

2.103 should be read subject to the substitution throughout of the words 'decree absolute of divorce' for the words 'divorce order'.

(e) Separation orders under the Family Law Act 1996

The provisions of the Family Law Act 1996 empowering the court to make separation orders 'providing for the separation of the parties to a marriage' have not been brought into force and are to be repealed: see Supplement para 2.72. In consequence, the provisions of the Matrimonial Causes Act 1973, s 17, dealing with decrees of judicial separation will remain in force. A petition may be presented at any time after the solemnization of the marriage alleging one or more of the 'facts' on which a divorce petition may be founded, as set out at Main Work para 2.73. If the court is satisfied of any such fact it is obliged to grant the decree; and the Matrimonial Causes Act 1973, s 17(2) specifically provides that the court is not to be concerned to consider whether the marriage has broken down irretrievably. **2.104–2.108**

A judicial separation decree relieves the parties of the duty to cohabit; but more important in practical terms is the fact that the court has power, on or after granting such a decree, to make financial relief and property adjustment orders: see Main Work para 2.154 and note (for an example of the utility of such a decree in founding jurisdiction to make substantial financial orders) *Le Foe v Le Foe and Woolwich plc* [2001] 2 FLR 970. Moreover, if one party to a marriage dies wholly or partially intestate whilst a judicial separation decree is in force, the property in question devolves as if the other party had died: Matrimonial Causes Act 1973, s 18(2).

C. The Legal Consequences of Family Relationships

(1) Rights in Respect of Property

(d) Determining beneficial ownership; the application of the doctrines of implied, resulting and constructive trusts

(i) Intention—actual, presumed or inferred

It should be noted, however, that in *Le Foe v Le Foe and Woolwich plc* [2001] 2 FLR 970 the court seems to have found that the wife had a beneficial interest in property by reason of her indirect contributions to mortgage payments notwithstanding the absence of any direct contribution by her. The same case also provides an example of the court applying a broad test to determining the parties' common intention: see further Main Work para 2.115 and note also *The Mortgage Corporation v Shaire* [2001] Ch 743. **2.114**

(2) Rights to Protection of the Home and Person

The Domestic Violence, Crime and Victims Bill, introduced by the government **2.127** into the House of Lords on 27 November 2003, is intended to add to the protection against domestic violence afforded by the legal provisions set out in this section.

(c) The Protection from Harassment Act 1997

2.144 n386: it appears that prosecutions under this Act are not uncommonly related to domestic relationships, but in *R v Hills* [2001] 1 FLR 580 the Court of Appeal asserted that the Act was intended to apply to 'stalking'; and that, whilst it might sometimes be appropriate to charge a person making a nuisance of himself to an estranged partner or wife with an offence under the Act, it would be inappropriate to invoke the harassment legislation when a couple were still involved in an ongoing relationship. See also *Lau v Director of Public Prosecutions* [2000] 1 FLR 799 (the fewer the incidents proved and the longer the period over which they were spread the less likely it was that a finding of harassment under the Act could reasonably be made) and *R v Colohan* [2001] EWCA Crim 1251 [2001] 2 FLR 757 (the test of harassment laid down in s 1(2) of the Act is objective, and accordingly the fact that the accused's perceptions are affected by mental illness does not constitute a defence).

(3) Rights to Financial Support

(a) Introduction: the common law duty to maintain, and the impact of the child support legislation on statutory remedies

2.147 The Child Support, Pensions and Social Security Act 2000 simplifies the formula used to calculate maintenance liabilities: the basic principle is that absent parents pay a percentage of their net income (up to £2,000 per week) for the support of each child. The Act also makes a number of other important changes intended to make the calculation and enforcement of child support obligations fairer as well as more efficient and effective. But the principles set out in the Main Work will remain unaffected.

2.148 The Child Support, Pensions and Social Security Act 2000 restricts the principle, stated in the Main Work, that the courts could continue to make consent orders which would effectively exclude the powers of the Child Support Agency. An order made after 5 April 2002 will only be effective in this way for a period of one year.

(b) The statutory framework for court ordered financial relief

2.150 n415: the following should be inserted at the beginning of this note. Children Act 1989, Sch 1, para 4, directs the court deciding whether to exercise its powers and if so in what manner, to have regard to all the circumstances including a number of specified matters.

The following should be added at the end of the note. Again, in *Re P (Child: Financial Provision)* [2003] EWCA Civ 837, [2003] 2 FLR 1054, the court ordered an unmarried father to provide a housing fund for his child amounting to £1 million, and to make periodical payments of £70,000 annually for the child's maintenance. These figures include an element for the support of the other parent, but only in her capacity as carer for the child.

(c) Private ordering of the financial consequences of divorce

In some societies it is common for parties to enter into agreements ('prenuptials') **2.151**
prior to their marriage dealing with the consequences of any future divorce; but English law refuses automatically to enforce the terms of such agreements and may regard them as being of only limited significance in influencing the court's approach to the resolution of financial issues between a divorcing couple. However, in appropriate cases the courts will give a prenuptial agreement evidential weight if its terms are relevant to an issue before the court in the exercise of its statutory jurisdiction: see *F v F (Ancillary Relief: Substantial Assets)* [1995] 2 FLR 45, 66; *N v N (Jurisdiction: Pre-Nuptial Agreement)* [1999] 2 FLR 745. Reference should be made to the case of *M v M (Prenuptial Agreement)* [2002] 1 FLR 654 where on the facts the terms of a prenuptial agreement were taken into account since to do otherwise would produce an unfair result. It is understood that formal prenuptial agreements are not infrequently made on professional advice in England and Wales in the belief that the existence of such an agreement would be regarded as relevant albeit not conclusive.

(d) Ancillary relief in divorce nullity and separation proceedings

It is now intended to repeal the relevant provisions of the Family Law Act 1996 **2.154**
(see Supplement para 2.72) and accordingly the reference to the changes intended to be made by that Act to the time at which financial arrangements are to be made should be deleted.

n429: the following should be added at the end of this note. The power to make orders for maintenance pending suit includes power (in a proper case) to make orders intended to finance the expenses of prosecuting the divorce proceedings: *G v G (Maintenance Pending Suit: Costs)* [2002] EWHC Civ 306, [2003] 2 FLR 71, and see *Wermuth v Wermuth (No 1)* [2002] EWHC 3049, [2003] 1 FLR 1022 and *Wermuth v Wermuth (No 2)* [2003] EWCA Civ 50, [2003] 1 FLR 1029 (where two-thirds of an order to pay maintenance pending suit of £150,000 per annum was intended for this purpose). It should also be noted that because the court's powers to make financial provision and property adjustment orders arise only on the grant of a decree absolute the court has power in certain circumstances when the petition is founded on separation to direct that a divorce be not made absolute unless and until the court is satisfied that the financial arrangements made are 'reasonable and fair' or 'the best that can be made in the circumstances': see Matrimonial Causes Act 1973, s 10(2). But before making such a direction the court will wish to be satisfied that the respondent would indeed be prejudiced by the termination of the marriage: see *Re G (Decree Absolute: Prejudice)* [2002] EWHC 2854, [2002] 1 FLR 870.

n430: the following should be added at the end of this note. Because of this rule, the personal representatives of a spouse who dies after decree nisi but before decree absolute cannot enforce a judgment previously given in ancillary relief proceedings: see *McMinn v McMinn (Ancillary Relief: Death of Party to Proceedings)* [2002] EWHC 1194, [2003] 2 FLR 865.

2.155 **n433**: the Welfare Reform and Pensions Act 1999 (the relevant provisions of which, referred to in Main Work n433, came into force on 4 December 2000) amends the Matrimonial Causes Act 1973 so as to give the court power, on granting a decree of divorce or a decree of nullity in respect of a petition presented after 1 December 2000 or at any time after granting such a decree, to make a pension sharing order. In effect, such an order transfers a percentage of one party's shareable pension rights to the other.

2.158 Here there should be added a reference to the fact that in *Mountney v Treharne* [2002] EWCA Civ 1174, [2002] 2 FLR 930 the Court of Appeal held that the making of a property adjustment order directing one party to transfer specific property to the other created an equitable interest over the property in question from the moment that the order took effect. This decision (as to the correctness of which members of the court expressed reservations) may be important where disputes arise involving third parties, such as the Trustee in Bankruptcy of husband or wife.

n444: the Welfare Reform and Pensions Act 1999, Sch 3, para 3, amends the definition of 'nuptial settlement' in the Matrimonial Causes Act 1973 so as to exclude from that definition pension schemes falling within the definition of 'pension arrangement' for the purpose of the 1999 Act. The intention is apparently to require applications to vary the provisions of an occupational pension scheme of the kind successful in *Brooks v Brooks* to be made exclusively under the 1999 Act. The decision in the *Brooks* case may, however, still have some residual importance as demonstrating the correct approach to the interpretation of the 'settlement' provisions of the 1973 Act.

It should be noted that in *C v C (Variation of Post-Nuptial Settlement: Company Shares)* [2003] EWHC 1222 (Fam) [2003] 2 FLR 493 it was not disputed that the court's powers to vary a settlement were unaffected by the settlement being located abroad or by the fact that the beneficial interests under the settlement were dependent on the exercise of the trustees' discretion.

(e) The exercise of the discretion to make financial orders

(ii) 'All the circumstances'

In *White v White* [2001] 1 AC 596 the House of Lords considered, in the context of a case involving assets amounting to some £4.5 million, the principles to be applied in the exercise of the discretion to make financial orders on the breakdown of marriage; and subsequently the Court of Appeal in *Lambert v Lambert* [2002] EWCA Civ 1685 [2003] 1 FLR 139 gave further guidance on the application of the statutory provisions. **2.162–2.163**

In the *White* case the House of Lords asserted that the objective implicit in the statutory provisions was to achieve (first consideration being given to the welfare of the children) a fair outcome in financial arrangements on divorce; and their Lordships considered that the court should in all cases have close regard to the language of the statute. For this reason, use of expressions such as 'reasonable requirements' (rather than the statutory 'needs') was to be deprecated.

Their Lordships' opinions emphasized that discrimination between husband and wife was incompatible with fairness; and that any division of labour between them should not affect the outcome: if each contributed equally (albeit in different spheres) to the family then in principle it mattered not which of them earned money as distinct from making contributions in other ways. When considering the division of assets, therefore, judges should depart from equality only if and to the extent that there was good reason for so doing; and the parties' financial 'needs' should not be regarded as a ceiling for the division of assets.

On the facts, the House of Lords refused to interfere with the (unequal) division of assets ordered by the Court of Appeal (against which both parties had appealed) holding that this had been within the proper ambit of the discretion conferred by the legislation. In the *Lambert* case (where the parties' assets exceeded £20 million) the Court of Appeal reiterated that the overarching principle of the legislation was to achieve a fair division of any assets which remained after provision had been made for appropriate housing for parents and children. The court asserted that it would only be in wholly exceptional cases that circumstances would make an unequal division of the remaining assets appropriate. The House of Lords refused leave to appeal in the *Lambert* case, and it appears that equal division of assets has thus become the norm in what are conventionally described as 'big money' cases. However, there remain difficult questions to be resolved (as, for example, about how far the principle of equal division is applicable where one party inherited substantial assets shortly before the breakdown or where the parties' relationship has not been as lengthy as it had been in the cases of *White* and *Lambert*: see *GW v RW (Financial Provision: Departure from Equality)* [2003] EWHC 611, [2003] 2 FLR 108 and compare *Foster v Foster* [2003] EWCA 565, [2003] 2 FLR 299, CA).

In Main Work para 2.163 the text to which nn461, 462, and 463 are attached should be deleted.

(4) Rights and Duties in Respect of Children

(a) **'Parental responsibility'**

(i) Who has parental responsibility?

2.171 Under the provisions of the Adoption and Children Act 2002 (see Supplement paras 2.10–2.32): (1) the father of an illegitimate child will also have parental responsibility if he and the mother are registered as the child's parents on the Register of Births; (2) a child's step-parent will also have parental responsibility for the child if the parent and step-parent have made a parental responsibility agreement; (3) a 'special guardian' appointed by the court under the provisions of the Children Act 1989, ss 14A–G will also have parental responsibility for the child. A 'special guardian' is entitled in the absence of any other relevant order to exercise parental responsibility to the exclusion of others with parental responsibility. (In this respect, the position of a 'special guardian' is incompatible with the general principle of the Children Act 1989 as stated in Main Work para 2.173, but this is said to be justified because of the distinctive needs which special guardianship is intended to meet: see Supplement para 2.179.)

2.176 Although there has been no statutory modification of the parental right to inflict corporal punishment on a child, it has been held in *R v H (Assault of Child: Reasonable Chastisement)* [2001] EWCA Crim 1024 [2002] 1 Cr App R 21 that a jury determining whether such punishment was 'moderate and reasonable' must be directed to take account of the factors identified by the European Court in *A v United Kingdom (Human Rights: Punishment of Child)* (1999) 27 EHRR 611 (n515 below); and see *Williamson v Secretary of State for Education and Employment* [2002] EWCA Civ 1926, [2003] 1 All ER 385.

2.177 It should be noted that judicial decisions have increasingly emphasized that parental rights and the powers which go with them exist to enable the parents to carry out their duties and responsibilities for the child, and are to be exercised in the best interests of the child: see eg *Williamson v Secretary of State for Education and Employment* [2002] EWCA Civ 1926, [2003] 1 All ER 385; and *Re A (Children)(Conjoined Twins: Surgical Separation)* [2001] Fam 147 (where the Court of Appeal upheld a decision authorizing surgery intended to separate conjoined twins, notwithstanding the fact that the procedure would necessarily result in the death of one of the two. The Court of Appeal regarded the purpose of the surgery as being to preserve the life of one twin, rather than to cause the death of the other).

But it should also be noted that the facts about a child's parentage are relevant to decisions on his or her upbringing, and it will normally be desirable to resolve any doubts there may be on this score: see *Leeds Teaching Hospitals NHS Trust v A* [2003] 1 FLR 1091.

(b) Court orders in respect of children's upbringing

The Adoption and Children Act 2002 will, when the relevant provisions are brought into force, empower the courts to make a 'special guardianship order' in certain circumstances. Such an order is intended to meet the needs of children for whom adoption is not appropriate but who would benefit by having greater security and permanence than could be provided under the Children Act 1989 as originally enacted. **2.179**

There should be added a reference to the statutory procedures intended to deal with cases of child abduction. The Child Abduction Act 1984 creates criminal offences applicable in cases in which a child has been removed from the lawful control of a person with (or entitled to exercise) such control; and the suspicion that such an offence has been committed may suffice to enable pre-emptive action to be taken by the police or immigration authorities. The Child Abduction and Custody Act 1985 gives effect to the Hague Convention on the Civil Aspects of International Child Abduction 1980 and to the European Convention on Recognition and Enforcement of Decisions concerning Children and on the Restoration of Custody of Children. The Family Law Act 1986 creates machinery for the recognition, registration and enforcement within the United Kingdom and the Isle of Man of certain orders relating to children. For a full consideration of these provisions and the relationship between them, reference may usefully be made to D Hershman and A McFarlane, *Children: Law and Practice* Division E.

(iii) Orders the court can make in family proceedings: (1) 'Section 8 orders'

Jurisdiction to make residence and contact orders is dependent on the child being habitually resident in England and Wales: see *Re G (Adoption: Ordinary Residence)* [2002] EWHC 1376, [2003] 2 FLR 994. **2.188**

(iv) Orders the court can make in family proceedings: (2) court directed investigations

The Criminal Justice and Court Services Act 2000 established the Children and Family Court Advisory and Support Service (usually known as CAFCASS). The functions of CAFCASS include safeguarding and promoting the welfare of children whose welfare is or may be in question in family proceedings; giving advice to the court about applications made in such proceedings; making provision for children to be represented; and providing information, advice and other support for the children and their families. In effect, CAFCASS has assumed the roles formerly allocated in these respects to probation officers, welfare officers and guardians ad litem. The legislation has been amended to substitute a reference to **2.189** 'an officer of the Service' for (in the present case) the reference to a probation officer. It is thought that in the context of the Main Work para 2.189 the change is rather one of terminology than of substance.

(v) When the court can make a section 8 order

2.199 **n585**: an illustration of the court's cautious approach in this regard is provided by *Re N (Contact: Minor Seeking Leave to Defend and Removal of Guardian)* [2003] 1 FLR 652 where the court held that an 11-year-old boy did not have sufficient understanding to consider all the implications of granting his application to remove the court appointed guardian and be allowed to continue a course of therapy and counselling.

(c) The decision whether to make an order: child's welfare paramount

2.210 For an illustration of the proposition that decisions on what is in the child's interests will often be dependent on findings of fact, see *Re C (Welfare of Child: Immunisation)* [2003] EWHC 1376, [2003] 2 FLR 1054 where a mother's opposition to immunization of her child was overridden in respect of immunization against certain diseases but not others.

n625: the following should be added. Where a dispute comes before the court, the court has a duty to resolve it and should not abnegate its responsibility: see eg *Re P (Parental Dispute: Judicial Determination)* [2002] EWCA Civ 1627, [2003] 1 FLR 286 (choice of school).

3

COMPANIES AND OTHER ASSOCIATIONS

A. Introduction

(2) Associations in English Law: An Overview

(c) Associative forms currently recognized by English law

The regulation of credit unions now falls within the ambit of the Financial Services Authority (FSA), acting in accordance with powers conferred by the Financial Services and Markets Act 2000. In 2003 the FSA published a specialist sourcebook of rules and guidance for credit unions, requiring them among other things to pass a basic solvency test, to maintain a minimum liquidity ratio, and to comply with FSA money-laundering regulations. *The Credit Union Specialist Sourcebook* is available online at: www.fsa.gov.uk/vhb/html/cred/CREDtoc.html. The Credit Union Act 1979, s 3, was amended by the Regulatory Reform (Credit Unions) Order 2003 (SI 256/2003), to prohibit organizations other than established credit unions from describing themselves as credit unions without FSA approval. The 1979 Act is criticized as over-restrictive, and an eloquent appeal is made for legislative reform, in N Ryder, 'Credit Unions in the United Kingdom: A Critical Analysis of **3.10** their Legislative Framework and its Impact upon their Development' [2003] JBL 45.

3.12 The fact that common law systems do not ascribe legal personality to charitable foundations was central to the resolution of *T Choithram International SA v Pagarani* [2001] 1 WLR 1, PC. Here, Lord Browne-Wilkinson held that a statement of intent to transfer property to a charitable foundation was legally meaningless, and so should be interpreted as a statement of intent to vest the property in the trustees of the charitable trust which had been established in order to bring 'the foundation' into being.

Following a consultation exercise, the course of which can be tracked through the papers and responses published online by the DTI at www.dti.gov.uk/cics, the government has decided to create a new type of registered company, the community interest company (CIC), for use by non-profit-distributing enterprises providing benefit to the community. To this end, the Companies (Audit, Investigations and Community Enterprise) Bill was introduced in the House of Lords in December 2003. It is intended that CICs will take the form either of a registered company limited by guarantee, or of a registered company limited by shares, with various superadded features including supervision by a new Regulator of Community Interest Companies and an asset-lock (ie they will ordinarily be prohibited from distributing profits to their members).

(d) The Human Rights Act 1998

(i) Article 11 of the European Convention on Human Rights

3.14 The requirement that Convention member states must permit and enable trade unions to take action for the protection of their members' interests (see Main Work text to n24) does not necessarily extend to granting them an unlimited right to strike: 'such a right, which is not expressly enshrined in Article 11, may be subject under national law to regulation of a kind that limits its exercise in certain instances'. See *National Union of Rail, Maritime and Transport Workers v London Underground Ltd* [2001] ICR 647, 664, CA (Robert Walker LJ), following *Schmidt v Sweden* [1976] 1 EHRR 632, ECHR. See too *National Union of Belgian Police v Belgium* [1975] 1 EHRR 578, ECHR.

In *RSPCA v AG* [2002] 1 WLR 448, 466, Lightman J held that in principle 'the freedom of association under Article 11 . . . embraces the freedom to exclude from association those whose membership [the RSPCA] honestly believes to be damaging to the interests of the society' (the RSPCA is a statutory corporation).

(iv) Articles 8, 9, and 10

3.17 n36: cf *R v Inland Revenue Commissioners, ex p Banque Internationale à Luxembourg SA* [2000] STC 708, 723 (Lightman J): to the extent that notices served on a bank under the Income and Corporation Taxes Act 1988, s 767C, requiring the disclosure of documents relating to a customer, interfered with the bank's and the customer's rights to privacy under Article 8(1), there was justification for this as required by Article 8(2).

n39: and see *Cable and Wireless (Dominica) Ltd v Marpin Telecoms and Broadcasting Company Ltd* [2001] 1 WLR 1123, PC, where Lord Cooke discussed *Antronic AG v Switzerland* at 1132.

(3) Persons and Personality in English Law

(c) **Artificial persons**

n50: see now also *Piggott v Aulton (Deceased)* [2003] EWCA Civ 24, [2003] RTR 540, [7] (Arden LJ), considering CPR 19.8(2): 'proceedings may be commenced against the estate of a deceased person but the proceedings so brought cannot be prosecuted until a person has been appointed to represent the estate of the deceased'. **3.21**

(e) **The use of the terms 'person' and 'personality' in English legal practice**

(i) The possession of personality does not entail the possession of a fixed set of legal capacities

n62: see too *R v Secretary of State for Health, ex p C* [2000] 1 FCR 471, 477, CA (Hale LJ), affirming the statement in 8(2) *Halsbury's Laws of England* (4th edn reissue, sv 'Constitutional Law and Human Rights', 101, n6), that 'at common law the Crown, as a corporation possessing legal personality, has the capacities of a natural person and thus the same liberties as the individual'. **3.24**

n63: see too *R v Hertfordshire CC, ex p Green Environmental Industries Ltd* [2000] 2 AC 412, HL. **3.25**

n65: however, while Bell J's order in the *McDonald's* case was varied on appeal, the Court of Appeal agreed with him that the respondent parent and subsidiary companies had each been equally injured by the appellants' defamatory statements, to the extent that these statements had in fact been defamatory: *Steel v McDonald's Corp* [1999] EWCA Civ 1144, [88] and [89]. In their Lordships' collective view, the two companies 'each have a related but distinct reputation and each have related but distinct goodwill', an analysis for which they derived support from *Habib Bank v Habib Bank AG Zurich* [1981] 1 WLR 1265, 1278, CA (Oliver LJ).

(ii) The anthropomorphizing quality of the term 'person'

In May 2003 the government announced that it would publish a draft Bill to introduce a new offence of corporate killing by the end of the year; however, **3.27** nothing was said about this in the Queen's Speech at the start of the 2003/04 Parliamentary Session.

B. Corporations

(1) Statutory and Chartered Corporations

(b) Historical background

3.45 It is incorrectly suggested in this paragraph that the principal reason why commercial associates could not act as corporate bodies without royal or statutory authority in the eighteenth and early nineteenth centuries was because the Bubble Act 1720 prevented them from doing so. The Bubble Act 1720 is often portrayed by historians as a piece of reactionary, anti-joint stock company legislation enacted as a panicky response to, and designed to suppress, the activities of both the South Sea Company and its competitors. But, in fact, the statute was a (misjudged) measure promoted by the directors of the South Sea Company itself, as one of a series of manoeuvres designed to blow the company's own bubble by suppressing competition for capital in the share market. If Parliament had truly been committed to the suppression of joint stock companies as a matter of general policy in 1720, it would not have needed to enact a statute to effect this, since associations were in any case illegal at common law (as noted in Main Work paras 3.05 and 3.06). Since the Glorious Revolution, the Orange administration had been unwilling to enforce the Royal Prerogative against evaders of the requirement that associates should obtain an Act or charter, because such enforcement had become politically identified with the bad old days of Stuart absolutism, exemplified by the trial following the revocation of the Corporation of London's charter in 1682 (*R v City of London* (1681–3) 8 Howell's State Trials 1039). But in 1720 the mechanism still existed at common law to suppress the joint stock companies which had proliferated since 1689—as indeed Lord Eldon was to stress much later in 1825 when his own (genuinely reactionary) efforts to block the Bubble Repeal Act in Parliament came to nothing. All this and much more is fruitfully discussed in Ron Harris's excellent new historical study, *Industrializing English Law: Entrepreneurship and Business Organization 1720–1844* (2000).

(d) How statutory and chartered corporations act

3.49 In the event that a chartered corporation is subsequently placed on a statutory footing, the statute may cut down the corporation's previously unlimited powers, as in, for example, *Jenkin v Pharmaceutical Society of Great Britain* [1921] 1 Ch 392, 400 (Peterson J), considered in *R (Mahmood) v Royal Pharmaceutical Society of Great Britain* [2002] 1 WLR 879, 897, CA (Chadwick LJ).

(2) Registered Companies

(a) Overview

In July 2001 the DTI Company Law Review Steering Group concluded its review of English company law and presented its final recommendations to the Secretary of State for Trade and Industry: *Modern Company Law for a Competitive Economy: Final Report* (2001). The Group recommended a major overhaul of the English companies legislation which, if enacted, should considerably simplify and streamline the rules of English company law, and should also effect many substantive changes to the content of these rules. In July 2002, the government issued a White Paper, stating that it had accepted many of the Steering Group's recommendations and intended to proceed with legislation, a draft form of which was included: *Modernising Company Law* (Cm 5553). In July 2003 the government announced that it was still in the process of drafting a final version of its new Companies Bill, and that in the meantime it planned to respond to recent major corporate failures (viz the collapse of the Enron and Worldcom corporate groups) by bringing forward early legislation to implement changes to the regulation of the accountancy and audit professions, and to enhance the regulatory authorities' powers to investigate companies. This process is now under way: in December 2003 the Companies (Audit, Investigations and Community Enterprise) Bill was introduced in the House of Lords. **3.50**

In Case C-212/97 *Centros Ltd v Erhvervs-og Selskabsstyrelsen* [2000] Ch 446, ECJ, two Danish nationals and residents bought an English registered company and then sought to register a branch office in Denmark. Their purpose was to avoid the minimum capital rules in Denmark, which are more restrictive than those in England. The Danish trade and companies board refused the registration, but the European Court of Justice held that this refusal infringed Articles 52 and 58 of the EC Treaty (which were renumbered Articles 43 and 48 by the Treaty of Amsterdam 1997). These articles give companies established in the EU the right to create secondary establishments in other member states in the form of branches, agencies, or subsidiaries (for general discussion see V Edwards, *EC Company Law* (1999), chs 16 and 17). In effect, the ECJ decided that they confer the right to register a company in one member state for the sole purpose of carrying on business through a branch office in another. The scope of the *Centros* decision was subsequently reviewed in Case C-208/00 *Uberseering BC v NCC Nordic Construction Company Baumanagement GmbH* [2002] OJ C323/12, where the ECJ effectively held that the EC principle of freedom of establishment trumps the 'real seat theory' that a company's governing law should be determined by its seat of administration. Hence, a company incorporated in the Netherlands which had not been reincorporated in Germany following the acquisition of its shares by German nationals, and relocation of its seat of administration to

Germany, was held by the ECJ to possess the legal capacity to mount legal proceedings in Germany notwithstanding the fact that German law deemed companies in this position to lack such capacity. Some have expressed fears that the *Centros* and *Uberseering* decisions will prompt businesses to shop around within the EU for the incorporation regime which requires least of them. Others believe that, on the contrary, market forces will stimulate a 'race to the top', as investors seek the protection of tough corporate governance regimes. Either development may well force EU member states into closer harmonization of their incorporation regimes.

(b) How registered companies are conceptualized

(i) Nineteenth-century developments

3.59 n151: cf *Flitcroft's Case* (1882) 21 Ch D 519, CA, affirmed in *Bairstow v Queens Moat Houses plc* [2001] 2 BCLC 531, CA: where the shareholders in general meeting declare a dividend on the basis of misleading accounts presented by the directors, the company can sue the directors for breach of duty. In Brett LJ's words (at 535): 'Even if the shareholders had all sanctioned what was done, and had remained the same throughout, still the company could have sued the directors for a breach of trust. They are trustees for the company not for the individual shareholders.'

(c) How registered companies act

(i) The 'primary' and 'special' rules of attribution

3.63 n172: the Court of Appeal's decision in the *Standard Chartered Bank* case has been reversed by the House of Lords: [2002] UKHL 43, [2003] 1 AC 959. At [23] and [41] respectively, Lord Hoffmann and Lord Rodger both considered that the *Williams* case lent no support to the view that the respondent in the *Standard Chartered Bank* case should escape personal liability because he should be 'identified' with the company for which he had acted. Moreover Lord Rodgers appeared to take the view at [40] that a defendant can never make this argument, holding that 'the maxim *culpa tenet suos auctores* may not be the end, but it is the beginning of wisdom in these matters. Where someone commits a tortious act, he at least will be liable for the consequences; whether others are also liable depends on the circumstances.'

(ii) Limitations on their powers to act and the position of third parties

3.68 The wording of s 35A was reviewed in *Smith v Henniker-Major & Co (a firm)* [2002] EWCA Civ 762, [2002] 2 BCLC 655, where the CA made heavy weather of the question whether the section protects third parties who have dealt with an inquorate board. Carnwath and Robert Walker LJJ took different approaches to this question, and their answers leave the law in some disarray. It must be hoped that the government will revisit cl 17 of the Draft Companies Bill contained in its White Paper (see annotation to para 3.50 above) with a view to ironing out this problem.

In *EIC Services Ltd v Phipps* [2003] EWHC 1507 (Ch), [2003] 1 WLR 2360, Neuberger J held that a shareholder who was mistakenly allotted bonus shares was 'a person dealing with a company' within the meaning of s 35A.

(d) Directors' duties and disabilities

(ii) Directors' duties: an overview

Although directors owe a range of duties to the company, they do not generally owe duties of skill and care or fiduciary duties directly to the shareholders, although circumstances can sometimes arise in which such duties are owed; for discussion, see *Peskin v Anderson* [2001] 1 BCLC 372, CA. Also, note that the DTI Company Law Review Steering Group has recommended in its final report (see Supplement para 3.50) that a statutory statement of directors' duties should be enacted, a draft version of which is contained in Vol 1, Annex C of the DTI final report. **3.71**

n193: see now also *Johnson v Gore Wood & Co (a firm)* [2002] 2 AC 1, HL. The courts have struggled to distinguish situations in which a shareholder is debarred by this rule from recovering 'reflective loss' from situations where he is not: C Mitchell, 'Shareholders' Claims for Reflective Loss' (2004) 120 LQR 457. **3.72**

It should also be noted in this paragraph that company directors are sometimes sued by company liquidators after their companies have gone into insolvency, for breaches of common law duties and/or analogous statutory duties imposed by the Insolvency Act 1986, as in, for example, *Cohen v Selby* [2001] 1 BCLC 176, CA. However, the courts' restrictive attitude towards a liquidator's ability either to assign his rights to third parties or to recover the costs of such actions out of the company's assets as an expense of the liquidation has had a chilling effect: *Re MC Bacon Ltd (No 2)* [1991] Ch 127; *Re Oasis Merchandising Services Ltd* [1997] 1 BCLC 689, CA; *Lewis v Inland Revenue Commissioners* [2001] 3 All ER 499, CA. **3.73**

n203: see now also *Re Bradcrown Ltd* [2001] 1 BCLC 547, esp 550–1 (Lawrence Collins J).

(iii) The duty of skill and care

Lord Browne-Wilkinson's comments in the *Henderson* case (see Main Work text to nn204 and 205) are interpreted differently—and persuasively—in S Worthington, 'The Duty to Monitor: A Modern View of the Director's Duty of Care' in FM Patfield (ed), *Perspectives on Company Law: 2* (1997) 181, 187–8. She **3.74** takes them to support her argument that 'directors clearly owe a (tortious) duty of care to the companies they serve', based on Lord Atkin's 'neighbour test' in *Donoghue v Stevenson* [1932] AC 562, 580, HL, and that the existence of this tort duty leaves no room 'for a concurrent general equitable duty of care'. She concludes that:

> . . . a wide, non-fiduciary, equitable duty—whatever its historical possibilities—can have no place where its only sensible description is that it must serve the same policy ends, demand the same standards of care, and impose the same measure of liability as the tort duty (whatever adjustments this might require to the remedy of equitable compensation) . . . [A] director's general duty of care must now be seen exclusively as a common law duty.

(iv) Fiduciary loyalties of fidelity and loyalty

3.76 Lord Millett has written extra-judicially that fiduciaries (including directors) must account for unauthorized profits not because they commit a wrong when they receive these profits, but because they are subject to a prophylactic equitable rule that disables them from receiving the profits for themselves: 'Book Review' (2002) 2 OUCLJ 291, 295. This view finds support in important authorities, eg *Furs Ltd v Tomkies* (1936) 54 CLR 583 (HCA) 592; *Scott v Scott* (1963) 109 CLR 649 (HCA); *Regal (Hastings) Ltd v Gulliver* [1967] 2 AC 134 (HL) 144. To the extent that it is correct, the discussion in the Main Work of a director's liability to account for unauthorized profits should appear under the heading 'Disabilities'. However, matters are complicated by the fact that in *Gwembe Valley Development Co Ltd* v *Koshy* [2003] EWCA Civ 1478, esp [43]–[45], [104], and [118], the CA has now held that *over and above* the rule identified by Lord Millett, a fiduciary is also subject to a second rule, which states that he must disgorge any profits that he makes when he commits the wrong of dishonestly breaching his fiduciary duty. Support for the existence of this rule can also be found in the case law: eg *New Zealand Netherlands Society 'Oranje' Inc* v *Kuys* [1973] 1 WLR 1126 (PC) 1129; *United PanEurope Communications NV* v *Deutsche Bank AG* [2000] EWCA Civ 166 [44]; *Walsh* v *Deloitte & Touche Inc* [2001] UKPC 58 [13]. The fiduciary's duty was formulated by Mason J, in *Hospital Products Ltd* v *United States Surgical Corp* (1984) 156 CLR 41 (HCA) 103, as 'an obligation not to promote his personal interest by making or pursuing a gain in circumstances in which there is a conflict or a real or substantial possibility of a conflict between his personal interests and those of the persons whom he is found to prefer'.

The decision in the *Gwembe* case raises some difficult questions. It is unclear what purpose is served by having two bases for liability when the first appears to encompass the second entirely. Moreover, it is unclear what different consequences can follow from analysing the fiduciary's liability to account as a primary duty or as a secondary, wrong-based obligation. The availability of equitable compensation as a remedy for dishonest breaches of fiduciary duty is one consequence, and indeed it is arguable that this remedy has only recently emerged because lawyers had formerly conceived of the relationship of trust and confidence in terms of disabling rules rather than duties. In the *Gwembe* case itself, which concerned a limitations point, the Court of Appeal drew back from following the distinction between the two bases of liability through to its logical conclusion. Perhaps in time the measure of disgorgement in a case of dishonesty will prove to be more generous than the measure awarded in cases involving less egregious misconduct.

n219: in *Plus Group Ltd v Pyke* [2002] EWCA Civ 370, [2002] 2 BCLC 201, the court narrowed the application of the *Mashonaland* rule to situations where a director of two competing companies has so nominal a connection with one of them that he is able to avoid conflicts of interest.

(v) Disabilities

n221: a director's duty to act in the best interests of the company, in contrast to the rule which disables a director from acting for an improper purpose, is assessed subjectively: ie it is breached only if the director does not himself honestly believe that his actions are in the company's best interests, regardless of whether anyone else might have formed a different opinion: see eg *Regentcrest plc (in liq) v Cohen* [2001] 2 BCLC 80. **3.77**

n223: Grantham's analysis is consistent with Lord Cooke's statement in *Equitable Life Assurance Soc v Hyman* [2002] 1 AC 408, 460 that the *Ampol Petroleum* case (see Main Work n222), concerned 'the principle that no legal discretion . . . can be exercised for purposes contrary to those of the instrument by which it is conferred'.

(f) The extent of the members' liability for the company's debts

The price for limited liability is disclosure: limited liability companies must file accounts and place other information about themselves on the public record, requirements from which unlimited companies are exempt. To put this the other way around, 'the advantage of secrecy can be obtained at the price of losing limited liability': *R v Crown Court at Warrington, ex p RPNB* [2001] 1 WLR 2239, 2248, CA (Otton LJ). **3.83**

(4) Building Societies

(a) Historical background

The costs of converting a building society into a registered company are capital expenditure for trade purposes, and are therefore deductible when computing the profits made by the new company for the purposes of assessing its corporation tax liability: *Halifax plc v Davidson (Inspector of Taxes)* [2000] STC (SCD) 251, Commissioners for the Special Purposes of the Income Tax Acts. **3.89**

(5) Industrial and Provident Societies

3.93–3.94 The discussion in the Main Work has been superseded by the enactment of the Co-operatives and Community Benefit Societies Act 2003. To understand the terminology used by this statute it must be appreciated that in practice two types of industrial and providential society have been registered under the Industrial and Provident Societies Act 1965: 'cooperatives' and 'community benefit societies'. Co-operatives are run by their members, for their members; community benefit societies are enterprises which also benefit the wider community (eg retail societies, agricultural societies, housing associations, and working men's clubs).

In relation to the latter it was felt that outside funders were deterred from providing them with funding by the fact that they could convert themselves into registered companies and then use the money in any way that they wished. Section 1 of the 2003 Act meets this concern by enabling the Treasury to bring forward secondary legislation under which the members of a community benefit society are permitted to vote for an 'asset lock-in regime'—ie to prohibit irrevocably the distribution of assets other than for the benefit of the community, or the conversion of the society to a registered company, or the transfer of its assets to another body that does not also have an asset lock-in regime.

In relation to both types of society, the problems created for a third party who enters an ultra vires transaction with an industrial and provident society are now met by ss 3 and 4 of the 2003 Act, which insert new sections into the 1965 Act which essentially mirror the Companies Act 1985, ss 35, 35A, 35B and 36C.

(6) European Economic Interest Groupings

3.95 On 20 December 2000, the European Union's Council of Ministers finally reached political agreement on a proposal first mooted in 1959, to introduce a further type of European corporation, the European Company, also known as the '*Societas Europaea*' or 'SE' (for historical background, see V Edwards, *EC Company Law* (1999) 399–404). In September 2001 the European Parliament gave its opinion on the two amended texts of the European Company Statute agreed to by the Council of Ministers, and on 8 October 2001 the Council of Ministers formally adopted the Regulation to establish a European Company Statute. This legislation is due to enter into force in October 2004. Its purpose is to give corporate groups operating in more than one EU member state the opportunity to establish themselves as a single corporate body governed by EC law, and the freedom to operate throughout the EU with a single set of rules and a unified management and reporting system, without having to comply with all the different national laws of each member state where its subsidiaries carry on business. Under the European Company Statute, a European Company can be set up by the creation of a holding company or a joint subsidiary or by the merger of companies located in at least two member states or by the conversion of an existing company set up under national law. It will have legal personality and its capital will be divided into shares. In October 2003 the DTI published a consultation document, *Implementation of the European Company Statute: The European Public Limited-Liability Company Regulations 2004*. This is available online at: www.dti.gov.uk/cld/ecs-consultation-document.doc.

C. Quasi-Corporations

(1) *Trade Unions*

(b) How trade unions act

In *National Union of Rail, Maritime and Transport Workers v London Underground Ltd* [2001] ICR 647, CA, Robert Walker LJ had to determine whether a trade union had disclosed all the membership information in its 'possession' to an employer in accordance with the Trade Union and Labour Relations Consolidation Act 1992, ss 226A and 234A. At 662–3, he reasoned by way of analogy with *Meridian Global Funds Management Asia Ltd v Securities Commission* [1995] AC 500, PC, that 'information was possessed by the defendant union if it was possessed by any official of the union who in accordance with the union's rules and normal operating procedures, was concerned with maintaining records kept for the union's purposes', but unless the case was an 'exceptional' one, he would not go further 'so as to bring within the information possessed by the union information known only to members' representatives, who are not only unpaid but are also . . . not formally elected'. Robert Walker LJ's invocation of the *Meridian* case in this context suggests that the 'special rules' of attribution outlined there by Lord Hoffmann may be pressed into service in future cases to fix trade unions with the knowledge of particular individuals and/or responsibility for their actions, but it is unclear when these rules should be preferred to the ordinary ('primary') rules of agency law (cf the discussion in Main Work paras 3.62–3.64). **3.100–3.102**

(3) *Limited Liability Partnerships*

The Limited Liability Partnerships Act 2000, the Limited Liability Partnerships Regulations 2001, SI 2001/1090, and the Limited Liability Partnerships (Fees) (No 2) Regulations, SI 2001/969, were all brought into force on 6 July 2001. Collectively, these provide that firms of partners can register as LLPs with Companies House and that the effect of their doing so is to bring a new legal entity into being which is separate and distinct from the partners individually or collectively. As anticipated, ss 1(5) and 5(1) of the 2000 Act provide that the principles of partnership law do not generally apply to LLPs. To the extent that the relationships between the members inter se, and between the members and the **3.107–3.108**

LLP, are not governed by the Act, they are governed either by agreements between the parties or, in the absence of such agreements, by the default provisions contained in the LLP Regulations 2001, reg 7. Also as anticipated, s 6 of the 2000 Act provides that an LLP is not bound by the unauthorized actions of a member dealing with a third party who knows of the member's lack of authority, or does not know or believe that he is a member. For a sceptical critique of this legislation, see V Finch and J Freedman 'The Limited Liability Partnership: Pick and Mix or Mix-Up?' [2002] JBL 475.

D. Unincorporated Bodies

(1) Partnerships and Limited Partnerships

(b) How partnerships are conceptualized

3.113 In 2000 the English and Scottish Law Commissions released a joint consultation paper, *Partnership Law* (LCCP 159, 2000; SLCDP No 111, 2000) in which they made many useful proposals to tidy up the law of partnership. Following a consultation exercise, they have now published a joint report, recommending legislation to implement most of these proposals: *Partnership Law* (Law Com No 283, 2003; Scot Law Com No 192, 2003). In Part V of the Report it is recommended that legislation be enacted to invest partnerships with legal personality, distinct from the personalities of their members; but at the same time partnerships are not to be treated as bodies corporate, as the Commissioners 'do not wish to import the often-antiquated rules of the common law of [chartered and statutory] corporations into partnership law' (para 5.38). Hence the legal entity created by this legislation would be sui generis, its characteristics to be determined by the terms of the partnership contract, and by the Commissioners' draft Partnerships Bill and the rules of common law and equity, to the extent that these are not excluded by the partners' contract (para 5.39). In the event that this proposed legislation is enacted, it seems to follow that partnerships would then belong under the heading 'Quasi-Corporations' in the classificatory scheme adopted in this chapter. In the Law Commissioners' view, the primary advantage of treating partnerships in this way would be that the legal framework within which partners operate would then enable them to enjoy business continuity notwithstanding changes to the membership of their firm, without having to make special contractual arrangements to secure this.

The Commissioners' Draft Bill provides that although the firm would be primarily liable for business debts contracted by the partners, individual partners would also owe an unlimited liability for the firm's debts (cl 23(1)). Curiously, it also provides that a partnership would have 'unlimited capacity' as a legal person (cl 7) but would lack the capacity to commit a criminal offence (cl 8), and that the firm would be a legal person (cl 1(3)) but that the firm's business would be carried on by the partners rather than the firm itself (cl 6).

n327: in their Consultation Paper on partnership law (see previous annotation) the English and Scottish Law Commissioners proposed the total abolition of the 20-member limit, and the government implemented this proposal in December 2002: Regulatory Reform (Removal of 20 Member Limit in Partnerships, etc) Order 2002 (SI 2002/3203).

When preparing their joint report on partnership law (see annotation to previous para), the Law Commissioners' original intention was for limited partnerships to acquire entity status under their proposed new legislation in just the same way as general partnerships. However, fears were then expressed that this might create difficulties for participants in the venture capital market who currently use the limited partnership form as a vehicle for European investment into the UK equities market. The Inland Revenue has agreed that treating limited partnerships as legal entities would not affect their tax status under UK law, but it was feared that this might still have adverse tax consequences overseas. Hence, the Commissioners have fallen back on the messy expedient of allowing those who use the limited partnership form to opt whether to acquire legal personality for their limited partnership or not: they propose that there should henceforth be 'limited partnerships' with legal personality and 'special limited partnerships' without it (Part XIX, and Draft Bill, cl 73 and Sch 10). **3.112**

n332: cf *Phillips v Symes* [2002] 1 WLR 853, 868 (Hart J): there is:

> . . . no basis in English law for distinguishing a partnership which is 'formally constituted' from one which is not. Subject to the qualifications made by statute and established by the case law, partnership is in English law simply 'the relation which subsists between persons carrying on a business in common with a view to profit': see section 1(1) of the Partnership Act 1890.

(2) Unincorporated Associations

(a) How unincorporated assocations are conceptualized

n342: see now also *Eastbourne Town Radio Cars Assoc v Customs and Excise Commissioners* [2001] 1 WLR 794, 802, HL (Lord Hoffmann). **3.115**

n346: but cf two sets of judicial dicta on the subject of changing an association's purposes that were quoted with approval in *Bank of New Zealand v Board of Management of the Bank of New Zealand Officers' Provident Association* [2003] UKPC 58 [19]–[20] (Lord Walker), [2004] 1 NZLR 577. According to Fisher J in *Waitakere City Council v Waitemata Electricity Shareholders Society Inc* [1996] 2 NZLR 735, 743:

> . . . the power to amend is not unlimited. A well-recognised limitation is that a society cannot amend its rules in a way which would conflict with its own fundamental objects . . . But for this purpose a wide scope is normally given to a society's fundamental objects . . . The matter is essentially one of contractual intent. A person joining a society must foresee rule changes in general but not those which would conflict with the very point of having the society in the first place. To find the point of the society its constitutional statement of principal objects is the first port of call.

And according to Millett J in *Re Courage Group's Pension Schemes, Ryan v Imperial Brewing and Leisure* [1987] 1 WLR 495, 506:

> . . . in the case of an institution of long duration and gradually changing membership like a club or pension scheme, each alteration in the rules must be tested by reference to the situation at the time of the proposed alteration, and not by reference to the original rules at its inception. By changes made gradually over a long period, alterations may be made which would not be acceptable if introduced all at once. Even the main purpose may be changed by degrees . . . So the main purpose of a club or pension scheme may be enlarged by appropriate amendments to the rules; and once it becomes too late to challenge the amendments, the enlarged purposes become the new basis by reference to which any further proposed changes must be considered.

(b) Members' liability

3.118 **n361**: see now also *Kearns v General Council of the Bar* [2003] EWCA Civ 331, [2003] 2 All ER 534, [3]–[4] (Simon Brown LJ).

It is incorrectly implied in the Main Work text to n362 that an unincorporated association of people who wish to employ others must create a management committee to act as employer. In fact, 'as between the association and its employees, the employer may be a nominated person, the committee, or the body of members as a whole': *Eastbourne Town Radio Cars Assoc v Customs and Excise Commissioners* [2001] 1 WLR 794, 803, HL (Lord Hoffmann). For discussion of the difficulties that may confront a claimant who wishes to sue an unincorporated association for breach of an employment contract, see *Ermogenous v Greek Orthodox Community of SA Inc* [2002] HCA 8, (2002) 187 ALR 92, [32]–[35], considering *President of the Methodist Conference v Parfitt* [1984] QB 368 (CA), *Davies v Presbyterian Church of Wales* [1986] 1 WLR 323 (HL), and *Diocese of Southwark v Coker* [1998] ICR 140 (CA).

4

PROPERTY: GENERAL PRINCIPLES

B. Property Rights in Land

(5) Leases

(b) Substantive requirements of a lease

(ii) The requirements

4.92–4.108 The text in the Main Work talks of three substantive requirements of a lease: exclusive possession; for a term; at a rent. The question recently arose whether there is in fact a fourth: a capable grantor. In *Bruton v Quadrant Housing Trust* [2000] 1 AC 406, HL, a person with a freehold title to a block of flats granted the defendant charity, whose aim was to find housing for the homeless, a temporary licence of the block. The defendants in turn granted what they thought was a licence to various homeless people. But despite its label, the second licence was held to have all the substantive requirements of a lease. An argument that it could still not amount to a lease because the grantor had no estate in the land out of which it could be carved was rightly rejected by the House of Lords.

(d) Relief against forfeiture

(iii) Exercise of the judicial discretion to relieve

4.130–4.134 To the list of persons able to apply for relief against forfeiture of a lease should now be added holders of statutory charging orders: *Bland v Ingrams Estate Ltd* [2001] Ch 767, CA.

(7) Profits à Prendre

4.154 For a recent case confirming the position adopted in the text that *profits à prendre* may exist in gross, see the decision of the House of Lords in *Bettison v Langton* [2002] 1 AC 27, HL.

(9) Restrictive Covenants

4.162 For a recent, restrictive, interpretation of s 79 of the Law of Property Act 1925 (text in Main Work n217), see *Morrells of Oxford Ltd v Oxford United FC* [2001] Ch 459, CA.

(11) Options to Purchase

4.167 The text in the Main Work adopts the position taken by the Court of Appeal in *Pritchard v Briggs* [1980] Ch 338 that a right of pre-emption over land is not a property right. In *Dear v Reeves* [2001] EWCA Civ 277, the Court of Appeal held that such a right was a property right, at least for the purposes of s 436 of the Insolvency Act 1986. It should, however, be noted that the Insolvency Act 1986 adopts an extraordinarily wide definition of the word 'property' (the provision is set out in Main Work para 4.217 n306). But outside the context of that Act, the Court of Appeal in the *Dear* case also threw doubt on the correctness of *Pritchard v Briggs*. For registered land, however, the position is now governed by the Land Registration Act 2002, which provides in s 115 that 'a right of pre-emption . . . has effect from the time of creation as an interest capable of binding successors in title . . .'.

(14) Licences: A Doubtful Case

(d) The present state of play

The argument made in the Main Work is that a licence to occupy land should not be included in the list of property rights over land. It notes, however, (para 4.185) that where the licence arises by 'estoppel', many think the right has proprietary status, even if it does not when arising by some different manner. The text attacks such thinking as nonsensical. However, it seems that the legislature has adopted just such an approach for, in relation to registered land, s 116 of the Land Registration Act 2002 now provides that 'an equity by estoppel . . . has effect from the time the equity arises as an interest capable of binding successors in title . . .'. **4.184–4.185**

D. Interests Held Under a Trust

(6) Substantive Requirements of Trusts

Presumed intention. The text argues that the effect of s 60(3) of the Law of Property Act 1925 was not to have abolished the presumption that a trust was declared where land is conveyed gratuitously to someone not the wife or child of a male transferor. This argument was rejected, obiter, in *Lohia v Lohia* [2001] WTLR 101, and the point was not dealt with on appeal: [2001] EWCA 1691. **4.292**

(8) The Duties of Trustees

The section dealing with the duties of trustees needs fleshing out with the provisions of the Trustee Act 2000, which concern the powers of trustees. The first major topic dealt with in the Act is the range of investments which trustees are empowered to make. In the past, these were dictated by the terms of the trust instrument and, in default, by the Trustee Act 1961. The Trustee Act 2000 now gives trustees generally the wide powers of investment commonly contained in a well-drafted modern trust. The second topic is delegation. The restrictive power of trustees to delegate their functions conferred by the Trustee Act 1925 has been considerably widened by the 2000 Act. And finally, the Act makes new and more generous provision for payment of trustees. **4.309–4.325**

Something which also needs adding is a discussion of the beneficiary's rights to see the trust documents. An important discussion of the basis of the trustee's duty to provide sight of the trust documents is now contained in the decision of the Privy Council in *Schmidt v Rosewood Trust Ltd* [2003] 3 All ER 76.

E. Co-Ownership

(7) Statutory Reforms of Co-owned Land: 1996

4.374 The text in the Main Work talks of s 12 of the Trusts of Land and Appointment of Trustees Act 1996 giving beneficiaries of trusts of land a right to occupy that land in certain circumstances. Where two or more beneficiaries have rights of occupation, then s 13 of the same Act allows trustees to exclude one or more beneficiaries from occupation. The Court of Appeal recently took the view that this section empowered the court to order a partition (physical division) of the land and to make it a condition of such partition that a beneficiary contribute to the cost: *Rodway v Landy* [2001] EWCA Civ 471, [2001] Ch 703, CA.

(8) Disputes Over Co-Owned Land

4.375 The text in the Main Work notes that disputes between co-owners of land are governed by a statutory regime (Trusts of Land and Appointment of Trustees Act 1996, s 14) but that at the time of writing there was little guidance as to how that provision would be interpreted. There was some speculation that the section simply codified the existing law, but that has since been rejected by Neuberger J in *Mortgage Corp v Shaire* [2001] Ch 743, who attached particular significance to the fact that the trust was no longer a trust *to sell*, which meant that pre-1996 cases had to be treated with caution.

F. Acquisition of Property Rights

(1) Consent

(a) Gifts

Acting on the intent: the law's requirements

4.385 *Real property.* The text speaks of the Land Registration Act 1925. This, and subsequent Acts of 1936, 1986, and 1997, have all been abolished and a new statute, the Land Registration Act 2002, enacted. Details of the operation of this statute can be found in R Smith, *Property Law* (4th edn, 2003) 218–75. This reference replaces that in n491 of the Main Work. More detail on the operation of the system of land registration will be contained in the next edition of the Main Work.

(ii) Transfer to trustees on trust

4.399 For a case which the Privy Council said fell halfway between the two methods of creating a trust outlined in *Milroy v Lord* (see Main Work para 4.402), see *Choithram Int v Pagarani* [2001] 1 WLR 1, PC. It must be asked, however, whether the decision in the case really is (as Lord Browne-Wilkinson claimed) consistent with Turner LJ's comments in *Milroy v Lord*.

(iv) Imperfect gifts

The correctness of the rule in *Re Rose* (which the Main Work argues to be wrong) was assumed in *Choithram Int v Pagarani* [2001] 1 WLR 1, PC, 11, while in *Pennington v Waine* [2002] 4 All ER 215, the Court of Appeal assumes that the basis of the rule in *Re Rose* is 'unconscionable behaviour' on the part of the donor. In doing so, they expand the rule to cover cases where the donor has not done all in his or her power to perfect the gift. The case comes dangerously close to an outright contradiction of *Milroy v Lord* (1862) 4 De GF & J 264. **4.406–4.408**

(2) Wrongs

In the section on wrongs might possibly come the case of *Car & Universal Finance Ltd v Caldwell* [1965] 1 QB 525, where the tort of deceit may have given rise to a common law power to revest title in fraudulently obtained goods. **4.423**

(d) Breach of fiduciary duty

The text in the Main Work notes that there are differing views as to whether the wrong of breach of fiduciary duty should generate proprietary restitutionary rights, as opposed to merely personal restitutionary rights. A recent decision of the Court of Appeal could possibly be seen as authority for the proposition that property rights can be awarded by courts as a response to this particular wrong: *Collings v Lee* [2001] 2 All ER 332, CA. It is not, however, clear whether the case is an example of restitution for wrongs or restitution of unjust enrichment. **4.428–4.438**

(3) Unjust Enrichment

The text in the Main Work notes that there are differing views as to whether the defendant's unjust enrichment should ever generate proprietary restitutionary rights, as opposed to merely personal restitutionary rights. A recent decision of the Court of Appeal could possibly be seen as authority for the proposition that property rights can be awarded by courts as a response to unjust enrichment: *Collings v Lee* [2001] 2 All ER 332, CA. It is not, however, clear whether the case is an example of restitution of unjust enrichment or restitution for wrongs. **4.439–4.444**

More generally, the section should probably also include cases where a power is given, either at law or in equity, to revest title, eg, in cases of misrepresentation, which arguably arise in response to unjust enrichment.

(4) Miscellaneous Other Events

(b) Taking possession

The leading authority on the acquisition of title to land by an act of possession **4.458** must now be the decision of the House of Lords in *JA Pye (Oxford) Ltd v Graham* [2002] UKHL 30, [2003] 1 AC 419. The case is discussed below, in the section on loss of title by lapse of time.

(g) Mixtures

4.470 For a useful and detailed discussion of the proprietary effect of a mixture of oil, see the decision of Moore-Bick J in *Glencore International AG v Metro Trading International Inc* [2001] 1 Lloyd's Rep 284. Consistent with the position adopted in the Main Work, his Lordship takes the view that a wrongdoing mixer, despite the wrongfulness of his conduct, acquires a proportionate share in the resultant mixture.

G. Property for Purposes

(1) Public Purposes

(a) Definition of charity

4.486 For governmental discussions on the proper scope of charity, see the reports by the Cabinet Office Strategy Unit, 'Private Action, Public Benefit: A Review of Charities and the Wider Not-For-Profit Sector' (2002) chs 3 and 4, available at www.number-10.gov.uk/su/voluntary/report/index.htm and that by the Home Office, 'Charities and Not-for-Profits: A Modern Legal Framework: The Government's Response to "Private Action, Public Benefit" ' (2003), paras 3.1–3.28, 3.35–3.38, available at www.homeoffice.gov.uk/docs2/charitiesnotforprofits.pdf

(c) Other purposes beneficial to the community

4.496 For a recent affirmation of the principle that 'general welfare' trusts are not charitable, see the decision of the Privy Council in *A-G of the Cayman Islands v Even Wahr-Hansen* [2001] 1 AC 75, PC.

(2) Private Purposes

(c) Exceptions

(iii) Execution of the purpose enures to the benefit of indentifable persons

4.537 In discussing the rule that trusts for private purposes are void, the text in the Main Work notices that a private purpose trust seems to have been enforced in *Barclays Bank Ltd v Quistclose Ltd* [1970] AC 567. The decision in that case was recently upheld by the House of Lords in *Twinsectra Ltd v Yardley* [2002] 2 AC 164, though the speech of Lord Millett does not utilize a purpose trust at all.

H. Loss of Property Rights

(2) Lapse of Time

(a) **Common law**

(i) Real property

An argument that the statutory scheme under the Limitation Act 1980, whereby property rights are extinguished where they have been slept on for long periods, was contrary to the Human Rights Act 1998 was rejected by the Court of Appeal in *JA Pye (Oxford) Ltd v Graham* [2001] EWCA Civ 117, [2001] Ch 804, CA. On appeal to the House of Lords ([2002] UKHL 30, [2003] 1 AC 419), it was conceded that the 1998 Act did not have retrospective effect, and the point was accordingly not pursued. More importantly, however, Lord Browne-Wilkinson's judgment is set to become the *locus classicus* of this area of the law. In it, he rightfully says that for the purposes of the extinction of title by the Limitation Act 1980, there is no need to show that the possessor's title is in any sense 'adverse' to that of the person dispossessed. **4.557**

A further point to note is that the scope for the extinction of title through lapse of time where that title is registered has been drastically reduced by the operation of the Land Registration Act 2002. This statute will be discussed in detail in the forthcoming edition of the Main Work.

5

SECURITY

A. Real Security Over Land

(1) Types of Security

(a) Legal mortgages

n11: for Land Registration Act 1925, s 27, see now Land Registration Act 2002, ss 23(1), 51. All legal charges of registered land now take effect as charges by way of legal mortgage. **5.05**

n15: for Land Registration Act 1925, s 27(1), see now Land Registration Act 2002, ss 23(1), 51. All legal charges of registered land now take effect as charges by way of legal mortgage.

(b) Equitable mortgages

n22: the Land Registration Act 2002 makes no mention of the creation of a lien by deposit of a certificate. This is primarily because (as discussed in the Main Work) since 1989 any advantages, in terms of convenience, of this kind of mortgage have been lost. It is also true that the Land Registration Act 2002 paves the **5.09**

way for electronic conveyancing and hence a much reduced role for documentary evidence of land titles. Charge certificates have been abolished and land certificates are merely evidence of the state of the register.

5.10 **n33**: on the scope of the charge arising under the Legal Aid Act 1988 where there has been a settlement, see *Morgan v Legal Aid Board* [2000] 1 WLR 1657.

(2) Creation

(a) **Formalities for creation**

5.11 It is no longer the case that a deed is required to create a legal charge on registered land. Under the new system, registration is not merely the recording of an interest created otherwise, but amounts to the creation of the charge: Land Registration Act 2002, s 27. This paves the way for fully electronic transactions. By s 91(5), an electronic document has the same effect as if it were a deed, and by s 51, a registered charge has the same effect as if made by deed. The references to deeds are required to activate the mortgagee's powers under LPA 1925, s 101, including the power of sale (see Main Work paras 5.38ff).

(c) **Registration**

5.14 The system of registered land has been fundamentally changed by the Land Registration Act 2002, which came into force on 13 October 2003. The powers of a registered proprietor are set out in s 23. The only kind of legal mortgage allowed is a charge by way of legal mortgage (s 51). A person holding a legal charge over land has the power to create a sub-charge. It is no longer generally true that if a legal mortgage is created but not registered, it takes effect only in equity. Under the new system, registration is not merely the recording of an interest created otherwise, but amounts to the creation of the charge (s 27). The terminology of 'minor interest' has been dropped.

It remains possible to create voluntarily a mortgage which is only equitable (s 23(1)(a)) but this is not of practical importance for the reasons discussed in the Main Work para 5.09 and Supplement para 5.09. It is also possible for a person to hold an equitable mortgage in registered land, where the mortgage arises by operation of law (see Main Work para 5.10). The system for the protection of interests which are not registrable has also been changed. Cautions are prospectively abolished. What remain are notices (ss 32–39) and restrictions (ss 40–47). Notices may be unilateral, which makes them similar to cautions under the Land Registration Act 1925 (cf Main Work n51). As under the previous legislation, a notice under the new Act does not mean that the interest noted has any validity; but, if it is valid, the notice will preserve the priority of the interest noted, in the face of subsequent dispositions (s 32).

n54: the Land Registration Act 2002 widens the triggers for compulsory registration of land (s 4), and empowers the making of rules which would further widen compulsory registration (s 5). It also widens the range of interests which may be registered (s 3). The goal is to bring more land and more interests in land into the registered land system. **5.15**

(3) Protection of the Mortgagor

(c) **Other doctrines**

(iii) Legislative intervention

In *Rahman v Sterling Credit Ltd* [2001] 1 WLR 496, CA, it was held that the limitation period for a claim under the Consumer Credit Act 1974, s 139, is 12 years. It was also held that such a claim could be made by the mortgagor even after a possession order had been granted to the mortgagee. **5.26**

In *Paragon Finance plc v Staunton* [2001] EWCA Civ 1466, [2002] 1 WLR 685, CA, the mortgage had a floating rate of interest. The mortgagors did not argue that the agreements were, at the outset, extortionate, but they argued that the failure of the mortgagees to lower the rates, as interest rates fell in the general lending market, made the agreements extortionate. The court agreed that the mortgagee's power to vary interest rates was not totally unfettered, but rejected the claim that the agreements had become extortionate.

As to the regulation by the Financial Services Authority of mortgage lending, see now the Financial Services and Markets Act 2000, ss 19, 22(1), and Sch 2, paras 1, 2(1), 10, 23. Contrary to the suggestion reported in the Main Work, it appears that the regulation extends to mortgage brokers and to mortgage advisers; see the Financial Services and Markets Act 2000 (Regulated Activities) Order 2001 (SI 2001/544). Note that article 90 of this order reduced overlap with the Consumer Credit Act 1974 by adding to that Act s 16(6C).

n97: on the requirements as to form imposed by the Consumer Credit Act 1974, see the discussion of *Wilson v First County Trust Ltd (No 2)* [2003] UKHL 40, [2003] 4 All ER 97, HL, in Supplement paras 5.56 and 8.75.

The Main Work suggests that interest rates may not be subject to scrutiny under the Unfair Terms in Consumer Contracts Regulations 1999. In *Director General of Fair Trading v First National Bank plc* [2001] UKHL 52, [2002] 1 AC 481, HL, decided under the earlier 1994 regulations (SI 1994/3159), it was argued on a similar basis that there could be no scrutiny of a term which provided that if the creditor obtained a judgment against the debtor, interest should be payable at the contractual rate until the judgment was fully paid. The argument was rejected and the term was assessed, although it was held to be valid. **5.27**

5.28 In *Paragon Finance plc v Staunton* [2001] EWCA Civ 1466, [2002] 1 WLR 685, CA, the mortgage had a floating rate of interest. The mortgagors argued that the failure of the mortgagees to lower the rates, as interest rates fell in the general lending market, was a violation of s 3(2)(b) of the Unfair Contract Terms Act 1977, which limits the ability of a party to be excused from performance of its obligations. The court rejected this argument on the basis that the setting of interest rates by the creditor is not a performance by the creditor.

(4) Enforcement

5.29 The distinctness of the personal obligation to repay was underlined in *Alliance and Leicester plc v Slayford* (CA, 12 October 2000), noted MP Thompson [2002] Conv 53. Even if the mortgage as such is unenforceable, the personal claim may lead to bankruptcy proceedings.

The limitation period on the personal obligation is 12 years (Limitation Act 1980, s 20), whether or not the mortgagee has exercised a power of sale over the mortgaged property; it is not the case that a new personal claim to the shortfall arises (with a new limitation period) when the property is sold: *Bristol & West plc v Bartlett* [2002] EWCA Civ 1181, [2002] 4 All ER 544, CA.

(a) Possession

5.31 **n111**: *Ropaigealach v Barclays Bank plc* [1998] EWCA Civ 1960, [2000] 1 QB 263, CA.

5.34 Under the Administration of Justice Act 1970, s 39(1), 'dwelling house' is defined as property 'used' for a dwelling. In *Royal Bank of Scotland v Miller* [2001] EWCA Civ 344, [2002] QB 255, CA, the mortgaged premises included a residential flat; at the time of the granting of the mortgage, this was unoccupied, but at the time that the mortgagee sought possession, it was alleged to be occupied, albeit by someone other than the mortgagor, which would be a breach of a term of the mortgage contract. Nonetheless, it was held that if it was established that the flat was occupied at the time possession was sought, s 36 would apply.

5.35 **n123**: *Governor and Company of the Bank of Scotland v Grimes* [1985] QB 1179, CA, was followed on this point in *Royal Bank of Scotland v Miller* [2001] EWCA Civ 344, [2002] QB 255, CA.

n125: *Ropaigealach v Barclays Bank plc* [1998] EWCA Civ 1960, [2000] 1 QB 263, CA.

(b) Sale

(i) Statutory power of sale

5.38 **n132**: the holder of a registered charge under the Land Registration Act 2002 will have the powers granted by LPA 1925, s 101, even if the charge is created electronically. By Land Registration Act 2002, s 91(5), an electronic document has the same effect as if it were a deed, and by s 51, a registered charge has the same effects as if made by deed.

The mortgagor has no cause for complaint if the first mortgagee pays itself less than it is owed and pays the balance to a subsequent mortgagee, even if the mortgagor takes the view that its position would have been better if the first mortgagee had paid itself all of what it was owed: *Raja v Lloyds TSB Bank plc* [2001] 19 EG 143, leave to appeal this point denied [2001] EWCA Civ 210, CA. **5.40**

n135: in *Corbett v Halifax plc* [2002] EWCA Civ 1849, [2003] 1 WLR 964, CA, the court confirmed that a purchaser who has notice of some impropriety in the mortgagee's exercise of the power of sale is not protected by s 104(2); on the other hand, the fact of sale at an undervalue is not enough to have the sale set aside. In the *Corbett* case, the property was purchased by an employee of the mortgagee, which was against the mortgagee's rules, but the mortgagee was not aware at the time of sale; it was held that this did not allow the mortgagor to have the sale avoided.

The Land Registration Act 2002 has changed the rule regarding the validity of dispositions, in relation to registered land. By its s 52, it makes clear that a purchaser's interest can be affected only by an interest which is registered or protected on the register. In any other case, the mortgagor's only remedy is against the mortgagee (unless perhaps the purchaser has committed an independently wrongful act, such as conspiracy or dishonest assistance in a breach of trust). This was specifically intended to ensure that the suggestion in *Lord Waring v London & Manchester Assurance Co Ltd* [1935] Ch 310, mentioned in the Main Work n135, would not apply to registered land: *Land Registration for the Twenty-First Century: A Conveyancing Revolution* (Law Com No 271, 2001), para 7.8.

n138: the Land Registration Act 2002, s 54, provides that for the purposes of LPA 1925, s 105, the mortgagee of registered land is taken to have notice of anything in the register immediately prior to the sale. In registered land, it is not generally the case that registration of an interest constitutes notice of it. That principle is overridden here in order to create a requirement that a selling mortgagee search the register for other mortgages before transferring any surplus proceeds to the mortgagor.

If the mortgagee breaches the duty to act reasonably in selling, the loss caused is to be measured by the difference between the sale price actually obtained and the price which would have been obtained had the mortgagee acted reasonably: *Skipton Building Society v Stott* [2001] QB 261, CA. For the effect of a breach on a guarantor providing personal security for the debt, see Supplement para 5.171. **5.41**

In *Adamson v Halifax plc* [2002] EWCA Civ 1134, [2003] 1 WLR 60, CA, the first mortgagee breached its duty by selling for £17,000 a property worth £23,000. There was a second mortgagee and after paying itself out of the proceeds, the first mortgagee accounted to the second mortgage (see Main Work para 5.40) and paid the second mortgagee the surplus amount of £22. The second mortgagee was still owed £5,000. The mortgagor brought proceedings against the first mortgagee but the trial judge awarded her only £1,000, on the basis that if the first mortgagee had acted reasonably and obtained £23,000, it would have accounted for £5,000 of that to the second mortgagee. The mortgagor appealed and before the appeal was heard, the limitation period for any claim by the second mortgagee against the first mortgagee (see Main Work para 5.41) expired. There was still some prospect that the second mortgagee could enforce its claim against the mortgagor. The Court of Appeal held that the mortgagor was entitled to £6,000.

Even though the mortgage itself is given by a deed, the duty to act reasonably in selling is imposed by law. Therefore an action based on the breach of that duty is not an action 'upon a specialty' (see Main Work para 19.101); the limitation period is six years: *Raja v Lloyds TSB Bank plc* [2001] EWCA Civ 210, CA.

(ii) Court-ordered sale

5.42 If property is held on a trust of land (see Main Work para 4.82), and a mortgage has been given by a beneficiary of that trust, and the mortgagee seeks an order for the sale of the land, the matter is governed by the Trusts of Land and Appointment of Trustees Act 1996, ss 14 and 15. Section 15(3) requires the court to have regard to 'the circumstances and wishes of any beneficiaries of full age and entitled to an interest in possession in property subject to the trust'. It was held in *Mortgage Corp v Shaire* [2001] Ch 743 that the 1996 Act changed the law considerably, granting the court a wider discretion than it previously had when considering an application for an order to sell.

(c) Foreclosure

5.43 **n154**: for Land Registration Act 1925, s 34(3), see now Land Registration Act 2002, s 65 and Sch 4; Land Registration Rules 2003, SI 2003/1417, r 112.

(d) Appointment of a receiver

5.45 **n164**: *Medforth v Blake* [2000] Ch 86, CA.

(5) Miscellaneous Features

(a) Leases

5.47 **n173**: there is, however, an exception in the case of agricultural land, to an unauthorized lease not being enforceable against the mortgagee, if the unauthorized lease was granted after 1 March 1948 but before 1 September 1995, and if the other requirements of the LPA 1925, s 99 are satisfied: *National Westminster Bank plc v Jones* [2001] 1 BCLC 98.

(d) Possession of title deeds

n179: compulsory registration has been widened: see now Land Registration Act 2002, ss 4–5. **5.50**

Under the Land Registration Act 2002, there are no charge certificates. The Act contemplates that land certificates will be optional (Sch 10, para 4) and their role will be greatly reduced. As a result, there is no longer any requirement to deposit the land certificate when a charge is registered. These changes pave the way for electronic conveyancing. **5.51**

The Land Registration Act 2002 makes no provision for mortgage by deposit of land certificate. See Supplement paras 5.09 and 5.51. **5.52**

(e) Consolidation

Land Registration Act 2002, s 57, provides that rules may be enacted making provision for consolidation in relation to registered charges. See Land Registration Rules 2003, SI 2003/1417, r 110. **5.53**

(6) Discharge

n189: it is no longer generally true that if a legal mortgage is created but not registered, it takes effect only in equity. Under the Land Registration Act 2002, registration is not merely the recording of an interest created otherwise, but amounts to the creation of the charge (s 27). **5.55**

n191: for Land Registration Act 1925, s 35, see now Land Registration Act 2002, s 65 and Sch 4.

B. Real Security Over Moveables

n194: under the Consumer Credit Act 1974, s 65, an agreement which does not satisfy the formal requirements is unenforceable without a court order; and under s 113, any security given is enforceable only to the extent of such an order; but under s 127(3), the court has no jurisdiction to make such an order unless the debtor signed a document which, even if it was not in the form prescribed by the regulations, contains the contractual terms which the regulations require. In *Wilson v First County Trust Ltd (No 2)* the debtor had borrowed money and given security in the form of a pledge of a car; the agreement did not **5.56**

contain the required terms. The Court of Appeal, [2001] EWCA Civ 633, [2001] 3 WLR 42, CA, made a declaration under the Human Rights Act 1998, s 4(2), that s 127(3) of the 1974 Act was incompatible with Article 6(1) of the European Convention on Human Rights (the right to a fair and public hearing) and with Article 1 of the First Protocol to the Convention (the right to the peaceful enjoyment of one's possessions). The House of Lords reversed this decision, [2003] UKHL 40, [2003] 3 WLR 568, holding that the Convention did not apply to agreements made before its implementation in English law; that, in any event, the scheme of the Consumer Credit Act 1974 was not inconsistent with the Convention; and (here applying *Dimond v Lovell* [2002] 1 AC 384, HL) that where an agreement was rendered unenforceable by a protective statute, the lender could not recover the principal amount in unjust enrichment, because allowing such a claim would be inconsistent with the statutory intention of protecting vulnerable borrowers.

(1) Legal Security

(c) **Legal Ownership as Security**

(ii) Retention of ownership

5.78 n274: *On Demand Information plc v Michael Gerson (Finance) plc* was affirmed by the Court of Appeal [2001] 1 WLR 155, but reversed on further appeal [2003] 1 AC 368, HL. The leased assets had been sold by agreement and the proceeds paid into court, before the application for relief against forfeiture was heard. This meant it was impossible to reconstitute the lease exactly as it had been before the forfeiture. The Court of Appeal held that this was fatal to the claim for relief. The House of Lords, reversing this decision, explained that the economic consequences of relief from forfeiture are not lost merely because specific reconstitution of the lease is impossible, at least not where this was due to a sale of assets under court order. Two other recent cases, although concerning leases of land and not moveables, underline the recognition that the function of relief against forfeiture is to ensure that a lessor's right to forfeit serves only a security function and cannot be used to capture a windfall; the reasoning is parallel to that discussed for mortgages in the Main Work para 5.04. See *Bland v Ingrams Estates Ltd (No 2)* [2002] Ch 177, CA; *Croydon (Unique) Ltd v Wright* [2001] Ch 318, CA. On the whole question, see L Smith, 'Relief Against Forfeiture: A Restatement' (2001) 60 CLJ 178.

(2) Equitable Security

(c) **Equitable charge**

(ii) Arising by consent

5.86 The last sentence of the paragraph in the Main Work, and the case cited to support it, may now be in some doubt following *Agnew v Commissioner of Inland*

Revenue [2001] UKPC 28, [2001] 3 WLR 454, PC, discussed in Supplement para 5.87.

The paragraph in the Main Work must now be read subject to the advice of the Judicial Committee of the Privy Council, on appeal from the Court of Appeal of New Zealand, in *Agnew v Commissioner of Inland Revenue* [2001] UKPC 28, [2001] 3 WLR 454. Although this is technically a decision of a New Zealand court, it has the highest persuasive value in English law (see Main Work para 1.100). Furthermore, even before the *Agnew* case, English law moved in the same direction in *Chalk v Kahn* [2000] 2 BCLC 361 and *Re ASRS Establishment Ltd* [2000] 2 BCLC 631, CA. **5.87**

In the *Agnew* case, *Re New Bullas Trading Ltd* [1994] 1 BCLC 485, [1994] BCC 36, CA, was said to be 'fundamentally mistaken', and as a result the line of authority described in the Main Work n303, is now effectively overruled. The Main Work describes a tension between freedom of contract and respect for the interests of third parties; the advice of the Privy Council comes down in favour of the latter value, and adopts the following approach. In order to decide whether a charge over book debts is fixed or floating, the court must first look at the instrument of charge and gather the intention of the parties. The court does not address whether the parties intended to create a fixed charge or a floating charge, but considers the rights and obligations they have created. Only then does the court go on to decide whether the charge is fixed or floating; this categorization is a matter of law, not freedom of contract. The fundamental test is whether the chargor is permitted to deal freely in the ordinary course of its business with the charged assets; or, in the case of book debts, whether it is permitted to deal freely in the ordinary course of its business with the proceeds of the charged assets, that is, the money collected when the debts are paid. Moreover, it is not enough to have a contractual stipulation that the proceeds are under the control of the chargee; the court will examine how the agreement operated in reality, and only if the chargee exercised factual control over the disposition of the proceeds can the charge be a fixed charge.

n302: in general, whether a charge is fixed or floating depends on whether the chargor is permitted to deal freely in the ordinary course of its business with the charged assets. In the case of book debts, the question is whether the chargor is permitted to deal freely in the ordinary course of its business with the proceeds of the charged assets, that is, the money collected when the debts are paid. This was confirmed in *Agnew v Commissioner of Inland Revenue* [2001] UKPC 28, [2001] 3 WLR 454, PC, and this was said ([45] and [46]) to be justified because a book debt is an asset which cannot be enjoyed *in specie*. The Board also noted (at [30]) that a trader does not hold its stock-in-trade for enjoyment *in specie;* like book debts, it was said, stock-in-trade is part of the trader's circulating capital. If the assimilation between book debts and stock-in-trade is taken to its logical conclusion, then the *Agnew* case implies, contrary to traditional doctrine, that it is possible to have a fixed charge over stock-in-trade, so long as the chargor is not permitted to deal freely in the ordinary course of its business with the proceeds of the stock-in-trade, which would require that the chargee retain factual control over the proceeds. It is, however, fair to say that in respect of both book debts and stock-in-trade, the test laid down in the *Agnew* case may mean that it will be commercially impracticable for creditors to take fixed charges in respect of either of these classes of assets. The requirements of factual control would be unworkable for most businesses. On the other hand, given the advantages of a fixed charge, this development may invite consideration of the US experience with 'field warehousing', in which stock-in-trade is kept physically separated from the trader's other assets, and subjected to control mechanisms under the supervision of an agent of the chargee.

5.89 An interesting point about crystallization was addressed in *National Westminster Bank plc v Jones* [2001] 1 BCLC 98 in relation to a floating agricultural charge under the Agricultural Credits Act 1928. If crystallization is caused by the chargor's ceasing to carry on business through a transfer of all of the business assets to another party, does the transferee acquire the assets before or after crystallization? It is not clear that anything turned on this (especially if one takes the third view of floating charges discussed in the Main Work para 5.88): the disposition was, in any event, out of the chargor's ordinary course of business and so not one which the chargor was at liberty to make, and the transferee was aware of all of the circumstances, so it seems that even if the charge was floating at the time of the transfer, the transferee would take subject to the charge (see Main Work paras 5.108, 5.109, and 5.137). In any event, the judge held that in such a case, the charge should be understood as crystallizing before the transfer, relying in part on *Abbey National Building Society v Cann* [1991] 1 AC 56, HL, discussed in the Main Work para 5.151. See, however, Supplement para 5.151.

n308: this also applies in the case of a floating agricultural charge under the Agricultural Credits Act 1928: *National Westminster Bank plc v Jones* [2001] 1 BCLC 98.

n309: the reference should be to Agricultural Credits Act 1928, s 7(1)(a)(iv).

5.94 The decision in *Agnew v Commissioner of Inland Revenue* [2001] UKPC 28, [2001] 3 WLR 454, PC is discussed in Supplement para 5.87. The Board held that the question whether a charge is fixed or floating is a matter of law, not a matter of choice for the parties. If this philosophy were to be adopted more generally, the facts of *Welsh Development Agency v Export Finance Co Ltd* [1992] BCLC 148, [1992] BCC 270, CA, described in Main Work para 5.94, might well give a different result.

n343: in *Arthur D Little Ltd (in administration) v Ableco Finance LLC* [2003] Ch 217, a Scottish company was in administration and a question arose as to the registrability of a charge held by a creditor over the Scottish company's shares in an English subsidiary. It was held that as a matter of English law, the provisions of the Companies Act 1985 dealing with the registration of charges in Scotland (Part XII, Ch 2) apply in such a case. The court rejected an argument that those provisions had no relevance in an English court. **5.97**

C. Priorities in Real Security

(1) Introduction

n366: when electronic conveyancing is fully implemented under the Land Registration Act 2002, an agreement altering priorities may need to be electronically registered in order to be effective in relation to registered land: Land Registration Act 2002, ss 93(1), (2), (6). For an existing requirement to notify the registrar if the alteration of priorities is to affect third parties, see Land Registration Rules 2003, SI 2003/1417, r 102. **5.103**

(2) General Principles

(b) Authority to grant later interest

n380: seemingly against the view that execution on a debt is a transaction in the ordinary course of business is *Crantrave Ltd v Lloyds Bank plc* [2000] EWCA Civ 127, [2000] QB 917, CA, when read with *Liggett (Liverpool) Ltd v Barclays Bank Ltd* [1928] 1 KB 48, which the CA distinguished. **5.109**

(3) Particular Priority Contests

(a) Registered land

(i) Where the mortgaged estate is legal

n427: for Land Registration Act 1925, s 29, see now Land Registration Act 2002, s 48. The statement in the note regarding 'searches with priority' is now superseded pursuant to Land Registration Act 2002, s 72, and the Land Registration Rules 2003, SI 2003/1417. Under the new system, a notice may be entered on the register in advance of an intended registrable disposition. This attracts a 'priority period' and if the disposition is indeed registered before the end of that period, it will have priority over any interest noted on the register during the period. See Land Registration Rules 2003, SI 2003/1417, rr 147–154. The priority period is generally 30 business days: r 131. **5.125**

Under the Land Registration Act 2002, a legal mortgage does not actually come into existence until registration (s 27). Equitable mortgages may still arise in some **5.126** cases (see Supplement para 5.14). The terminology of 'minor interest' has been dropped.

n430: inhibitions and cautions have been prospectively abolished by the Land Registration Act 2002. The new concept of 'unilateral notice' performs a similar function to a caution (see Supplement para 5.14).

5.127 **n431**: for Land Registration Act 1925, ss 20(1), 23(1), see now Land Registration Act 2002, ss 29–30.

n432: for Land Registration Act 1925, s 27(3), see now Land Registration Act 2002, ss 29–30. Cautions have been prospectively abolished by the Land Registration Act 2002. The new concept of 'unilateral notice' performs a similar function to a caution (see Supplement para 5.14).

Under Land Registration Act 1925, s 70(1)(g), the right of a person in actual occupation of the land was an overriding interest. In *Collings v Lee* [2001] 2 All ER 332, CA, the claimant was tricked by Lee into transferring an estate to him, supposedly as the claimant's agent to sell it. Lee charged the estate to a building society and the claimant, who was always in occupation, sought rectification of the register. The building society argued that while the claimant might have a right to avoid the transfer to Lee, this did not constitute an interest in land which could be protected by s 70(1)(g). It was held that since there was never any intention to transfer the estate to Lee, he held it on trust for the claimant, whose interest was therefore protected by s 70(1)(g).

The concept of overriding interests continues under the Land Registration Act 2002 (ss 29–30; Sch 3) although the number of such interests has been reduced. Persons in actual occupation continue to be protected (Sch 3, para 2). The Act makes it clear (s 116) that a power to avoid a contract and revest an interest in land (a 'mere equity') is, itself, an interest in land, and so too is an 'equity by estoppel'. A person holding such a right or power, and remaining in actual occupation, is therefore protected without notation on the register.

n433: under the Land Registration Act 2002 the basic principle that priority goes to the interest created first in time is now in s 28, and this is subject to the rules in ss 29–30 by which a later interest which is registered can take priority over an earlier one which is not protected by an entry in the register.

n435: the criticisms noted here are now out of date in the light of the sweeping reforms introduced by the Land Registration Act 2002.

(ii) Where the mortgaged estate is equitable

5.128 **n436**: for Land Registration Act 1925, s 2(1), see now Land Registration Act 2002, s 2.

(b) Unregistered land

(i) Where the mortgaged estate is legal

n449: it was held in *Birmingham Midshires Mortgage Services Ltd v Sabherwal* (CA, 17 December 1999), noted C Harpum (2000) 116 LQR 341, that there was nothing in the Trusts of Land and Appointment of Trustees Act 1996 to change the result laid down in the *City of London Building Society* v *Flegg* case; furthermore, any rights a claimant may have arising under the doctrine of proprietary estoppel (see Main Work paras 8.60–8.62) are also overreached if the statutory conditions are met. 5.132

n450: land Registration Act 1925, s 70(1)(g) has been repealed. Under the Land Registration Act 2002, the concept of overriding interests remains operative (ss 29–30; Sch 3) although the number of such interests has been reduced. Persons in actual occupation continue to be protected (Sch 3, para 2). See Supplement para 5.127.

(c) Moveables

(i) Company charges

Companies Act 1985, s 395(1), makes a registrable but unregistered charge 'void against the liquidator or administrator and any creditor of the company'. In *Re Cosslett (Contractors) Ltd* [1998] Ch 495, CA, discussed in the Main Work, the creditor's interest in machinery belonging to Cosslett (Contractors) Ltd was held to be a floating charge and therefore registrable, but it had not been registered. As mentioned in the Main Work, the creditor/chargee's right to make use of the machinery after Cosslett (Contractors) Ltd defaulted and went into administration was held not to be part of the charge, and so this right was not affected by the failure to register. By the time of the hearing in the Court of Appeal, however, the chargee had sold the machinery. The power of sale *was* part of the charge, and since the charge was void, the administrator brought new proceedings in conversion against the chargee. This second round of proceedings was instituted by the administrator in his own name, because the wording of s 395(1) does not say that the unregistered charge is void against the company, but rather against 'the liquidator or administrator'. In *Smith (as Administrator of Cosslett (Contractors) Ltd) v Bridgend County Borough Council* [2001] UKHL 58, [2002] 1 AC 336, it was held that in the case of a liquidation or administration, the wording of s 395(1) did not mean that the liquidator or the administrator must act personally. 'Void against the liquidator or administrator . . . of the company' must be read to mean 'void against the company in liquidation or administration'. The claim succeeded. 5.135

(4) Future Advances

Under the Land Registration Act 2002, there is a fourth way in which A will have 5.146

priority over B in respect of funds advanced by A after the registration of B's security. This is where A's security interest was in respect of a maximum amount of credit, and this maximum amount was noted in the register. A will have priority over B for further advances up to this amount: Land Registration Act 2002, s 49(4).

n492: for Land Registration Act 1925, s 30, see now Land Registration Act 2002, s 49. The possibility that the common law rule governs where A has not even made his initial advance still seems to exist under the new Act.

5.147 **n493**: for Land Registration Act 1925, s 30, see now Land Registration Act 2002, s 49(6), which expressly provides for variation of priorities by agreement. When electronic conveyancing is fully implemented under the Land Registration Act 2002, an agreement altering priorities may need to be electronically registered in order to be effective in relation to registered land: Land Registration Act 2002, ss 93(1), (2), (6). For an existing requirement to notify the registrar if the alteration of priorities is to affect third parties, see Land Registration Rules 2003, SI 2003/1417, r 102.

5.148 As described in the Main Work, the system for giving notice to A under Land Registration Act 1925 depended in theory on a notification by the Registrar. Land Registration Act 1925, ss 30(1)–(2) has now been replaced by Land Registration Act 2002, s 49(1)–(2), in which the responsibility for notification to A is not on the Registrar but on B. This change was intended to replicate the *de facto* practice under the earlier Act: see Law Commission, *Land Registration for the Twenty-First Century: A Conveyancing Revolution* (Law Com No 271, 2001), paras 7.18–7.27, 7.30. Under the old Act, A was entitled to a notice from the Registrar, and to an indemnity from the Registry if A suffered loss because the Registrar's notice failed to reach A before A made a further advance (see Main Work para 5.148 n499). Lenders in the position of B, not having control over the Registrar's business, generally made direct contact with A to ensure that A had actual notice of B's interest, thereby ensuring B's priority. The new Act not only enshrines this practice, but shifts the risk of any postal mishap onto A; if A suffers a loss because the notice was not received in good time, the loss falls on A (s 49(2)). As noted in the Main Work para 5.148 n498, it is true that if B's interest was not one which could be registered or noted, there would be no obligation on the Registrar to notify A. The new Act makes no distinction based on the nature of B's interest. But under the old system, the risk of a failure of notice fell either on the Land Registry or on B. It is expected that with the advent of electronic conveyancing, B will be able to notify A reliably and instantly at the moment of B's registration.

5.149 **n500**: for Land Registration Act 1925, s 30(3), see now Land Registration Act 2002, s 49(3). The obligation to make further advances must itself be registered, for the protection of B. Again, the new Act makes no distinction based on the nature of B's interest; the provison of the old Act only applied if B's interest was also registered.

(5) *After-Acquired Property and Purchase Money Finance*

5.151 In discussing *Abbey National Building Society v Cann* [1991] 1 AC 56, HL, the Main Work notes that the 'agreement' aspect of the decision may limit its potential as the foundation of a general rule regarding purchase money security interests. This aspect of the case, however, was not emphasized in *National Westminster Bank plc v Jones* [2001] 1 BCLC 98, in relation to the crystallization of a floating agricultural charge under the Agricultural Credits Act 1928. Crystallization was caused by the chargor's ceasing to carry on business through a transfer of all of the business assets to another party, and the question was whether the transferee acquired the assets before or after crystallization. It was held that the crystallization occurred first (see Supplement para 5.89). The judge relied in part on *Abbey National Building Society v Cann,* even though there was of course no agreement between the transferee and the chargee which might justify the analogy.

D. Personal Security

(1) *Types of Security*

(a) Guarantees and indemnities

5.152 In *Actionstrength Ltd v International Glass Engineering IN.GL.EN SpA* [2001] EWCA Civ 1477, [2002] 1 WLR 566, CA, the claimant had claims against a third party. Its allegation was that the defendant promised that if the third party defaulted, the defendant would withhold payments due from the defendant to the third party, and instead pay to the claimant. The claimant argued that this promise did not amount to a guarantee, because the defendant was not imposing a liability on all of its assets. This argument was rejected and the alleged promise was held to be a guarantee. This argument was not made in the further appeal to the House of Lords, on which see Supplement para 5.163.

(b) Other personal securities

5.154 Another transaction whose features are very similar to those of a guarantee is a policy of indemnity insurance issued against the risk of a debtor's default: *Arab Bank plc v John D Wood Commercial Ltd* [2000] 1 WLR 857, CA, noted D Friedmann (2000) 116 LQR 365. Friedmann notes that the characterization can be important for at least two reasons. If the contract is one of indemnity insurance, as it was held to be in the *Arab Bank* case, then any recovery from the insurer does not reduce the claim against the primary debtor (although the insurer would have a claim against the creditor for any surplus recovery) (see Main Work para 15.227).

Another reason is that the creditor's disclosure obligations are traditionally more onerous in the case of insurance (see Main Work para 8.192) than in the case of a guarantee (see Main Work para 5.162). Friedmann argues that this is misconceived and the distinction should be between a professional insurer or guarantor, on the one hand, and one who acts for personal reasons, on the other.

n513: if a bank itself resists a claim on a 'demand guarantee' on the basis that the agreement itself is voidable for fraud, and the claimant seeks summary judgment, the test to be applied is whether the bank has shown 'a reasonable or real prospect' that the relevant bond was voidable: *Solo Industries UK Ltd v Canara Bank* [2001] EWCA Civ 1041, [2001] 1 WLR 1800, CA.

(2) Creation

(b) Formation

(iii) Vitiating factors

5.161 The law on this point was restated in *Royal Bank of Scotland v Etridge (No 2)* [2001] UKHL 44, [2001] 4 All ER 449, HL, discussed in Supplement para 8.206.

(v) Formalities

5.163 In *Actionstrength Ltd v International Glass Engineering IN.GL.EN SpA* [2003] UKHL 17, [2003] 2 AC 541, a guarantee was allegedly given without any note or memorandum and the creditor sought to enforce it. The creditor argued that it had relied to its detriment on the promise made, and that the guarantee should be enforceable under the principle of estoppel (on which see Main Work paras 8.51–8.54). The argument was rejected on the basis that estoppel could not be used to circumvent completely the requirement of writing.

5.164 **n535**: on the requirements as to form imposed by the Consumer Credit Act 1974, see the discussion of *Wilson v First County Trust Ltd (No 2)* [2003] UKHL 40, [2003] 4 All ER 97, HL, in Supplement paras 5.56 and 8.75.

(3) Scope of Liability

(b) Discharge

(ii) Discharge by creditor's conduct

5.171 If the creditor holding real security over property breaches the duty owed to the guarantor to act reasonably in selling the property, the guarantor is not discharged absolutely, but only to the extent of the loss caused, which is to be measured by the difference between the sale price actually obtained and the price which would have been obtained had the creditor acted reasonably: *Skipton Building Society v Stott* [2001] QB 261, CA.

The last word in the Main Work paragraph should be 'shown'. 5.172

(5) Guarantor's Rights Against Co-Guarantors

In *Hampton v Minns* [2002] 1 WLR 1 the claimant and the defendant were co-guarantors of the debts of a company. The claimant discharged the debt and sought contribution. The defendant argued that he should be liable only as to 20 per cent, since he held 20 per cent of the shares of the debtor company, while the claimant held 80 per cent. The court held that the normal rule of equal contribution applied. The claimant also argued that the right to contribution was governed by the Civil Liability (Contribution) Act 1978 which (under the Limitation Act 1980, s 10) has a two-year limitation period. The court held that it was a matter of construction whether any particular guarantee created a claim in debt against the guarantor, or a claim for damages for non-performance by the primary debtor, which is a possible interpretation even if the non-performance by the primary debtor was a failure to pay a debt (see Main Work paras 5.165, 5.167). In the latter case, which is probably the most common case, the Civil Liability (Contribution) Act 1978 would indeed govern any ensuing contribution claims. Here the judge held that the guarantees created a liability in the guarantors to pay a debt, not damages, to the creditor; the ensuing contribution claim therefore attracted a six-year limitation period (Limitation Act 1980, s 5). 5.176

n575: this case reference should be '126 ER 1276'.

6

INTELLECTUAL PROPERTY

B. Patents for Inventions

(9) Patent Procedures: Future Developments

6.42A The patent systems through which a patent for the United Kingdom is currently granted remain a cumbersome compromise between the purely national tradition and complete Europeanization. The same is true for other European Union states. National offices for the most part survive and grant national patents in accordance with principles largely prescribed in the EPC and the CPC. The EPO grants patents in standard form for such of its contracting states as are designated by the applicant. Enforcement after grant (and EPO opposition) takes place in national tribunals, as do challenges to the validity of the grant. So far the Community patent, which would give a unitary right across the entire Single Market, has been held back by an inability to agree, for instance, on an acceptable limitation to the languages in which it must be published. However, in March 2003 the European Commission and Council committed themselves to a plan to introduce a version of the CPC by means of a Community Regulation. This is intended to lead to the grant of Community Patents by 2010. For this it will be necessary to settle the issue over languages of publication and also to work out in detail the proposed system of first instance and appellate courts for Community patent litigation. These are intended to be new Community institutions, the latter consisting of a specialist body within the Court of First Instance of the European Court of Justice. Progress on this initiative has already run into difficulties.

The Commission is also contemplating the introduction of a second-tier registration system for technical improvements, broadly on the lines of the utility model, petty patent and short-term patent systems which exist already within various countries of the European Union. The protection would be granted without prior examination for novelty or inventive step, but would last for a shorter term (perhaps six, perhaps ten years). The possibility of converting the right into a full patent is likely to be preserved, making the scheme a route attractive to parts of large industry, as well as to the new market entrants for whom it is primarily intended by politicians.

C. Confidential Information

(2) Protectable Subject Matter

6.45A The breach of confidence action is one of the legal bases on which proceedings to protect personal privacy can be realized. It is accordingly a vital element in fulfilling the country's obligation under the European Convention on Human Rights, Article 8, to accord respect for private and family life, home and correspondence—now given effect through the Human Rights Act 1998. Since that Act took effect in 2000, celebrities, and sometimes others, have asserted with increasing frequency that breach of privacy should be recognized as a separate wrong or that breach of confidence should be broadened to encompass invasions of privacy that were previously not actionable. The House of Lords has rejected any cause for action for invasion of privacy that goes beyond the *Wilkinson v Downton* tort of *intentionally* inflicting physical harm or psychiatric illness: *Wainwright v Home Office* [2003] 4 All ER 969 (a decision under the pre-Human Rights Act position). At the same time, the Court of Appeal has refused invitations to re-cast breach of confidence simply in terms of breach of privacy: see *Douglas and Zeta-Jones v Hello (No 1)* [2001] QB 967 (although Sedley LJ showed some inclination to do so). In cases of prying by the media, the court has been ready to stress the countervailing interest of freedom of expression, guaranteed by the Convention, Article 10, and the adjunct provision in the 1998 Act, s 12, which severely limits the power of a court to grant interim injunctions against the press by way of 'prior restraint': *Naomi Campbell v MGN* [2003] EMLR 39. How far an individual will have such an action to prevent true revelations about his or her private life therefore calls for an assessment of all the particular circumstances, including the effect of revelation on innocent third parties, such as the wife of an adulterous footballer in the case of *A v B and C* [2002] 2 All ER 545.

D. Copyright

(11) Copyright, Digital Format and the Internet

The coming of digital technology led to computer programs being treated as literary works for copyright purposes (see Main Work para 6.55). The expansion of the Internet over recent years to encompass a host of uses, notably on the World Wide Web, provides a medium in which copyright material can be transmitted for viewing, downloading and transferring on to others. Interactive exchanges are commonplace and text and images can be endlessly modified—all with remarkable speed and accuracy. Authors and entrepreneurs are therefore in danger that there will be widespread taking of copyright material without payment or acknowledgement. This conduct may also be greatly assisted by those who run search engines and the like. Hence the litigation in the United States, the Netherlands and elsewhere against Napster and its successors for providing linking programs and directories to MP3 music files of the websites of others and against websites which provide programs for evading protective codes on DVD. **6.78A**

Already in 1996, the World Intellectual Property Organization (a United Nations organ) had fostered the signing of two treaties which were designed to adjust national laws on authors' copyright (WIPO Copyright Treaty) and the related rights of performers and sound recording producers (WIPO Performances and

Phonograms Treaty), particularly in relation to digitization. These international instruments are now operative, but before that, the EU took a major step towards being able to ratify them in Directive (EC) 01/29 on Copyright and Related Rights in the Information Society [2001] OJ L167/10. EU member states are required to have in their law a reproduction right which extends to temporary copying by any means and in any form, and a right of communication to the public which covers digital systems giving individual choice over access (Articles 2 and 3). UK law has now been redrafted to some extent in order to meet these new standards: see the Copyright and Related Rights Regulations, SI 2498/2003. As a result, the concept of 'broadcasting' has been defined more broadly, so as to eliminate 'cable-casting' as a separate category in defining what are works and what constitutes an infringing act. Broadcasting has now to be distinguished from communicating to the public in response to an individual request: as where material is retrieved on the Internet (see CDPA, 1988, ss 6, 7, 20, 21).

Whether digital material is placed on the Web or provided in hard copy such as a CD or DVD, electronic measures may be built in by the provider which aim to prevent the making or retransmission of multiple copies. The threat to such technical barriers is that others will devise ways of circumventing them. Under the Directive, national laws must give the provider rights to attack those who make these means of circumvention available. The provisions in the CDPA 1988 have been expanded to meet the Directive's complex requirements (see s 296ZG). This section has needed some considerable re-writing in order to comply with the Directive's complex requirements on the matter (see its Article 6). At the same time, the CDPA has acquired new provisions to protect systems for electronic rights management in accordance with the Directive (Article 7). Under these severe regimes, a person may be denied access to material which he is entitled to copy without authorisation by virtue of an exception to copyright. The person seeking access is not, however, entitled to a direct exception from these types of liability, but is only given a right to complain to the relevant Minister for remedial action to be taken, if indeed there is no voluntary channel for securing access: see CDPA 1988, s 296ZE.

The Information Society Directive also takes the harmonization of copyright law in the EU an important stage further, since it lays down criteria which limit the extent to which national law can contain exceptions and limitations to copyright. The governing criterion is the hazy 'golden formula': any exception must be for a special case, must not conflict with normal exploitation and must not prejudice legitimate expectations (Article 5.5). A measure of protection must be accorded to Internet Service Providers and the like, so far as they are involved in transient or incidental copying purely in the course of an Internet transmission from one third party to another (Article 5.1, implemented in

CDPA 1988, s 28A). This does not apply to a host ISP, which is liable for providing copyright material without licence after notification. In consequence, discussions are under way for the introduction of Notice and Take Down procedures of the type already in considerable use in the United States.

While Article 5.1 is a mandatory requirement, the other provisions on specific exceptions and limitations define the maximum permissible in national law relating to the reproduction right alone or to that right and the right of public communication (Articles 5.2, 5.3). The United Kingdom has had to make relatively few adjustments to its long list of copyright exceptions (for which, see Main Work paras 6.66 and 6.67), though it has been obliged to confine the fair dealing exception for research to research that is 'non-commercial'. Perhaps the most controversial issue has been whether an exception covering use for private purposes (such as home recording from CDs and broadcasts) should be introduced, subject to the Directive's requirement of 'fair compensation'. This, typically, would be through a levy on the sale of recording equipment and media, such as blank tape. Levies of this type have been resisted in the United Kingdom and no change has been made in the course of implementing the Directive. In such matters, the Directive is only a halfway station on the road to harmonization of EU copyright laws.

E. Industrial Designs

(2) Registered Designs

The existing paragraph is replaced with the following:

(a) The EU's Designs Directive and Designs Regulation

From the early nineteenth century European countries began to introduce **6.82** schemes for protecting the design elements included in mass-produced industrial products. In Britain a design registration system has been developing since the 1830s, acquiring over time some family resemblance to the patent system. Each scheme across Europe differed somewhat in its detailed requirements. A good case therefore arose for harmonization of the different national laws, and the subject matter was considered important enough also to justify the introduction of a Community Registered Design as an alternative to national registrations. Since 2003, the two schemes have operated upon the same principles, the national design registration having been reshaped according to the requirements laid down in the EU Designs Directive (98/71), and the Community Right being governed by the Community Designs Regulation (reg 6/2002). The UK system is found in the Registered Designs Act 1949, which was substantially amended, first, by the CDPA 1988, Part IV and now, by virtue of the

Designs Directive as implemented by amendments to the Registered Designs Rules 1995. Registration is effected through the Designs Registry of the UK Patent Office. The Registry no longer conducts an ex officio search for prior art. For A Community Registered Design, application is made by applying to the EU's OHIM—the Office for the Harmonization of the Internal Market (Trade Marks and Designs), quartered in Alicante, Spain.

The existing paragraph is replaced with the following:

(b) Protectable designs

6.83 Both the Community and the UK registered design are available for terms of five years from application, up to a maximum of 25 years in all. Registered design will be effective, not just against copyists, but against third parties who independently arrive at much the same design. They can be obtained for the design of a product, ie 'the appearance of the whole or part of a product resulting from the features of, in particular, the lines, contours, colours, shape, texture or materials of the product or its ornamentation': Designs Regulation, Article 3, RDA 1949, s 1(2). In a number of respects, this is a more embracing definition than before. As a counterbalance, the right can be accorded only to designs that are both novel and have individual character at the priority date accorded to them: Designs Regulation, Articles 5–7, RDA 1949, s 1B. Novelty (as in patent law) is a question of sameness; individual character falls to be judged by comparing the overall impression upon a person viewing each design. The prior art for this purpose may be found in a design for any kind of item. From it are excluded: confidential disclosures, disclosures by the applicant or associates within the previous 12 months, and disclosures that could not reasonably have become known to specialists in the European Economic Area. The last of these exceptions is likely to prove difficult to apply in marginal cases.

While the definition of 'design' is broad enough to cover elements of appearance which arise out of the technical purpose for adopting it, this is followed by an exclusion of designs that are solely dictated by function. It remains to be seen whether the courts (and ultimately the European Court of Justice) will read this exclusion narrowly, so as only to operate when the shape is the one form that will achieve the technical result—a condition which can only arise rarely); or whether it will be considered to keep out functional elements of design more generally. Under the previous law, the House of Lords adopted the second type of construction, thus leaving it to the patent system to protect technological shapes where they constituted inventions: see *AMP v Utilux* [1972] RPC 103. The issue is one that will determine how far registered designs can provide exclusive rights over the shape of mechanical products, an issue which remains contentious—particularly in relation to spare parts for engines and such like.

The legislation also specifies that the design cannot consist in 'must fit' elements of an item which is designed to be incorporated or attached to something else. See further below, para 6.84.

The existing paragraph is replaced with the following:

(c) Infringement

The owner of a registered design may object to any unauthorized act which uses the design in manufacturing, or in then marketing, an item of any kind, not just the item in respect of which it is registered: Designs Regulation, Articles 11, 41–44; RDA 1949, s 7. For a UK registered design, the acts must occur in the United Kingdom; for a Community design, in the EU. The definitions of the types of act covered and of exceptions to infringement are drawn from those relating to patents. The right is exclusive and there are no longer provisions for compulsory licensing of registered designs in the UK legislation. Crown use provisions survive. Whether the design has been used is tested by a curious negative: does the alleged infringement not produce on an informed user a different overall impression, taking account of the designer's degree of freedom in developing his design? **6.84**

It is in relation to infringement that the inability to resolve the issues of design registration and spare parts is most apparent. The temporary concordat in the EU legislation is that a registered design for a component in a complex product (one with at least two components permitting disassembly and re-assembly) is not infringed where the component is to be used to repair the whole. The European Commission is required to report on the issue by the end of 2004.

(c) Community Unregistered Design Right

The EU Designs Regulation, as well as establishing the Community Registered Design, also creates a transitional unregistered right which has direct effect under Community law throughout the Single Market: Designs Regulation, Article 11. Like the British unregistered right it is operative only against those who are proved to have copied the claimant's design, but beyond that it differs considerably. It is intended (alongside the one-year grace period already mentioned) to give more leeway over the designer's own product launch and it therefore lasts for three years from that point in time. It must satisfy the requirements for a registrable 'design' in the Community law sense: appearance, novelty and individual character, after taking account of the exceptions. In addition to the requirement of copying, it is infringed under the Community law rules on the subject. It is therefore not available for purely technical designs or where the 'complex products' limitation applies. This amounts to a considerable variance from the UK right. **6.88A**

F. Trade Marks and Names

(2) Common Law Liability: Passing Off

(c) Likelihood of damage

6.100 n158: the long-standing reluctance to allow passing off to control the reputation of celebrities in their image has been overcome by the Court of Appeal in *Eddie Irvine v Talksport* [2002] FSR 943, [2003] EMLR 538, CA. The objection that there could be no protection where claimant and defendant did not share a 'common field of activity' can no longer be sustained. There may still be arguments in future over what will constitute misrepresentation. In the *Irvine* case, a photograph of the claimant, a front-rank racing driver, was deliberately altered so as to suggest that he was endorsing the defendant's radio service.

G. Registered Trade Marks

The spate of case law interpreting the European trade mark Regulation and Directive continues at both the national and the European levels. Key decisions are referred to in what follows.

(4) What can be a 'Trade Mark'?

6.109 The requirement of graphic representation has made it difficult to register smells as marks, the ECJ having found against doing this by setting out a chemical formula or a loose description, or by depositing an odour sample: *Sieckmann's Application* [2003] ETMR 466.

(5) 'Absolute' Grounds of Objection

6.111 The ECJ exhibited considerable lenience when it allowed a mark with some descriptive content ('Baby-Dry', for nappies) onto the Community register without evidence of use: *Procter & Gamble v OHIM* [2002] RPC 369. In the face of professional unease, it has now adopted a more cautious tone in disallowing 'Doublemint' for chewing gum: *OHIM v Wm Wrigley* [2004] ETMR (9) 121; and see *DKV v OHIM* [2003] ETMR 241 ('Companyline' for insurance services; not registrable without evidence of use). Other problems concern single colours, which must almost always require proof of use: *Libertel v Benelux Merkenbureau* [2003] ETMR (63) 807. For the degree to which surnames can be registered, see *Nichols plc's Application* [2003] RPC 301 now referred to the ECJ.

6.112 The ECJ supported the restrictive view of the English courts in *Philips v Remington* [2003] RPC 14 concerning the danger of allowing a product shape to be monopolized by registering a mark for it; re-affirmed in *Linde AG's Application* [2003] ETMR (28) 354.

(6) 'Relative' Grounds of Objection

(b) Dilution

n113: in a confusing decision, *Davidoff v Gofkid* [2003] ETMR (42) 534, the ECJ has recognized that in the law of member states it is permissible to interpret this category of objection widely so as to include circumstances which involve no confusion of the public, but merely association. It is difficult to know how far this qualifies the result reached in *Sabel v Puma* (Main Work para 6.114, n182), an issue which the court is examining in *Adidas-Salomon v Fitnessworld* (for the Advocate-General's opinion, see [2003] ETMR (91) 1127. **6.115**

(7) Removal of Marks from the Register

(b) Revocation

(i) Non-use

In assessing whether a use is genuine, rather than merely token, the amount of use is only one factor, but particular care will be taken to examine the evidence where only a few instances are cited: see, eg, *Laboratoire de la Mer Trade Marks* [2002] FSR 790; *Gerber Products v Gerber Foods* [2002] ETMR 882; *Ansul v Ajax* [2003] ETMR (85) 1032, ECJ. **6.117**

(8) Infringement of a Registered Mark

(a) The types of case

Since in cases of the first type, the claimant does not have to establish any likelihood of confusion, it has been accepted that the identity of the marks and the goods or services must be strictly demonstrated: *LTJ Diffusion v Sadas* [2003] ETMR (83) 1005. But where the defendant's sign is in this category ('Arsenal' on sportswear, registered by the football club for those goods) there will be infringement if some buyers must be deemed to be confused about the source of his products, even if the vast majority merely treat the name as a badge of undying loyalty: *Arsenal FC v Reed* [2003] RPC 144, ECJ; [2003] ETMR (73) 895, CA. **6.120**

(d) Parallel importing

n196: the ECJ has ruled that there is no implication from failure to place an export embargo on goods, that impliedly they may be moved by a parallel importer into the EEA: *Zino Davidoff v A&G Imports* [2002] RPC 403. However, when they are discovered in trade within that area, the trade mark owner has to provide evidence (eg from goods numbers) that they were first marketed outside the territory and that there has been no breach of their arrangements for dividing markets: *Van Doren + Q v Lifestyle Sports* [2003] ETMR (75) 922, ECJ. **6.125**

(9) Domain Names on the Internet

6.126 Trade marks are not the only signs of identification for which a registration system exists. The names of registered companies, for instance, can give rise to conflicts with one another and with trade marks. Registration of a corporate name may therefore be refused or removed: see the Companies Act 1985, ss 26–34; *Glaxo v Glaxowellcome* [1996] FSR 388. As noted in the Main Work para 6.98, cybersquatting has become a widespread practice and can be the subject of a passing off injunction where the name in a top-level domain name (as in 'audi.com') is someone else's established trade mark. So rampant has the practice of registering such domain names been that registration services which allot domain names have an arbitral procedure by which the registration contract is a condition of the registration. Under the Dispute Resolution Policy of the US body ICANN, for instance, the owner of a trade mark or similar identifier (such as an author's or performer's name) may seek to have the domain name registration transferred to him or her if (a) the public is likely to be confused by the identity or similarity between the mark and domain name, (b) the domain name registrant has no right or legitimate interest in it, and (c) he or she has registered and used it in bad faith. In this way, for example, those who register the <.com> domain for a famous mark may be thwarted in their wish to sell it on to the mark owner for far more than it cost to obtain. One institution providing a Dispute Resolution procedure for ICANN is the Arbitration and Mediation Center of the World Intellectual Property Organization. Thousands of decisions have been published since the introduction of the system in January 2000.

7

SUCCESSION

A. Introduction

(a) Jointly owned property

In *Re Woolnough, Perkins v Borden* [2002] WTLR 595 it was held that a beneficial joint tenancy would be severed not only where the parties made mutual wills (see Main Work para 7.116) but also where, each knowing that the other had done so, they made simultaneous wills purporting to deal with their interests in the jointly owned property. **7.02**

(b) Property held in trust

7.03 n5: see now Hanbury & Martin, *Modern Equity* (16th edn, 2001). The relevant chapters remain chapters 11 and 12.

C. Wills

(1) The Nature and Contents of Wills

(b) Conditional wills

7.41 In *Nathan v Leonard* [2003] 1WLR 827 it was held that a condition in a home-made codicil—whereby if one beneficiary contested the will, both he and other beneficiaries who had not contested it might forfeit interests given to them by the will—was, as drafted, too uncertain to be enforced and so invalid. Nevertheless, such a condition was not intrinsically void for repugnancy and would have been upheld had it not failed the test of certainty.

(c) Solicitor's duty of care in preparation of will

(ii) Solicitor's duty to beneficiary under will

7.44 In *X v Woolcombe Yonge* [2001] WTLR 301 it was held that there was no breach of duty by a solicitor who took a week to prepare a will for a client who was in hospital suffering from cancer. At the time when the solicitor took instructions, the hospital, the client and the solicitor all believed that the client had two months or so to live. She died, unexpectedly, within the week.

In *Trusted v Clifford Chance* [2000] WTLR 1219 it was held that the duty owed (in tort) by the solicitor to an intended beneficiary and the duty owed (in contract) by the solicitor to his client are for all practical purposes one and the same. Unless the solicitor is in breach of his (contractual) duty towards his client, he cannot be in breach of his (tortious) duty towards an intended beneficiary. It follows that no tortious duty of care will arise in favour of an intended beneficiary unless and until the client has decided to confer on the intended beneficiary a particular testamentary benefit; and has retained the solicitor for that purpose.

It is suggested in Supplement paras 7.86 and 7.87 that a finding of lack of knowledge and approval generally implies misconduct by someone involved in the preparation of the will. Where a will has been prepared by, or its execution has been supervised by, a professional will draftsman, and it is subsequently held that the testator lacked knowledge and approval, it is possible that an action might be brought against the draftsman, seeking the recovery of the costs involved in setting the will aside. There is, as yet, no record of such an action having succeeded in England. Where the will is set aside, then, if an action is to be brought against the draftsman, it should be brought not by those who benefit under an earlier will, or intestacy, as the case may be, but by the personal representatives on behalf of the estate. See the New Zealand case of *Knox v Till* [2002] WTLR 1147 and the English case of *Worby v Rosser* [1999] Lloyd's Rep P N 972, CA.

(3) The Making of Wills: Capacity

(c) Delusions

The rule in *Parker v Felgate* has been applied in *Clancy v Clancy* [2003] WTLR 1097. **7.79**

(f) Rectification

For the inter-relationship between applications for rectification and actions for negligence, see *Walker v Medlicott* [1999] 1 WLR 727 and *Horsfall v Haywards* [1999] 1 FLR 1182. It is suggested that these two decisions of the Court of Appeal are difficult to reconcile and that the decision in the *Horsfall* case is to be preferred. See [2003] 62 CLJ 750–770. **7.83**

n207: see now for extension of the time limit, *Chittock v Stevens* [2000] WTLR 643.

(h) Challenging a purported will

It is said in Main Work para 7.86 that someone who is considering challenging a purported will finds himself in a position of some difficulty and it is said in Main Work para 7.87 that it seems that those who are considering challenging wills are now being encouraged to plead lack of knowledge and approval, rather than fraud or undue influence. The difficulties faced by those minded to challenge wills are illustrated by a number of recent cases. In *Ewing v Bennett* [2001] WTLR 249 a will made by a solicitor for a woman who was very deaf, suffered from dizziness and memory loss, and who was in the early stages of senile dementia with periodic forgetfulness, was upheld by the trial judge: and the Court of Appeal refused to interfere with his decision. In *Re Dabbs* [2001] WTLR 527 a will prepared on the principal beneficiary's computer for a testator, who died in circumstances which caused the coroner's jury to return a verdict of unlawful death, was also upheld. **7.86–7.87**

Where a testator suffers from some degree of incapacity, and where the will is challenged on the grounds both of lack of capacity and of lack of knowledge and approval, it appears that a finding of lack of knowledge and approval generally implies, though does not clearly state that there has been, misbehaviour by someone involved in the preparation of the will. Findings of lack of knowledge and approval are routinely linked with references to 'suspicious circumstances'.

If the trial judge does not want to suggest any form of improper conduct, he may set the will aside simply on the ground of lack of capacity, *Brown v Deacy* [2002] WTLR 781. If he believes that there was some degree of impropriety, he will generally opt for lack of capacity combined with lack of knowledge and approval, *Richards v Allan* [2001] WTLR 1031 and *Tchiingirian v Ouzounian* [2003] WTLR 709. A finding of lack of knowledge and approval alone implies a greater degree of misconduct. There are two recent examples. In *Buckenham v Dickenson* [2000] WTLR 1083 the testator was 'very deaf and partially blind' and the trial judge held that the reading over of a will to him, by a solicitor, was an 'idle ceremony'. In *d'Eye v Avery* [2001] WTLR 227 the testator had had a massive stroke, was a patient of the Court of Protection and executed his will in a bank when the principal beneficiary was present.

But the problem for someone challenging a will is that these findings of lack of knowledge and approval appear to be applicable only in cases where there is also a degree of lack of capacity. They hint at misconduct, but do not appear to have a significant effect on the outcome of the cases.

In *Fuller v Strum* [2002] 2 All ER 87 the will was written out by one of the principal beneficiaries and, though the trial judge did not accept the evidence of a handwriting expert that the testator's signature had been forged, he followed the *Wintle v Nye* approach of referring to a 'suspicion' and found that the testator had not known and approved of almost the entire contents of the will. The Court of Appeal set aside the judge's order and pronounced in favour of the will. This is a case where the person challenging the will had pleaded lack of knowledge and approval, when the honest plea would have been fraud. It is not easy to see what the trial judge was referring to when he talked about a 'suspicion' in this case. If neither fraud nor undue influence was pleaded, what could the 'suspicion' be a 'suspicion' of? Given the way the case was pleaded and fought, the decision of the Court of Appeal appears to be correct—and yet this means that there is remarkably little protection for those who are disinherited in circumstances where others assist in the preparation of wills under which they take significant benefits. Judges remain very reluctant to reach findings which indicate clearly that they believe that there had been improper conduct by beneficiaries or by those who have overseen the execution of wills.

The contrast between the attitude of the courts in will cases, and in cases relating to lifetime gifts, is clear. In cases of lifetime gifts, the courts apply a presumption of undue influence. An example is *Hammond v Osborn* [2002] WTLR 1125 where, shortly before he died, an elderly man, living alone, gave away most of his investments to a neighbour who was helping to look after him. The gifts were discovered after his death. The trial judge found no undue influence, but the Court of Appeal presumed it and set the gifts aside.

It is suggested that the courts should approach the will cases with more circumspection and that they should apply presumptions of fraud and undue influence in all cases where beneficiaries are directly or indirectly involved in the preparation of wills.

CPR Part 49, para 9, which laid down the rules applicable to the contents of pleadings in contentious probate cases, has now been replaced by CPR 57.7. The new rule, which came into force on 15 October 2001, still appears to require that a plea of lack of knowledge and approval should not be used as a cloak for a plea of fraud or undue influence, but the wording is less clear than it was.

(4) Revocation, Alteration, Revival and Republication of Wills

(a) Revocation

(iii) Revocation by destruction

In *Re Dickson, Dickson v Dickson* [2002] WTLR 1395 the Court of Appeal reversed the trial judge and followed the approach taken in *Sugden v Lord St Leonards*—granting probate of a missing will. The solicitor draftsman had retained a photostat copy. **7.100**

(5) Mutual Wills

(d) The property bound

In *Healey v Brown* [2002] WTLR 849 the judge followed an approach suggested obiter by one of the judges (who cited no authority for the proposition) in the Court of Appeal in *Re Goodchild* and held that the constructive trust to which the survivor was subject applied only to property acquired from the deceased and not to property already owned by the survivor. It is suggested that this is wrong in principle and that the constructive trust should apply according to the terms of the agreement between the parties. **7.122**

(6) Secret Trusts

(b) Enforcement of secret trusts

In *Kasperbauer v Griffith* [2000] WTLR 333 the claimants originally suggested that the testator, their father, had created a secret trust with the intention of deceiving the Revenue. The Court of Appeal thought that the suggestion was 'unattractive' and were glad when it was not persisted in. In the event, the Court of Appeal upheld the trial judge's finding that there was no secret trust. The problem of the interrelationship between secret trusts and illegality did not, therefore, need to be faced. **7.126**

D. Construction

(1) The General Principles of the Construction of Wills

(b) Section 21 of the Administration of Justice Act 1982

7.134 In *Re El-Kaisi's Estate, Midland Bank v MacLeod* [2001] WTLR 817 the Jersey Royal Court (Probate Division) had to decide whether the words in the testator's will 'assets within the United Kingdom' included assets in Jersey. The court held that assets in Jersey were included, because this is what the testator intended the words to mean. It is submitted that an English court would also have adopted this approach. In fact, the case concerned a testator domiciled in Scotland; so the Jersey Court was applying Scottish Law. *Quaere* whether this was good law for Scotland—Scotland still applies Wigram's literal approach.

In *Re Bowles; Hayward v Jackson* [2003] Ch 422 the court, in construing the terms of an option contained in a will, adopted a straightforwardly intentional approach. For the construction of a will, the starting point is the testator's intention; the court should not follow previous cases in such a way as to override it.

(2) Specific Rules of Construction

(c) Gifts to children

(i) Adopted children

7.140 n341: see now *Theobald* (16th edn, 2001) 406. See also *Hawkins on the Construction of Wills* (5th edn, 2000) 171.

(e) Rules for ascertaining classes

7.144 n352: see now *Theobald* (16th edn, 2001) ch 32.

E. Failure of Gifts by Will or of Interests on Intestacy

(1) Ademption

(b) Change in substance, not in name or form

7.162 In *Re Viertel* [2003] WTLR 1075 the Supreme Court of Queensland had to deal with a case similar to *Re Dorman* and came to the same result, but by a different route. The court held that there would be no ademption where there was a sale by an attorney under an enduring power of attorney. This case implies that, in Queensland, ademption is a question of the testator's intention and is not a rule of law. *Quaere* whether this may become the position in England, where ademption has been regarded as a rule of law.

(c) Ademption by contract or option

In *Pennington v Waine* [2003] WTLR 1011 it was held that the rule in *Lawes v Bennett* does not apply to a gift of shares in a private company where owners of other shares in the company have a right of pre-emption over them. This is a welcome refusal to extend an illogical rule. 7.163

(3) Beneficiary or Spouse is an Attesting Witness

(a) General rule

The Trustee Act 2000, s 28(4) reverses the presumption that any payment to which a trustee is entitled in respect of services is to be treated as a gift for the purposes of the Wills Act, s 15, so a will which contains a charging clause can now be witnessed by the trustee without his losing the benefit of that clause. 7.166

(7) Murder or Manslaughter

(a) Forfeiture rule

Re DWS [2001] Ch 568, CA concerned the entitlement to the share forfeited by a child who had killed his intestate parent and who himself had issue. Did his share pass to the child's issue, or to the deceased's brothers and sisters? The Court of Appeal held, by a majority, that it passed to the brothers and sisters. The result appears wrong; and it is submitted that it is. The child's issue should have taken, not by a literal reading of the intestacy rules, but by way of a constructive trust. See 117 LQR (2001) 371. The Law Commission has published a Consultation Paper (No 172) *The Forfeiture Rule and the Law of Succession* which considers whether the law needs to be amended to cope with the problem. 7.175

(8) Disclaimer

A disclaimer made before the testator's death is ineffective, unless supported by consideration: *Re Smith* [2001] 1 WLR 1937. 7.177

F. Executors and Administrators

(1) Executors

(a) Appointment of executors

(i) Express appointment by will

n416: see now Williams, Mortimer and Sunnucks, *Executors, Administrators and Probate* (18th edn, 2000) 18. 7.180

G. Family Provision

(1) Introduction

7.198 For Family Provision generally, see S Ross, *Inheritance Act Claims* (2nd edn, 2000).

n450: where the deceased dies domiciled in England and Wales, the court is entitled to take account of any property he owned abroad when considering the 'reasonableness' of the provision made by him: *Bheekhun v Williams* [1999] 2 FLR 229, CA.

(3) Categories of Applicant and Matters to which Court must have Regard

(a) The deceased's wife or husband

(i) The surviving spouse standard

7.204 See *Re Adams, Adams v Lewis* [2001] WTLR 493. Any tentative view formed by the judge should be checked against the yardstick of equality of division. As a general guide, equality of division should be departed from only if there is good reason. This follows from the decision of the House of Lords in the (divorce) case of *White v White* [2001] 1 AC 596 discussed at Supplement para 2.158.

(b) Deceased's former wife or husband

Matters to which the court must have regard

7.208 **n473**: see now also *Barrass v Harding & Newman* [2001] 1 FLR 138, CA.

(c) A cohabitant

7.209 **n476**: *Fitzpatrick v Sterling Housing Association* is now reported in [2001] 1 AC 27, but has been distinguished in *Ghaidan v Godin-Mendoza* [2003] Ch 380, CA. These cases both concern succession to statutory tenancies, but the *Ghaidan* case construes the UK legislation post the enactment of the Human Rights Act 1998.

n477: *Re Watson* is now reported in [1999] 1 FLR 878.

(d) A child of the deceased

(i) Matters to which the court must have regard

7.211 An *infant* child does not need to show some special circumstance in order to obtain provision under the 1975 Act: *Re Robinson* [2001] WTLR 267.

(f) A dependant of the deceased

(iii) Form of dependency

n496: *Re B (dec'd)*—where the carer mother was held to have been a dependant of her child—is now reported in [2000] Ch 662, CA. **7.218**

(4) Orders the Court may make

(a) The net estate

See now also *Bheekhun v Williams* [1999] 2 FLR 229, CA discussed at Supplement para 7.198 n450. **7.220**

8

CONTRACT: GENERAL RULES

B. Constituent Elements

(1) Agreement

(a) Reaching agreement: offer and acceptance

(i) Offer

8.06 Advertisements relating to the sale or supply of goods can also give rise to contractual liability under legislation for the protection of consumers.[23a]

n20: where a supplier of goods or services indicates their availability on a website, the offer (if any) likewise comes from the customer. This is implicit in Electronic Commerce (EC Directive) Regulations 2002, SI 2002/2013, reg 12.

n21: the auctioneer may be liable to the highest bidder on a collateral contract if he refuses to accept that person's bid: *Barry v Davies (t/a Heathcote Ball & Co)* [2001] 1 WLR 1962.

(ii) Acceptance

8.10 **n41**: in the case of web-site trading, the Electronic Commerce (EC Directive) Regulations 2002, SI 2002/2013 state that communications in this medium are 'received' when the addressee is 'able to access them' (reg 11(2)(c)); but this does not necessarily answer the question when the contract is made. See also the Law Commission's paper of December 2001 on *Electronic Commerce: Formal Requirements in Electronic Communications.*

8.12 A consumer who is bound by a contract under the common law rules stated in Main Work paras 8.10 and 8.11 may have a 'right to cancel' the contract under the Consumer Protection (Distance Selling) Regulations 2000, SI 2000/2334. The effect of the exercise of this right is, however, not the same as the effect of saying that no contract has been made under the common law rules stated in the above paragraphs of the Main Work.

[23a] Under implied terms or consumer guarantees: Sale of Goods Act 1979, s 14 (2D); Sale and Supply of Goods to Consumers Regulations 2002, SI 2002/3045, reg 15.

(iii) Termination of offer

Problems of the kind discussed in the Main Work para 8.21a likewise cannot arise in the case of a limited liability partnership incorporated under the Limited Liability Partnerships Act 2000 since such bodies corporate[90a] have 'unlimited capacity.'[90b] **8.21A**

(b) Vagueness, uncertainty and incompleteness

(ii) Failure to specify vital terms

n97: see also *Baird Textile Holdings Ltd v Marks & Spencer plc* [2001] EWCA Civ 274, [2002] 1 All ER (Comm) 737, discussed in full at Supplement para 8.69. **8.23**

(iii) Terms to be agreed

n100: in *Mamidoil-Jetoil Greek Petroleum Co SA v Okta Crude Oil Refinery AD* [2001] EWCA Civ 406, [2001] 2 Lloyd's Rep 76 a distinction was drawn between cases in which a fee (for services) was to be agreed before the *conclusion* of a contract, and those in which such agreement was needed for the *continued operation* of an existing long-term contact. In the latter case a term was to be implied for the payment of a reasonable fee. **8.24**

(c) Conditional agreements

n125: see also *Jolley v Carmel Ltd* [2000] EGLR 153 where a failure by a purchaser of land to secure planning permission within a reasonable time was held not to be a breach of his duty to make reasonable efforts to that end. **8.28**

(2) Consideration

(a) Introduction

(i) Nature of the doctrine

n132: for certain electronic documents as deeds, see Land Registration Act 2002, s 91(5) and (9). In *Shah v Shah* [2001] EWCA Civ 527, [2002] QB 35 the signer of a deed was estopped from relying on a temporal defect in the witnessing requirements laid down in s 1 of the Law of Property (Miscellaneous Provisions) Act 1989. **8.29**

(b) Adequacy

n148: the principle that the law does not investigate the adequacy of consideration is recognized by the Unfair Terms in Consumer Contracts Regulations 1999, **8.36**

[90a] Limited Liability Partnerships Act 2000, s 1(2).
[90b] ibid, s 1(3).

SI 1999/2083, reg 6(2): see *Director General of Fair Trading v First National Bank plc* [2001] UKHL 52, [2002] 1 AC 481 at [12].

8.37 The rule that equity will not aid a 'volunteer', while preventing the enforcement of gratuitous *promises,* does not affect the validity of a *completed gift*: *Pennington v Waine* [2002] EWCA Civ 227, [2002] 1 WLR 2075.

(c) Past consideration

8.38 Where the guarantee is a 'consumer guarantee' within regulations for the protection of consumers, it 'takes effect . . . as a contractual obligation owed by the guarantor'[155a] by force of the regulations; there is no further requirement of consideration.

(e) The value of consideration

(iii) Compromises and forbearances

8.42 In the absence of 'clear language' the court is 'slow to infer' that a compromise is intended to cover claims of which a party 'was unaware and could not have been aware': *Bank of Credit & Commerce SA v Ali* [2001] UKHL 8, [10], [2001] ICR 337.

(g) Rescission and variation

(v) Distinguished from estoppel by convention

8.55 **n214**: for further discussion of the distinction between the various kinds of estoppel discussed in Main Work paras 8.51, 8.55 and 8.60, see *Johnson v Gore Wood & Co* [2002] 2 AC 1, 33, 38–40 and *Baird Textile Holdings Ltd v Marks & Spencer plc* [2001] EWCA Civ 274, [2002] 1 All ER (Comm) 737, at [36], [50], [83]–[85].

n217: in *Johnson v Gore Wood & Co* [2002] 2 AC 1 Lord Bingham regarded the requirements of estoppel by convention as having been satisfied; but his view on this point was not shared by Lords Goff and Millett.

Add new footnore at end of para 8.55:

n221a: the view that estoppel by convention does not give rise to a cause of action is also supported, though with some hesitation, by Lord Goff in *Johnson v Gore Wood & Co* [2002] 2 AC 1 at 40.

[155a] Sale and Supply of Goods to Consumers Regulations 2002, SI 2002/3045, reg 15(1).

(i) Proprietary estoppel

n261: for the flexibility of the remedy in cases of proprietary estoppel, see further *Jennings v Rice* [2002] EWCA Civ 159, [2002] WTLR 367 where it was said at [36], [56] that there must be 'proportionality' between the expectation and the detriment. **8.62**

(3) Contractual Intention

(b) Proof of contractual intention

At **n275**: 'text' is a misprint for 'test'.

n275: the objective test was applied in *Edmonds v Lawson* [2000] QB 501 where acceptance of an offer of pupillage was held to give rise to a contract between the pupil barrister and the members of the chambers from which the offer had come. **8.65**

n279: a statement in an advertisement that a product is 'foolproof' is probably not one as to its 'specific characteristics' so as to give rise to liability under Sale of Goods Act 1979, s 14(2D); nor would such a statement be a 'consumer guarantee' within Sale and Supply of Goods to Consumers Regulations 2002, SI 2002/3045, regs 2 and 15. **8.66**

(c) Illustrations

In *Baird Textile Holdings v Marks & Spencer plc* [2001] EWCA Civ 274, [2002] 1 All ER (Comm) 737, B had for 30 years supplied clothing to M & S, but B's claim that this relationship gave rise to an implied contract not to terminate except on reasonable notice failed for want of contractual intention since (i) M & S had deliberately refused to enter into a long-term contract and (ii) the alleged implied contract was too uncertain to be enforced under the rules stated in Main Work para 8.23. **8.69**

(4) Form

(c) Effect of non-compliance

n306: in *Wilson v First County Trust* [2003] UKHL 40, [2003] 4 All ER 97, the House of Lords has held that s 127(3) of the Consumer Credit Act 1974 (which provides that a contract contained in a regulated consumer credit agreement cannot be enforced against a debtor who has not signed it) was not incompatible with the European Convention for the Protection of Human Rights, which has the force of law by virtue of the Human Rights Act 1998. Where no enforcement order is made, the debtor is not liable to make restitution to the creditor in respect of benefits received under the agreement : *Dimond v Lovell* [2002] AC 384 at 398. **8.75**

(e) Electronic communications

8.79A Most of the formal requirements described above can be satisfied by electronic communications and signatures: eg where a contract is made on a website or by an exchange of e-mails.[314a] Some such requirements (eg the requirement that copies of consumer credit agreements must be sent to the debtor by post)[314b] cannot be so satisfied. An EC Directive requires member states to ensure that contracts can be made by electronic means;[314c] but this requirement does not extend to contracts for the sale of interests in land or to contracts of guarantee.[314d]

C. Contents

(1) Express Terms

(c) The parol evidence rule

8.82 **n320**: for statements of the policy underlying the parol evidence rule, see also *AIB Group plc v Martin* [2001] UKHL 63, [2002] 1 WLR 94 at [4] and *Shogun Finance Ltd v Hudson* [2003] UKHL 62, [2004] 1 All ER 215, at [49].

(d) Qualifications

8.85 **n326**: evidence is not admissible to *contradict* the document so as to show that the contract is between persons other than those expressly named in it as the parties to it: *Shogun Finance Ltd v Hudson* [2003] UKHL 62, [2004] 1 All ER 215 at [49].

n327: the parol evidence rule does not exclude evidence of an antecedent *contract* between the parties, though if that contact is intended to be superseded by the later contract, then such evidence will be of little use: *HIH Casualty General Insurance Ltd v New Hampshire Insurance Co* [2001] EWCA Civ 735, [83], [2001] 2 All ER (Comm) 39.

(2) Implied Terms

(a) Terms implied in fact

8.89 **n344**: it follows from the words 'must have intended' in the passage quoted in the Main Work that the intention in question may be an imputed (as opposed to an actual) one: *Equitable Life Assurance Society v Hyman* [2002] 1 AC 408.

[314a] See Law Commission paper on *Electronic Commerce: Formal Requirements in Commercial Contracts* (December 2001).

[314b] eg, Consumer Credit Act 1974, ss 63(3), 64(2).

[314c] Directive 2000/13/EC.

[314d] ibid, Art 9; for electronic conveyancing, see Land Registration Act 2002, Part 8.

n345: the fact that an allegedly implied term was reasonable may help to show that the parties would have agreed to it: *Paragon Finance Ltd v Nash* [2001] EWCA Civ 1466, [2002] 1 WLR 685 at [36].

D. Standard Terms

(1) Exemption Clauses at Common Law

(a) Incorporation

(ii) Notice

n368: see also *O'Brien v MGN Ltd* [2001] EWCA Civ 1279, The Times, 8 August 2001 where rules of a newspaper competition were incorporated by reference even though the claimant had not read the document in which they were contained. **8.94**

(b) Construction

(iii) Seriousness of breach

n405: *The Chanda* [1989] 2 Lloyd's Rep 494 has been disapproved so far as it relates to the effect of carriage on deck on the carrier's limitation of liability under Article IV(5) of the Hague Rules: *The Kapitan Petko Voivoda* [2003] EWCA Civ 451, [2003] 1 All ER (Comm) 801; but this disapproval does not affect the dictum from *The Chanda* cited in para 8–102 of the Main Work. **8.102**

(c) Other common law limitations

n416: it is an open question whether a party can exclude liability for the fraud of his own agent; and even if this can be done the intention to exclude such liability must be expressed 'in clear and unmistakable terms': *HIH Casualty & General Insurance Ltd v Chase Manhattan Bank* [2003] UKHL 6, [2003] All ER (Comm) 349, at [16]; cf ibid at [24], [82], [92] and [122]. **8.105**

(2) Other Standard Terms at Common Law

n424: it has been doubted whether the requirement of a high degree of notice of unusual terms applies where the term is contained in a document signed by the party alleged to be bound: *HIH Casualty & General Insurance Ltd v New Hampshire Insurance Co* [2001] EWCA Civ 735, [209], [2001] 2 All ER (Comm) 39; for incorporation by signature, see Main Work para 8.93. **8.106**

n423: for the view that the unreasonableness of a standard term is not, of itself, a ground of invalidity, see *Amiri Flight Authority v BAE Systems Ltd* [2002] EWHC 2481, [2003] 1 Lloyd's Rep 50 at [14]. On appeal, the question was left open: [2003] EWCA Civ 1447, [2003] 2 Lloyd's Rep 767, at [15].

(3) Legislative Limitations on Effectiveness

(a) The Unfair Contract Terms Act 1977

(i) Terminology

8.108 **n429**: the requirement stated in the Main Work that the goods must be of a type ordinarily supplied for private use or consumption, no longer applies where the goods are supplied to an individual: Unfair Contract Terms Act 1977, s 12(1A).

The concluding sentence of this note in the Main Work should, in consequence of amendments to s 12(2) of the 1977 Act made by the Sale and Supplies of Goods to Consumers Regulations 2002, SI 2002/3045, reg 14(3), read: 'Except in certain cases where the buyer is an individual, sales by auction or competitive tender are excluded by s 12(2).'

(ii) Structure of the Act

8.112 **n455**: a decision that a term was unreasonable may, however, be reversed on appeal where that decision was based on a wrong principle of law, eg, on a misconstruction of the term, as in *Granville Oil & Chemicals Ltd v Davies Turner & Co Ltd* [2003] EWCA Civ 570, [2003] 1 All ER (Comm) 819; cf *Watford Electronics Ltd v Sanderson Ltd* [2001] EWCA Civ 317, [2001] 1 All ER (Comm) 696. Terms incorporated in a contract after negotiations between parties 'of equal bargaining power' (ibid at [55]) are unlikely to be struck down for unreasonableness; but even between such parties a term may fail to satisfy the requirement of reasonableness where it was incorporated without negotiations between them and would affect 'matters which the parties would have regarded as fundamental': *Bacardi-Martini Beverages Ltd v Thomas Hardy Packaging Ltd* [2002] EWCA Civ 549, [2002] 2 All ER (Comm) 335 at [26]; *Britvic Soft Drinks Ltd v Messer UK Ltd* [2002] EWCA Civ 548, [2002] 2 All ER (Comm) 321 at [26].

(b) The Unfair Terms in Consumer Contracts Regulations 1999

(iii) Unfairness and good faith

8.120 The House of Lords has described the requirement of good faith in the Regulations as 'one of fair and open dealing'.[489a] Openness here refers to the way in which the terms are set out and fairness to matters of substance.[489b]

8.121 **n490**: the decision in *Director General of Fair Trading v First National Bank* [2000] 3 WLR 1297, has been reversed: [2001] UKHL 52, [2002] 1 AC 481. The House of Lords has upheld the view of the Court of Appeal that a provision in a regulated

[489a] *Director General of Fair Trading v First National Bank* [2001] UKHL 52, [2002] 1 AC 481 at [17].

[489b] ibid.

consumer credit agreement for the payment of interest after judgment for repayment of the principal sum was not a 'core provision' since it was merely ancillary to the principal obligation of the borrower; but further held that, contrary to the view of the Court of Appeal, the provision was not 'unfair' or contrary to good faith within the Unfair Terms in Consumer Contracts Regulations 1994, now superseded (without material change on this point) by the 1999 Regulations.

(4) Other Legislative Techniques

A variety of techniques for protecting consumers is used in the Consumer Protection (Distance Selling) Regulations 2000, SI 2000/2334. These include (in the case of contracts to which the Regulations apply) a requirement for the supply of specified information to the consumer, provisions for the exercise of rights of cancellation by the consumer and consequent rights of restitution, provisions against inertia selling, the avoidance of contract terms inconsistent with provisions for the protection of the consumer, and provisions for the Office of Fair Trading to intervene to secure compliance with the Regulations. **8.128**

n507: the Fair Trading Act 1973, ss 2 and 14 have been repealed by the Enterprise Act 2002, so that the text of the Main Work at this point should be amended accordingly. The functions of the Director General of Fair Trading are transferred to the Office of Fair Trading (OFT) by s 1 of the 2002 Act. By s 8 of that Act, the OFT is to promote 'good practice in carrying out activities which may affect the economic interests of consumers'.

n509: the Fair Trading Act 1973, ss 35 and 37 have been repealed by the Enterprise Act 2002 so that the text of the Main Work at this point should be amended accordingly.

nn510, 511: the legislation referred to in these notes remains in force under the Enterprise Act 2002.

E. Mistake

Recent developments (described in para 8.136 of this Supplement) have considerably reduced the scope of equitable intervention on the ground of mistake. **8.129**

(1) Mistakes Nullifying Consent

(a) Fundamental mistake at common law

(i) Types of mistake

n519: cf *Great Peace Shipping Ltd v Tsavliris Salvage (International) Ltd (The Great Peace)* [2002] EWCA Civ 1407, [2003] QB 697 where ship A had been chartered **8.131**

to provide escort services to ship B, which was in distress at sea, in the mistaken belief that A was in close proximity to B. This mistake was not fundamental at common law as A could, in spite of it, have provided 'several days of escort service' (at [165]).

(ii) Effects of mistake

8.132 **n529**: for another situation in which relief on the ground of mistake was refused to a party who had by the terms of the contract taken the risk of the alleged mistake, see *Kalsep Ltd v X-Flow BV* The Times, 3 May 2001.

(b) Mistakes for which equity gives relief

(i) Types of mistakes

8.132 **nn531, 532**: the relief given in the cases cited in these notes of the Main Work would no longer now be available in view of the development discussed in para 8.136 of this Supplement.

8.134 **n536**: the view that a mistake in law can, after the *Kleinwort Benson* case, [1999] 2 AC 349, make a contract void at law is supported by *Brennan v Bolt Burden* [2003] EWHC 2493, The Times, 20 November 2003; but contrast the view expressed in *S v S* [2002] EWHC 223, [2003] Fam 1, at [70] that the *Kleinwort Benson* decision was 'specific to the law of restitution and . . . not intended to apply across the board of every branch of the law'.

n537: for the view that the contract in *Cooper v Phibbs* (1867) LR 2 HL 1049 should now be regarded as void at law, see *Great Peace Shipping Ltd v Tsavliris Salvage (International) Ltd (The Great Peace)* [2002] EWCA Civ 1407, [2003] QB 697, at [126]–[128] and see Supplement para 8.161.

(ii) Effects of mistake

8.136 The authorities which formerly supported the view that there was an equitable jurisdiction to rescind contracts for mistake which were not sufficiently 'fundamental' to make the contract void at law were reconsidered in *The Great Peace.*[545a] The Court of Appeal there concluded that there was in such cases no power in equity to rescind the contract. It emphasized the difficulty (mentioned in the Main Work) of reconciling such an equitable power with the common law requirement that a mistake affects the validity of the contract only if it is 'fundamental'. Its conclusion was based on the need to restore doctrinal coherence to this branch of the law.[545b] No attempt was made to evaluate previous cases which had exercised the

[545a] *Great Peace Shipping Ltd v Tsavliris Salvage (International) Ltd (The Great Peace)* [2002] EWCA Civ 1407, [2003] QB 697.
[545b] ibid at [157].

equitable jurisdiction to rescind on their merits or to meet the point that its exercise was 'on occasion . . . the passport to a just result'.[545c]

(2) Mistakes Negativing Consent

(a) Types of mistake

(iii) As to the person

The difficulty of distinguishing between a mistake as to identity of the other party and one as to an attribute is further illustrated by the difference of judicial opinion on the point in *Shogun Finance Ltd v Hudson.*[557a] A rogue (X) obtained possession of a car under a written hire-purchase agreement by pretending to be Y, producing Y's driving licence (which X had improperly obtained) and forging Y's signature. The agreement was expressed to be between Y and Z, a finance company which had checked Y's address and credit-rating before entering into the agreement. These investigations, in the view of a majority of the House of Lords, showed that Z intended to deal only with Y so that there was no contract between X and Z; alternatively, evidence that X was a party to the contract was inadmissible under the parol evidence rule as it contradicted the written agreement.[557b] It followed that a person who had in good faith bought the car from X acquired no title to it. The dissentients were prepared to depart from earlier House of Lords authority[557c] on the issue of mistake and took the view that there was a contract, though one that was voidable for fraud, between X and Z. **8.140**

(c) Effects of mistake

(ii) In equity

The equitable power to rescind where the mistake was not fundamental in the common law sense does not seem to have survived *The Great Peace* [2002] EWCA Civ 1407, [2003] QB 697, see Supplement para 8.136. That case was, indeed, concerned with a mistake which was alleged to have *nullified*, while our present concern is with one which is alleged to have *negatived*, consent. But the reasoning of the case was that doctrinal coherence would be destroyed by allowing contracts which were valid at law (in spite of the mistake) to be rescinded in equity (see Supplement para 8.136) and this reasoning applies as much to mistakes alleged to have negatived as to those alleged to have nullified consent. Cases such as *Torrance v Bolton* (1872) 8 Ch App 118 (Main Work n572) can perhaps be explained on the ground of misrepresentation. **8.146**

545c *West Sussex Properties Ltd v Chichester DC*, 28 June 2000, CA, at [42].

557a [2003] UKHL 62, [2004] 1 All ER 215.

557b Above. Para 82 n20 of this Supplement.

557c ie, *Cundy v Lindsay* (1878) 3 App Cas 459, Main Work, n553. In the *Shogun* case, Lord Millett (dissenting) and Lord Walker (one of the majority) also regarded *Ingram v Little* [1961] 1 QB 31 (Main Work n557) as having been wrongly decided.

F. Misrepresentation

(1) The Representation

(c) Statements of Law

8.161 Misrepresentation of law is likely to be a ground for relief in the same way as misrepresentation of fact: see *Pankhania v Hackney LBC* [2002] EWHC 2441, [2002] NLJ 1884; cf Supplement para 134 n536.

(2) Other Conditions of Liability

(c) Reliance

8.164 **n621**: on the same principle, it was held that a person who had acquired contractual rights from the original victim of the fraud by novation (Main Work para 8.325) was entitled to damages in respect of the misrepresentation: *Clef Aquitaine SARL v Laporte Materials (Barrow) Ltd* [2001] QB 488.

n623: a claim for relief on the ground of fraud is not barred by the fact that, in addition to the misrepresentation, the representee relied also on some other, though irrational, belief: *Standard Chartered Bank v Pakistan National Shipping Corp (No 2)* [2002] UKHL 43, [2003] 1 AC 959 at [14]–[15].

n626: for the rights of a representee who was influenced partly by fraud and partly by other inducements, see also *Standard Chartered Bank v Pakistan National Shipping Corp (No 2)* [2002] UKHL 43, [2003] 1 AC 959.

(3) Damages

(a) Fraud

8.165 **n628**: new provisions for compensation in respect of untrue or misleading statements in 'listing particulars' are made by Financial Services and Markets Act 2001, s 90. The Financial Services Act 1986 is repealed by the Financial Services and Markets Act 2000 (Consequential Amendments and Repeals) Order 2001, SI 2001/3649.

n630: *Standard Chartered Bank v Pakistan National Shipping Corp (No 2)* [2000] 1 Lloyd's Rep 218 has been reversed in part [2002] UKHL 43, [2003] 1 AC 959, but not on the point for which it is cited in n630 in the Main Work.

(f) Content of the right to damages

8.171 **n564**: see also *Clef Aquitaine SARL v Laporte Materials (Barrow) Ltd* [2001] QB 488 where a buyer who had been induced to enter into a contract by fraud recovered the difference between what he had paid and the lower amount that he would, but for the fraud, have paid.

(h) Criminal Compensation Orders

n666: the provisions formerly contained in Powers of Criminal Courts Act 1973, s 35 have been repealed and are replaced by Powers of Criminal Courts (Sentencing) Act 2000, s 130. For Financial Services Act 1986, ss 47, 61 (now repealed: see Supplement para 8.165 n628) substitute Financial Services and Markets Act 2000, s 397. **8.173**

n667: the provisions formerly contained in Powers of Criminal Courts Act 1973, s 38 have been repealed and are replaced by Powers of Criminal Courts (Sentencing) Act 2000, s 134.

(4) Rescission

(f) Non-disclosure

(i) General rules

n707: for further provisions applicable to 'insider dealing', see the prohibition of 'market abuse' in Financial Services and Markets Act 2000, s 118. **8.189**

(ii) Exceptional cases

n718: the duty of disclosure here under discussion is one which exists in the negotiations *before* the conclusion of the contract of insurance. It is distinct from any duty of disclosure which may be imposed by the terms of the contract in relation to events or claims *after* the contract was made: *Manifest Shipping Co Ltd v Uni-Polaris Insurance Co Ltd (The Star Sea)* [2001] UKHL 1, [2003] AC 469. **8.192**

n729: new provisions imposing a statutory duty of disclosure in 'listing particulars' are made by Financial Services and Markets Act 2000, s 80. For the repeal of the Financial Services Act 1986, see Supplement para 8.165 n628. **8.198**

G. Improper Pressure

(2) Undue Influence

(a) Actual pressure

n746: the view that in cases of actual pressure the victim need not show that the transaction was to his disadvantage is supported by *Royal Bank of Scotland v Etridge (No 2)* [2001] UKHL 44, [12], [2002] 2 AC 773, *per* Lord Nicholls, with whose speech Lords Bingham and Clyde agreed. **8.202**

(b) Presumed undue influence

The principles relating to presumed undue influence have been restated by the **8.203**

House of Lords in *Royal Bank of Scotland v Etridge (No 2)*[758a] the following conclusions (based mainly on the leading speech of Lord Nicholls)[758b] may tentatively be drawn. The presumption arises where two facts are established by the party seeking to impugn the transaction. These are[758c] that (1) the relationship between two parties, A and B, is such that A has reposed trust and confidence in B and (2) the transaction is one which 'calls for explanation' (eg because it is a substantial transfer of property, as opposed to a moderate Christmas gift). The second of these requirements replaces or reformulates that (stated in some of the earlier authorities)[758d] of a transaction which is 'disadvantageous' to A. In a number of situations, moreover, 'the law presumes, irrebuttably'[758e] that A has reposed trust and confidence in B. This is the position where the relationship between A and B falls into the first of the two groups described in the Main Work:[758f] eg where B is A's parent, trustee or solicitor. The effect of establishing facts (1) (either by evidence or by means of the irrebuttable presumption) and (2) above[758g] is to give rise to 'a rebuttable evidential presumption of undue influence'[758h] so that the court will infer 'that in the absence of a satisfactory explanation, the transaction can only have been procured by undue influence'.[758i] This presumption[758j] can be rebutted in the way described in the Main Work[758k] or by other evidence that A's will was not in fact 'overborne'.[758l] The above principles are subject to some modification where the relationship between B and A is that of husband and wife living together in a successful marriage.[758m] In such a relationship each party will normally repose trust and confidence in the other[758n] (though the relationship is not one to which the irrebuttable presumption described above applies).[758o] But even a substantial gift by A to B or a guarantee by A of B's business debts will not 'in the ordinary case'[758p] call for explanation since in such a relationship it can plausibly be accounted for by motives of affection or joint interest.[758q] But there is a 'minority

[758a] [2001] UKHL 44, [2002] 2 AC 773.
[758b] With which Lords Bingham and Clyde agreed: see at [3], [91].
[758c] At [14].
[758d] See Main Work para 8.203 n748; *Barclays Bank plc v Coleman* [2000] 1 All ER 385 was affirmed in *Royal Bank of Scotland v Etridge (No 2)* (n758a above): see n758t below.
[758e] *Royal Bank of Scotland v Etridge (No 2)* (n758a above) at [18].
[758f] Main Work para 8.203 at nn749–51.
[758g] After n758c above.
[758h] *Royal Bank of Scotland v Etridge (No 2)* (n758a above) at [16].
[758i] ibid at [14].
[758j] Unlike the irrebutable presumption stated at n758c above.
[758k] Main Work para 8.203 n758.
[758l] *Royal Bank of Scotland v Etridge (No 2)* (n758a above) at [162].
[758m] Or of parties living together in an analogous relationship without being married.
[758n] *Royal Bank of Scotland v Etridge (No 2)* (n758 above) at [159].
[758o] ibid, at [19].
[758p] ibid, at [30].
[758q] ibid, at [159].

of cases'[758r] in which a husband may take advantage of his wife's 'vulnerability'[758s] and in which the law will protect the wife against such conduct,[758t] though it is not clear whether this result is to be explained on the ground of actual[758u] or of presumed[758v] undue influence. The further point, that in such cases the party to whom the guarantee of B's debts is given must take steps to safeguard A against the *risk* of undue influence on A's part, is discussed in para 8.206 of the Main Work and of this Supplement.

(c) Unconscionable bargains

n763: Fair Trading Act 1973, s 17 has been repealed by Enterprise Act 2002. Some of the legislative restrictions discussed in paras 8.108–8.128 are designed to prevent, or to redress, the abuse of superior bargaining power: eg Unfair Contract Terms Act 1977, s 11 (2) and Sch 2, para (a). **8.204**

(d) Bars to relief

(i) General

n767: where a wife had by affirmation lost her right to avoid a transfer against her husband on the ground of alleged undue influence, she was held also to have lost her secondary right of avoidance against a bank (under the rules stated in Main Work para 8.206): *First National Bank v Walker* [2001] FLR 505. **8.205**

(ii) Third party rights

n774: there is no invariable requirement for the bank to hold a separate meeting with C: *Royal Bank of Scotland v Etridge (No 2)* [2001] UKHL 44, [55], [2002] 2 AC 773; and cases in which A has to ensure that the solicitor's advice is actually taken by C will be extremely rare: see at [58]–[63]. **8.206**

The law relating to cases in which A (usually a bank) lends money to B for the purposes of his business and the loan is guaranteed, or charged on property wholly or partly owned by C (often B's wife) is extensively reviewed in *Royal Bank of Scotland v Etridge (No 2)*.[777a] The use of the phrase 'constructive knowledge' in this context is discouraged: instead the question is whether A is 'put on inquiry'. This

---

758r ibid, at [37].

758s ibid, at [36]; cf [163] ('vulnerable surety wives').

758t As in *Barclays Bank plc v Coleman* (n758d above) where the actual decision was that the wife lost her case against the third party lender as the latter had taken reasonable steps of the kind described in Supplement para 8.206.

758u *Royal Bank of Scotland v Etridge (No 2)* (n758a above) at [130].

758v ibid, at [291].

777a [2001] UKHL 44, [2002] 2 AC 773.

is a convenient[777b] (if not strictly accurate)[777c] phrase to indicate that A must take reasonable steps[777d] to reduce the risk of C's entering into the transaction as a result of undue influence exerted by B. There is no need for A itself to investigate this question[777e] or for one of its representatives to hold a personal meeting with C.[777f] It will[777g] suffice for A to communicate directly[777h] with C to the effect that A will require a solicitor acting for C (who may also act for A or B or both of them in the transaction)[777i] to confirm to A in writing that the solicitor has explained to C the nature and effects of the documents to be signed by C, containing the transaction;[777j] this explanation must be given at a face to face meeting between the solicitor and C, in the absence of B.[777k] A must also supply the solicitor with the financial information relating to the transaction which he needs for the purpose.[777l] These guidelines will apply to all relationships (whether marital, sexual though non-marital,[777m] or not)[777n] in which trust and confidence are likely to be reposed by C in B; they will, moreover, apply, where C *acts as surety* for B's debts, whenever the relationship between them is a non-commercial one.[777o] They do not, by contrast, normally apply to the case of a joint loan made by A to B and C: in such a case, A is not 'put on inquiry' unless A knows that the loan is made solely for B's purposes, as distinct from the joint purposes of B and C.[777p]

H. Illegality

(1) Contracts Contrary to Law

(a) Making of contract forbidden by law

8.208 **n780**: for an account of the legislative changes made with regard to 'conditional' (as opposed to 'contingent') fees, see *Callery v Gray* [2001] EWCA Civ 1117, [2001] 1 WLR 2112, affirmed [2002] UKHL 28, [2002] 1 WLR 2000; *Sharratt v London Central Bus Co Ltd* [2003] EWCA Civ 718, [2003] 4 All ER 590.

[777b] ibid, at [44]; references in this and the following footnotes are to the speech of Lord Nicholls, with which Lords Bingham and Clyde agreed.
[777c] ibid, at [41].
[777d] ibid, at [54].
[777e] ibid, at [53].
[777f] ibid, at [55]; though taking such a step may be sufficient: ibid at [50]
[777g] See the reference to 'the future' in ibid, at [50]
[777h] ibid, at [79].
[777i] ibid, at [74].
[777j] ibid, at [79].
[777k] ibid, at [66].
[777l] ibid, at [79].
[777m] ibid, at [47].
[777n] ibid, at [83].
[777o] ibid, at [87].
[777p] ibid, at [48]; Main Work para 8.206 after n774.

(c) Method of performance contrary to law

n793: the policy stated in the Main Work in the sentence ending with n 793 is continued by Financial Services and Markets Act 2000, ss 20 and 26–30. The Financial Services Act 1986 has been repealed: see Supplement para 8.165 n628. **8.213**

(d) Performance contingent on unlawful act

n801: see also *Charlton v Fisher* [2001] EWCA Civ 112, [2002] QB 578, motorist not entitled to be indemnified by his insurer where he had caused criminal damage to another's car by deliberately backing his own car into it in a car park. **8.215**

(2) Contracts Contrary to Public Policy

(b) Types of contract contrary to public policy

(i) Sexual immorality

n815: see also *Ghaidan v Godin-Mendoza* [2002] EWCA Civ 1533, [2003] Ch 380 (same sex partner entitled to succeed to statutory tenancy). **8.218**

(2) Contracts Contrary to Public Policy

(c) Restraint of trade

(i) Sale of a business and employment

n876a: in *Dranez Anstalt v Hayek* [2002] EWCA Civ 1729, The Times, 3 December 2002 a restraint on an inventor of a medical device to prevent him from competing with a manufacturer of such devices was held invalid, mainly because it was contrary to the public interest. **8.239**

(v) Other agreements

n892: in *World Wide Fund for Nature v World Wrestling Foundation* [2002] EWCA Civ 196, [2002] UKCLR 338 the restraint of trade doctrine was held to apply to an agreement to settle an intellectual property dispute, but the agreement was upheld as the party resisting its enforcement failed to show that it was unreasonable. **8.243**

(vi) Competition Law

Under the 1998 Act, claims for monetary compensation are available to persons who have suffered loss or damage as a result of an infringement of its provisions (s 47A); where such persons are 'consumers,' such claims can be brought on their behalf by a 'specified body' (s 47B). **8.244**

(3) Effects of Illegality

(a) Enforcement

(ii) Position of innocent party

8.247 **n906**: for new provisions on the enforceability of contracts by (and at the discretion of the court against) members of a protected class, see Financial Services and Markets Act 2000, ss 20 and 26–30. For repeal of the Financial Services Act 1986, see Supplement para 8.165 n628.

(d) Restitution

(ii) Exceptions

8.253 **n923**: for power to order restitution in favour of a person to whom financial services are provided by a person lacking the requisite licence, see Financial Services and Markets Act 2000, ss 26(2), 27(2) and 28(3)–(6).

I. Lack of Capacity

(1) Minors

(b) Voidable contracts

8.267 **n972**: if a minor were to become a member of a limited liability partnership, his legal relations with the other members would be governed by the Limited Liability Partnerships Act 2000, ss 4 and 5. These sections contain no reference to minority.

(3) Drunken Persons

8.276 **n1003**: habitual drunkenness or drug addiction does not of itself deprive a person of contractual capacity: *Irvani v Irvani* [2000] 1 Lloyd's Rep 412 at 425.

J. Plurality of Parties

(1) Promises by More than One Person

(b) Similarities

8.280 **n1011**: where A and B are not joint, or joint and several, debtors, but have entered into entirely separate contracts with C, each of which has been broken, an agreement between A and C for the release by C of all claims against A may be expressed to cover loss suffered by C by reason, not only of A's, but also of B's breach. It is then a question of the construction of the agreement to what extent it was intended to cover C's claims against B (whether arising from breach of the contract between them or otherwise): *Heaton v Axa Equity and Law Life Assurance Society plc* [2002] UKHL 15, [2002] 2 AC 329.

K. Third Parties

(1) Benefiting Third Parties

n1039: under Sale and Supply of Goods to Consumers Regulations 2002, SI 2002/3045, reg 15, contractual liability under 'consumer guarantees' can arise even though the common law requirements of a 'collateral contract' are not satisfied. **8.289**

(a) Privity of contract at common law

(i) Operation of the contract

n1049: the promisee can claim the agreed sum if the contract on its true construction is one to pay the third party or as the promisee may direct: *Tradigrain SA v King Diamond Shipping SA (The Spiros C)* [2001] 2 Lloyd's Rep 319, 331. **8.292**

n1055: on the same principle, an executrix was able to recover substantial damages from a firm of solicitors whom she had instructed to act for her in administering the estate and whose failure to take steps to that end caused loss of income to the estate: *Chappell v Somers & Blake* [2003] EWHC 1644 (Ch), [2003] 3 All ER 1076; it made no difference that the executrix was not a beneficiary under the will.

(ii) Scope of the doctrine

n1070: a solicitor engaged by one party to a transaction may, in exceptional circumstances, owe a duty of care in tort to the other: *Dean v Allin and Watts* [2001] EWCA Civ 758, [2001] 2 Lloyd's Rep 249. **8.295**

n1075: for the time at which C must have acquired a proprietary or possessory interest in the damaged thing so as to enable him to sue A in tort, see *Homburg Houtimport BV v Agrosin Private Ltd (The Starsin)* [2003] UKHL 12, [2003] 2 WLR 711 at [40], [64], [90], [139].

n1081: where the negligent solicitors had settled the disappointed beneficiary's claim, it was held in *Corbett v Bond Pearce* [2001] EWCA Civ 531, [2001] 3 All ER 769 that they were not liable to the testatrix's estate for the costs of an action successfully brought by beneficiaries under an earlier will to challenge the validity of the will in favour of the former (ie the disappointed) beneficiary. **8.296**

n1082: for an application of the principle of the disappointed beneficiary cases outside the testamentary context, see *Gorham v British Telecommunications plc* [2000] 1 WLR 2129 where negligent advice by an insurance company in relation to pension arrangements, causing loss to the dependants of the assured, but not to the assured himself, gave the dependants a right of action in tort against the company.

(b) Exceptions to the doctrine

(ii) Contracts (Rights of Third Parties) Act 1999

8.300 **n1094**: in *Nisshin Shipping Co Ltd v Cleaves & Co Ltd* [2003] EWHC 2602, [2004] 1 Lloyd's Rep 38, a third party was held to be able to enforce a term of a contract by virtue of s 1(2)(b) of the 1999 Act in circumstances in which, before the Act, he could have done so as the beneficiary of a trust of the promisor's promise (see Main Work, para 8.299).

(iii) Other statutory exceptions

8.310 **n1131**: for further discussion of rights of third parties against the Motor Insurers' Bureau, see *White v White* [2001] UKHL 9, [2001] 1 WLR 481.

8.311 **n1134**: the exact ground on which Law of Property Act 1925, s 56 was said to be applicable in *OTV Birwelco Ltd v Technical & General Guarantee Co Ltd* [2002] EWHC 2240, [2002] 4 All ER 668, at [12] is not clear from the reported facts.

(3) Exemption Clauses and Third Parties

(a) Benefiting third parties

(ii) Himalaya clauses

8.317 **n1157**: the third party is not, at common law, protected where the provision in the Himalaya Clause on which he relies is invalid under other rules of law: *Homburg Houtimport BV v Agrosin Private Ltd (The Starsin)* [2003] UKHL 12, [2003] 2 WLR 711. The same result would follow under the 1999 Act (see Main Work at n1159) by virtue of s 3(6) of that Act.

(b) Binding third parties

8.321 **n1163**: an alternative explanation of such cases is that C's consent to the terms of the sub-bailment to A gives rise to an implied contract between A and C: *Sandeman Coprimar SA v Transitos y Transportes Integrales SL* [2003] EWCA Civ 113, [2003] QB 1270, at [63]–[65].

L. Transfer of Contractual Rights

(6) Consideration

(b) Further acts to be done by assignor

8.336 **n1202**: vesting the subject matter in one of a number of trustees was held to complete the gift in *T Choithram International SA v Pagarani* [2001] 1 WLR1. In *Pennington v Waine* [2002] EWCA Civ 227, [2002] 1 WLR 2075 the execution of an instrument of transfer of shares in a company, with the intention to make a gift of them, was held to have completed the gift, even without delivery of the instrument to either the donee or the company, since any further steps necessary to complete the gift could have been taken by the donee and the donor had constituted himself the donee's agent for the purpose of taking such steps by telling the donee that nothing more needed to be done to that end.

(10) Vicarious Performance

n1243: C's performance of A's obligation to B will not necessarily discharge A: eg payment by a bank of its customer's debt does not discharge the debt unless the payment is authorized or ratified by the customer: *Crantrave Ltd v Lloyd's Bank plc* [2000] QB 917. **8.349**

M. Performance

(1) Method of Performance

(a) When performance is due

n1253: for legislation requiring a demand before performance is due, see also Commonhold and Leasehold Reform Act 2002, s 166. **8.352**

(2) Rescission for Failure to Perform

(a) Introduction

n1266: for use of the term 'rescission' in this context, see also Sale of Goods Act 1979, ss 48A(2)(b)(ii), 48C and 48D(1)(a) and (2)(a), all referring to a remedy available to a buyer who deals as consumer in respect of non-conformity of the goods. **8.356**

(d) Exception to the requirement of substantial failure

(i) Express provisions

n1296: for restrictions on a landlord's right to forfeit certain leases, see also Commonhold and Leashold Reform Act 2002, ss 167–170. **8.365**

(iii) Conditions, warranties and intermediate terms

n1130: for the judicial tendency not to be 'too ready' to classify a previously unclassified term as a 'condition', see also *Universal Bulk Carriers Ltd v André & Cie* [2001] EWCA Civ 588, [2001] 2 Lloyd's Rep 65. **8.373**

n1336: the 'additional rights' conferred on a buyer who deals as consumer by ss 48A–48C of the Sale of Goods Act 1979 include a right to rescind for non-conformity. This right is subject, under s 48E, to restrictions; but these restrictions do **8.374**

not affect the consumer's right (preserved by s 15A) to reject under the rules stated in paras 8.369–8.371 of the Main Work.

8.378A **Consumer sales.** Under Sale of Goods Act 1979, ss 48A and 48C, a buyer who deals as consumer has in certain circumstances the right to rescind the contract in respect of non-conforming goods. Non-conformity here includes breach of an express term (s 48F) which may be a warranty. The buyer's right to rescind for breach of such a warranty is, however, subject under s 48E to the power of the court to award another remedy, such as price reduction.

(e) Limitations on the right to rescind

8.383 **n1360**: for the distinction between the two types of waiver described in para 8.383 of the Main Work, see also *Glencore Grain Ltd v Flacker Shipping Ltd (The Happy Day)* [2002] EWCA Civ 1068, [2002] 2 Lloyd's Rep 487 at [64], [65], [68].

N. Breach

(1) What Amounts to Breach?

(c) Standard of duty

(i) Strict liability

8.409 **n1446**: an element of fault enters into the seller's liability in respect of public statements relating to the goods. Under Sale of Goods Act 1979, s 14(2E)(a) there is no such liability if, when the statement was made, the seller 'was not, and could not reasonably have been, aware of the statement'.

(3) Repudiation Before Performance is Due

(c) Effect of not accepting the breach

8.433 **n1512**: the view stated in the Main Work text to n1512 (that affirmation does not bar the right to rescind in the face of a continuing refusal to perform) is accepted in *Stocznia Gdanska SA v Latvian Shipping Co (No 3)* [2001] 1 Lloyd's Rep 537 (disagreeing in this respect with the case of the same name cited in Main work n1512). On appeal [2002] EWCA Civ 889, [2002] 2 Lloyd's Rep 436 it was not necessary to decide the point as it was held that there had been no affirmation; but the Court of Appeal at [96]–[100] inclined to the view that affirmation would not be a bar to later rescission for anticipatory breach, nor necessarily in cases of actual breach.

9

AGENCY AND REPRESENTATION

A. General Considerations

(1) Introduction

(c) Commercial agents

n9: see also *Mercantile International Group plc v Chuan Soon Huat Industrial Group Ltd* [2002] EWCA Civ 288, [2002] 1 All ER (Comm) 788. **9.06**

(3) The Boundaries of Agency

(b) Indirect representation

n22: but compare *Triffit Nurseries v Salads Etcetera Ltd* [1999] 1 All ER (Comm) **9.19**

110, [2000] 1 All ER (Comm) 737, CA, where the first instance judgment in particular suggests that indirect agency reasoning may be required.

(d) Companies: agent and organ

9.22 **n31**: the *Meridian* case is in fact a Privy Council (PC) case, not HL as stated in the Main text of this footnote. Also, caution as to the proper extent of the more recent line of reasoning mentioned in Main Work para 9.22 (ie that the acts of certain persons are regarded as the acts of the company itself) is, however, expressed by Buxton LJ in *Odyssey Re (London) Ltd v OIC Run-Off Ltd* [2001] LRLR 1, CA; and see Watts (2000) 116 LQR 525.

(f) Lack of significance of types of agent

9.24 **n34**: the *Dun & Bradstreet* case is reported at [1998] 2 EGLR 175, CA.

B. Formation of Agency

(1) Conferring of Authority

(a) Significance of agreement

9.28 **n46**: there is valuable discussion on these issues by Finn J in *South Sydney DRLFC v News Ltd* (2000) 177 ALR 611 at 645ff, affirmed without reference to this point [2003] HCA 415, (2003) 77 ALJR 1575.

9.29 **n47**: this case is, however, not accepted as authority for such reasoning in American Law Institute, *Restatement, Third, Agency*, Tentative Draft No 2 (2001), Reporter's Note to para 3.01.

(2) Ratification

(d) Retroactivity of ratification

9.38 **n64**: see the general problem discussed by Tan Cheng-Han (2001) 117 LQR 626.

9.40 The following should be added to the Main Work:

Two recent cases adopt a general approach, of which the property cases are only to be taken as examples, that ratification is not permitted where to allow it would be unfairly prejudicial to the third party.[73A]

n73A: *Smith v Henniker-Major & Co* [2002] EWCA Civ 762, [2002] Ch 182; *The Borvigilant* [2003] EWCA Civ 935, [2003] 2 Lloyd's Rep 520.

C. The External Effects of Agency

(1) *Express and Implied Authority*

(c) Other considerations

n81: see *Heinl v Jyske Bank (Gibraltar) Ltd* [1999] Lloyd's Rep Bank 511 especially at 519–21, CA; though there are contrary dicta in *Macmillan Inc v Bishopsgate Investment Trust plc (No 3)* [1995] 1 WLR 978 at 984. **9.53**

(2) *Actual and Apparent Authority*

(b) Apparent authority

(i) Basis of doctrine

n89: it appears, however, that the understanding in the United States is that the principal can sue. See *Restatement, Third, Agency*, Tentative Draft No 2 (2001) at 167, 183, 205. **9.60**

n96: *Hirst v Etherington* is reported in [1999] Lloyd's Rep PN 938, CA. **9.62**

(3) *Doctrine of the Undisclosed Principal*

(b) Limitation and exclusion of the doctrine

n122: in the United States it seems that the doctrine is clearly regarded as one facilitating the principal's concealed entry into a market, for example, to accumulate parcels of land. See Hynes, *Agency, Partnership and the LLC* (5th edn, 1998) at 377ff. **9.72**

(c) Other difficulties of the doctrine

n132: the reference to *Bowstead and Reynolds on Agency* should now be to the 17th edn (2001). **9.76**

n133: as to Canada see *Lang Transport Ltd v International Trucking Ltd* (1997) 143 DLR (4th) 672.

(5) *Delegation of Agency Functions*

n151: cf *Pangood Ltd v Barclay Brown & Co Ltd* [1999] PNLR 678, CA. It has been held that the Commercial Agents Regulations do not apply as between principal and subagent: *Light v Ty Europe Ltd* [2003] ECWA Civ 1238, [2003] Eur LR 858. **9.87**

(6) Agency of Necessity

9.90 n157: the traditional approach was, however, followed in England in *The Pa Mar* [1999] 1 Lloyd's Rep 338.

(7) Termination of Authority

(a) External position

9.96 n164: contrast *Schindler v Brie* [2003] EWHC 1804 (Ch), [2003] WTLR 1361.

(b) Internal position

9.99 n173: the reference to *Bowstead and Reynolds on Agency* should now be to the 17th edn (2001). A recent discussion appears in *Alpha Lettings Ltd v Neptune Research and Development Ltd* [2002] EWCA Civ 704, citing *Crawford Fitting Co v Sydney Valve and Fittings Pty Ltd* (1988) 14 NSWLR 438.

(c) Commercial agents

9.100 n174: the reference to *Bowstead and Reynolds on Agency* should now be to chapter 11 of the 17th edn (2001).

9.101 n178: *King v T Tunnock Ltd* was decided in the (Scottish) Court of Session on the basis of French law as understood by the court: 2000 SC 424. Scepticism as to such an approach is expressed in *Duffen v Frabo SpA* (see Main Work, this note) and in *Barret McKenzie v Escada (UK) Ltd* [2001] ECC 50, [2001] Eur LR 567; it was viewed favourably in *Ingmar GB Ltd v Eaton Leonard Technologies Inc* [2001] EWHC 3 (QB), [2001] Eur LR 755, but doubts were cast on this in *Tigana Ltd v Decoro Ltd* [2003] EWHC 23 (QB), [2003] Eur LR 189.

D. The Agent and Third Parties

(1) Rights and Liabilities on the Main Contract

(b) Agent of undisclosed principal

9.107 n190: *Alfred McAlpine Ltd v Panatown Ltd* is now reported at [2001] 1 AC 518, HL. See also *L/M International Construction Inc (now Bovis International Inc) v The Circle Ltd Partnership* (1995) 49 Con LR 12, CA.

9.108 n192: the reference to *Bowstead and Reynolds on Agency* should now be to the 17th edn (2001).

(c) Oral and written contracts

9.109 n194: the reference to *Bowstead and Reynolds on Agency* should now be to the 17th edn (2001). A recent example of such a dispute is *Internaut Shipping GmbH v Fercometal SARL (The Elikon)* [2003] 2 Lloyd's Rep 430.

(2) *Liability of the Unauthorized Agent*

n198: such reasoning now derives support from the judgment of Arden LJ in *Braymist Ltd v Wise Finance Co Ltd* [2002] EWCA Civ 127, [2002] Ch 273. **9.110**

n199: this case deals with a contract on behalf of a company not yet formed. Problems of this sort are now regulated by s 36C(1) of the Companies Act 1985, which implements the first EEC Directive on company law. For discussion of cases on it see *Bowstead and Reynolds on Agency* (17th edn, 2001) 511 and see more recently *Braymist Ltd v Wise Finance Co Ltd* [2002] EWCA Civ 127, [2002] Ch 273 (agent has right to sue).

n202: For a recent more straightforward example, see *Habton Farms v Nimmo* [2002] EWCA Civ 68, [2004] QB 1. **9.111**

(3) *Agent's Liability in Tort*

n206: see now also *Merrett v Babb* [2001] QB 1174, CA (surveyor); *Dean v Allin & Watts* [2001] 2 Lloyd's Rep 249, CA (solicitor). **9.113**

n207: eg *Fairline Shipping Corporation v Adamson* [1975] QB 180 (contract); *Standard Chartered Bank v Pakistan National Shipping Corp (No 2)* [2002] UKHL 43, [2003] 1 AC 959 (deceit); contrast *Trevor Ivory Ltd v Anderson* [1992] NZLR 517 and *Williams v Natural Life Health Foods Ltd* [1998] 1 WLR 830, HL, where liability in negligence was not imposed. These cases raise difficult questions as to the extent to which the acts of the agent of a company should be regarded as those of the company and thus not giving rise to personal liability at all. See Reynolds, 'Personal Liability of Company Directors in Tort' (2002) 33 HKLJ 51 and literature there cited.

n212: a recent example is *Marcq v Christie, Manson & Woods* [2003] 3 WLR 980.

(4) *Restitution*

n216: the reference to Goff and Jones, *Law of Restitution*, should now be to the 6th edn (2002), ch 40. **9.114**

n218: the reference to Goff and Jones, *Law of Restitution*, should now be to the 6th edn (2002) paras 40-014ff; that to Burrows, *Law of Restitution*, should now be to the 2nd edn (2002) 597ff.

E. The Use of Agency Reasoning in Non-contractual Situations

(2) Agency Reasoning Used Against the Principal in Tort Cases

9.127 **n233**: the reference should now be to *Clerk and Lindsell on Torts* (18th edn, 2001) paras 5-23ff.

n234: the reference should now be to paras 5-48ff (ie of the 18th edn).

9.128 **n239**: difficulties can occur where the act of the agent is said not to be a wrong at all. See Main Work para 9.113, n206 as updated by this Supplement.

n240: the words 'make the agent liable on a statement' should read 'make the principal liable on a statement by the agent that'.

(3) Notification, Notice and Knowledge

9.131 **n243**: see an elaborate discussion of the problems in *Permanent Trustee Australia Co Ltd v FAI General Insurance Co Ltd* (2001) 50 NSWLR 679 (revised without reference to this point [2003] HCA 25, (2003) 77 ALJR 1070); see also Watts (2001) 117 LQR 300.

F. The Internal Relationship Between Principal and Agent

(1) Duties of the Agent Towards the Principal

(b) Equity: fiduciary duties

(i) Scope of the duties

9.138 **n263**: a recent example is *Re Bhullar Bros* [2003] 2 BCLC 241.

n264: see now also *Fyffes Group Ltd v Templeman* [2000] 2 Lloyd's Rep 643, and comment by Mitchell (2001) 117 LQR 207.

9.139 **n269**: assurances were also accepted in *Halewood International Ltd v Addleshaw Booth & Co* [2000] Lloyd's Rep PN 298.

(ii) Exclusion of fiduciary duties

9.140 **n270**: the Act of 2000 has been brought into effect by stages during 2001. The part of it most relevant here became effective on 18 June 2001 (SI 2001/1820).

(iii) Remedies

9.141 **n274**: the reference to Goff and Jones, *Law of Restitution*, should now be to the 6th edn (2002) ch 2.

n275: but see a useful discussion by Conaglen (2003) 119 LQR 246; *JJ Harrison (Properties) Ltd v Harrison* [2002] 1 BCLC 162.

n281: *Coulthard v Disco Mix Club Ltd* is now reported in [2000] 1 WLR 707; see now also *Cia de Seguros Imperio v Heath (REBX) Ltd* [2001] 1 WLR 112, CA. See also *Gwembe Valley Development Co Ltd v Koshy* [2003] EWCA Civ 1478. **9.142**

n282: a recent example is *Hilton v Barker Booth and Eastwood* [2002] Lloyd's Rep PN 500.

n283: there is also valuable discussion in *Pilmer v Duke Group Ltd* (2001) 207 CLR 165, HCA.

n284: but a more moderate view was taken in *Cadbury Schweppes Inc v FBI Foods Ltd* [1999] 1 SCR 142.

n288: in *Dubai Aluminium Co Ltd v Salaam* [2003] 2 AC 366 at [142] Lord Millett preferred 'accountable in equity' to 'accountable as constructive trustee'. **9.144**

(2) Rights of the Agent Against the Principal

(a) Commission

n292: for a recent example see *Harding Maughan Hambly Ltd v Cie Européenne de Courtage d'Assurances et de Réassurances SA* [2000] 1 Lloyd's Rep 316. **9.147**

(b) Reimbursement

n297: for a recent discussion of the right to indemnity see *Linklaters v HSBC Bank plc* [2003] EWHC 1113 (Comm), [2003] 2 Lloyd's Rep 545. **9.148**

10

SALE OF GOODS

A. The Statutory Regime

(1) Introduction

n1: the reference to PS Atiyah, *The Sale of Goods* should now be to the 10th edn (2001) and the reference to *Benjamin: Sale of Goods* should now be to the 6th edn (2002). See also E McKendrick (ed), *Sale of Goods* (2000). **10.01**

n10: the reference to *Benjamin: Sale of Goods* should now be to the 6th edn (2002) paras 1-008 and 1-009. **10.02**

(c) **Consumer sales**

The application of the Sale of Goods Act 1979 to consumer sales must now be modified in the light of Council Directive (EC) 1999/44 on Certain Aspects of the Sale of Consumer Goods and Associated Guarantees [1999] OJ L171/12 which has been implemented in English law in the form of the Sale and Supply of Goods to Consumers Regulations 2002 (SI 2002/3045). The Directive has as one of its aims the creation of a common set of minimum rules of consumer law and it applies to contracts made by a consumer buyer with a professional seller. The Directive should have been implemented into UK law no later than 1 January 2002 but the Regulations did not in fact come into force until 31 March 2003. The Regulations have modified the application of ss 13–15 of **10.04A** the Sale of Goods Act 1979 to consumer sales. They have also introduced a more elaborate remedial regime than that originally contained in the Sale of Goods Act 1979. The Regulations are discussed in more detail in a supplement to the 6th edition of *Benjamin: Sale of Goods* published in 2003. See more generally M Bridge, 'What is to be done about Sale of Goods?' (2003) 119 LQR 173.

(2) The Scope of the Sale of Goods Act 1979

(b) Goods

(i) Distinguished from services or work and material

10.07 n24: the reference to *Benjamin: Sale of Goods* should now be to the 6th edn (2002) paras 1-041–1-047.

(ii) Definition

10.08 n28: the reference to *Benjamin: Sale of Goods* should now be to the 6th edn (2002) paras 1-092–1-094.

(d) Transfer of property

10.12 n43: the reference to PS Atiyah, *The Sale of Goods* should now be to the 10th edn (2001) 309. See now also G Battersby, 'A reconsideration of 'Property' and 'Title' in the Sale of Goods Act' [2001] JBL 1.

B. Transfer of Property and Risk

(1) The Passing of Property

10.13 n46: the reference to Atiyah should now be to 314–15 (of the 10th edn, 2001).

(2) Transfer of Title by a Non-Owner

(b) Exceptions to the *nemo dat* rule

10.23 n101: the reference to *Benjamin: Sale of Goods* should now be to the 6th edn (2002) ch 7.

n112: replace *Forsythe International (UK) Ltd v Silver Shipping Co Ltd* [1994] 1 WLR 1334, QBD with *Michael Gerson (Leasing) Ltd v Wilkinson* [2001] QB 514, CA, noted by Ulph (2001) 64 MLR 481.

(3) Risk of Loss or Damage

(b) Goods that have already perished when the contract is made

10.25 n130: the reference to *Benjamin: Sale of Goods* should now be to the 6th edn

(2002), para 1-032 and the reference to PS Atiyah, *The Sale of Goods* should now be to the 10th edn (2001) 93–8.

C. The Contract

(1) The Terms of the Contract

(a) Implied terms about title

(i) Right to sell the goods

n144: the reference to *Benjamin: Sale of Goods* should now be to the 6th edn (2002) para 4-006. **10.27**

(c) Satisfactory quality and fitness for purpose

(i) Of satisfactory quality

The definition of 'satisfactory quality' has been amended in the case where the buyer deals as a consumer. In such a case the factors to be taken into account also include any public statements on the specific characteristics of the goods made about them by the seller, the producer or his representative, particularly in advertising or on labelling. However, a public statement is not to be taken into account if the seller shows that (a) at the time the contract was made, he was not, and could not reasonably have been, aware of the statement, (b) before the contract was made, the statement had been withdrawn in public or, to the extent that it contained anything which was incorrect or misleading, it had been corrected in public, or (c) the decision to buy the goods could not have been influenced by the statement (see ss 14(2D)–(2F) of the Sale of Goods Act 1979). These provisions were inserted into the 1979 Act by the Sale and Supply of Goods to Consumers Regulations 2002 (SI 2002/3045). **10.34**

n177: the reference to *Benjamin: Sale of Goods* should now be to the 6th edn (2002) paras 11-032–11-043

n187: the reference to PS Atiyah, *The Sale of Goods* should now be to the 10th edn (2001) 167–8 and the reference to *Benjamin: Sale of Goods* should now be to the 6th edn (2002) para 11-057.

(2) Performance of the Contract

(a) Delivery

n215: the reference to *Benjamin: Sale of Goods* should now be to the 6th edn (2002) para 19-069. **10.40**

D. Remedies

(1) The Importance of Termination

(a) The pursuit of certainty

10.45 **n241**: but a court today might take a more relaxed approach: see *Truk (UK) Ltd v Tokmakidis GmbH* [2000] 1 Lloyd's Rep 543, 550–1.

(b) Restrictions on the right to reject: s 15A of the 1979 Act

10.46 **n248**: the reference to G Treitel, *The Law of Contract* should now be to the 11th edn (2003) 801–2.

(c) Waiver and acceptance

10.48 **n254**: See also *Clegg v Andersson* [2003] EWCA Civ 320; [2003] 2 Lloyd's Rep 32 at [57]–[60].

n260: the Court of Appeal in *Clegg v Andersson* [2003] EWCA Civ 320; [2003] 2 Lloyd's Rep 32 at [63] concluded that *Bernstein v Pamson Motors (Golders Green) Ltd* no longer represents the law. Hale LJ stated at [76] that 'if a buyer is seeking information which the seller has agreed to supply which will enable the buyer to make a properly informed choice between acceptance, rejection or cure, and if cure in what way, he cannot have lost his right to reject' See further FMB Reynolds 'Loss of the right to reject' (2003) 119 LQR 544.

(2) Remedies of the Seller

(b) Personal remedies

(i) Action for the price

10.58 **n293**: the reference to PS Atiyah, *The Sale of Goods* should now be to the 10th edn (2001) 484–6.

n297: the reference to *Benjamin: Sale of Goods* should now be to the 6th edn (2002) paras 16-027 and 16-028.

(ii) Damages for non-acceptance

10.59 **n303**: the reference to *Benjamin: Sale of Goods* should now be to the 6th edn (2002) paras 16-058–16-066.

n305: the reference to *Benjamin: Sale of Goods* should now be to the 6th edn (2002) paras 16-071–16-072.

(3) Remedies of the Buyer

(d) Consumer buyers

Consumer buyers have been given additional remedies as a result of the insertion of 'Part 5A' into the Sale of Goods Act 1979 by the Sale and Supply of Goods to Consumers Regulations 2002 (SI 2002/3045). These remedies are only available to a buyer who 'deals as consumer' (see s 48A of the 1979 Act). The phrase 'deals as consumer' is defined in s 61(5A) of the 1979 Act and s 12 of the Unfair Contract Terms Act 1977. The consumer buyer is given a qualified right to (a) require the seller to repair or replace the goods (see s 48B of the 1979 Act), (b) reduce the price (see s 48C(1)(a) of the 1979 Act) or (c) rescind the contract (see s 48C(1)(b) and 48C(2) of the 1979 Act). The consumer buyer is also given the benefit of a presumption that goods which do not conform to the contract within six months from the date of delivery did not conform to the contract at the time of delivery (see s 48A(3) and (4)). In other words, the consumer buyer is relieved of the burden of proving that goods did not conform to the contract where the non-conformity occurs within six months of delivery; in such a case it is for the seller to prove that the goods did conform to the contract at the time of delivery. **10.67**

A number of points should be noted about these new provisions. First, they introduce a more elaborate remedial regime into English law and the buyer is, in principle, given the right to select from this remedial menu. Secondly, the right of the buyer to choose is not, however, an unqualified one. To give one example, the buyer cannot require the seller to repair or replace the goods if it would be impossible for the seller to do so or if it would be 'disproportionate' to require the seller to do so ('disproportion' is further defined in s 48B(2) and (3)). The language of 'proportionality' is new to English law in this area and may be said to introduce a degree of uncertainty into the law. That said, repair and replacement are commonly used in practice in consumer sales and the change may be one that has implications in the realm of legal theory rather than practice. Thirdly, these provisions accord a higher priority to specific performance (here using the phrase specific performance to encompass the remedies of repair and replacement) than is traditionally to be found in English law (see further D Harris, 'Specific performance—a regular remedy for consumers?' (2003) 119 LQR 541). In this respect, the provisions reveal a civilian rather than a common law orientation. Fourthly, these provisions introduce into English law the remedy of price reduction. Once again, the consequence may be more apparent at the level of theory than practice given that the remedy of damages frequently reaches results that are very similar to, if not identical with, the result that is reached through reliance on the remedy of price reduction. Finally, the new provisions purport to relegate 'rescission' of the contract to a lowly place in the remedial hierarchy (see s 48C(2)). The meaning of the word 'rescind' in this context is not immediately obvious. It could mean **10.68** either the prospective or the retrospective setting aside of the contract. Prospective discharge is the consequence which an English lawyer would expect to flow from a breach of contract but it may be that it is discharge having retrospective effect which the framers of the Directive had in mind. However, the point may not prove to be an important one in practice. The reason for this is that this new remedial regime does not purport to take away the existing common law or other statutory rights of consumer buyers. Given that consumer buyers had a wide right to reject non-conforming goods prior to the enactment of Part 5A of the 1979 Act (see Main Work and Supplement paras 10.45 and 10.46), buyers who wish to reject are more likely to rely on their existing rights than seek to invoke the additional remedies to be found in Part 5A. The relationship between these new remedies and existing remedies is, however, likely to prove to be an uneasy one and calls for rationalization of the present legal framework are likely to increase in the near future (see, for example, M Bridge, 'What is to be done about Sale of Goods?' (2003) 119 LQR 173). The changes introduced into English law by Part 5A of the 1979 Act are discussed in more detail in a supplement to the 6th edition of *Benjamin: Sale of Goods* published in 2003.

11

CARRIAGE OF GOODS BY SEA

A. Introduction

(1) General

n3: see also Reynolds, 'Maritime and Other Influences on the Common Law' [2002] LMCLQ 182. **11.03**

B. Charterparties

(1) Types of Charterparties

(b) The time charterparty

n11: this decision of the Court of Appeal was, however, reversed by the House of **11.17**

Lords [2001] 1 AC 638, where it was held that such an order was commercial. Reluctance to interfere with the conclusions of arbitrators was stressed.

(2) The Regime Under Which the Goods are Carried

(a) General common law principles

(i) Duty to furnish a seaworthy vessel

11.26 Lines 4–5: for 'lading' read 'loading'.

(3) Remedies for Breach of the Contract Duties

(b) Termination of the contract

(i) Condition or warranty

11.35 n44: for a recent case raising such issues see *The Seaflower* [2001] 1 Lloyd's Rep 341.

(iii) Repudiation or renunciation

11.38 n55: the reference to *Chitty on Contracts* should now be to the 29th edn (2004) vol 1, paras 25-017ff.

(4) Deviation

11.45 n87: the reference to Goff and Jones, *Law of Restitution*, should now be to the 6th edn (2002), paras 20-053 – 20-054.

11.48 n97: it is now clear, however, in England at least, that it does not do so: *The Kapitan Petko Voivoda* [2003] EWCA Civ 451, [2003] 2 Lloyd's Rep 1, CA, overruling *The Chanda. The Pembroke*, being a New Zealand decision, stands in that jurisdiction, but may perhaps deserve reconsideration.

C. Carriage Under a Bill of Lading

(4) The Hague-Visby Rules

11.61 n114: some forms of this clause are puzzling. One form is elucidated in *The Starsin* [2003] UKHL 12, [2003] 2 WLR 711.

11.65 n123: the English approach is reaffirmed in *The Jordan II* [2003] EWCA Civ 144, [2003] 2 Lloyd's Rep 87 (now subject to appeal).

(6) The Present Situation

Add at end of main text:

11.68 At the end of 2001 the CMI (Comité Maritime International) completed a Draft

Instrument on Transport Law, which deals not only with the regime under which goods are carried by sea, but also with the documents used and their transfer, and electronic communication. It has been under consideration by UNCITRAL since that time.

D. Bill of Lading for Goods in a Chartered Ship

(2) Bills of Lading Given to Other Shippers

(a) The 'identity of carrier' problem

n137: Delete second sentence and substitute: In *The Starsin* [2003] UKHL 12, [2003] 2 WLR 711, however, the House of Lords held that a clear indication on the face of the bill that the charterer was carrier overrode a demise clause (below, n138) on the reverse and a further similar clause indicating (not without obscurity caused by miscopying) that the owner was carrier. Thus the charterer was carrier. **11.75**

(b) The 'actual carrier' problem

n142: the question of when the loss or damage is to be regarded as occurring for this purpose is considered in *The Starsin* [2001] 1 Lloyd's Rep 437, 457, CA ('when more than insignificant damage was caused by [the] negligence to the goods'): approved [2003] 2 WLR at [37]–[40], [64]. **11.78**

n145: Substitute as follows:

The Starsin, above, n137, went on to determine also the liability of the owner as actual carrier. The bill of lading contained a Himalaya clause which in addition to incorporating the Hague Rules purported to exempt the actual carrier completely. This part of it was, by a majority, held void under Article III.8 of the Rules, though the majority was not in agreement as to the exact reasons for this. The complications were caused by the way in which the operation of the Himalaya clause is explained in English law (see above, para 11.61).

n149: for a more recent example of similar reasoning see *The Rigoletto* [2001] 1 Lloyd's Rep 437, CA.

E. Freight

The first and second complete sentences on p 291of the Main Work are misleading and require redrafting. They should read: **11.79**

If the goods only arrive in part or arrive damaged, and the cause of this is within the carrier's responsibility, he is entitled to freight but liable in damages, which will include the lost freight.[154] But if the goods do not arrive, and the cause is an excepted peril, though the carrier is not liable, he earns no freight.[155]

F. The Functions of the Bill of Lading and Other Documents

(a) The bill of lading

11.85 **n166**: it has been held that delivery against a forged bill of lading does not discharge the carrier: *Motis Exports Ltd v Dampskipsselskabet AF 1912* [1999] 1 Lloyd's Rep 837.

(2) Receipt for the Goods

11.94 **n190**: the matter is, however, now fully discussed in a court of first instance in *The David Agmashenebeli* [2002] EWHC 104 (Admlty), [2003] 1 Lloyd's Rep 92 ('reasonable assessment of the master').

(3) Document of Title

11.97 **n198**: the reference to *Benjamin's Sale of Goods* should now be to the 6th edn (2002) paras 18-006ff.

11.99 **n200**: in *The Rafaela S* [2002] EWCA Civ 556, [2003] 2 Lloyd's Rep 114 the Court of Appeal decided that a document headed as a bill of lading, not referring to delivery to 'order', but containing at the end a requirement for surrender of one of the bills in exchange for the goods, was a bill of lading or similar document of title for the purposes of the application of the Hague Rules. This, if correct, recognizes a third type of document intermediate between a transferable bill of lading and a waybill, which is nevertheless a bill of lading. An appeal seems likely. See Treitel (2003) 119 LQR 698.

Transfer of the contract

11.103 **n208**: the reference to *Benjamin's Sale of Goods* should now be to the 6th edn (2002), paras 18-078ff.

Replace existing text to n213 with the following:

The Act is a complicated piece of draftsmanship but there is now a valuable decision of the House of Lords explaining its background and present operation.[213]

Replace existing n213 with the following:

n213: *Borealis AB v Stargas Ltd (The Berge Sisar)* [2001] UKHL 17, [2002] 2 AC

205; for another important decision on the Act see *East West Corporation v DKBS 1912* [2003] EWCA Civ 83, [2003] 1 Lloyd's Rep 239 (deploying bailment reasoning in favour of a shipper who had parted with the bill of lading).

(4) Other Documents Used in Connection with Sea Carriage

(a) Non-negotiable sea waybills[215]

n215: the reference to *Benjamin's Sale of Goods* should now be to the 6th edn (2002) paras 18-124ff. **11.105**

(b) Ship's delivery orders[221]

n221: the reference to *Benjamin's Sale of Goods* should now be to the 6th edn (2002) paras 18-143ff. **11.107**

(d) Mate's receipts[227]

n227: the reference to *Benjamin's Sale of Goods* should now be to the 6th edn (2002) paras 18-135ff. **11.111**

12

EMPLOYMENT

A. Definition, Sources, and Scope of the English Private Law of Employment

(1) Definition

The general definition of the English private law of employment

12.04 **n5**: the reference to S Deakin and GS Morris, *Labour Law* should now be to the 3rd edn (2001) 1.

(2) Sources

(a) Common law and equity

12.08 **n14**: the reference to *Clerk & Lindsell on Torts* should now be to the 18th edn (2000) paras 30.17–30.20.

(b) English statute law

12.12 The prediction made in this paragraph that the Human Rights Act 1998 would become one of the sources of the private law of employment has started to be realized, as in *Pay v Lancashire Probation Service* [2004] ICR 187 where its provision determined the outcome of a claim for unfair dismissal.

(c) European Community law

12.14 The proposition in this paragraph about the shaping effect of European Community measures concerning equal pay and opportunity between women and men at work should now be regarded as extending to Community measures concerning discrimination on the grounds of race, religion or belief, disability, sexual orientation, and age—see further Supplement para 12.40.

n21: Council Directive (EEC) 77/187 [1977] OJ L061/26 has since been amended and consolidated into Council Directive (EC) 2001/23, [2001] OJ L082/16.

(3) The Range and Classification of Work Relationships Falling Within the English Private Law of Employment

(b) The meaning of 'personal' in the context of work relationships

12.18 **n29**: the exclusive approach taken in those cases has now been followed in *Wolstenholme v Post Office Ltd* [2003] ICR 546.

(4) The Distinctions Between the Different Types of Personal Employment Contracts

12.19 **n31**: the difference between 'employees' and 'workers' is now elaborated in *Byrne Brothers (Formwork) Ltd v Baird* [2002] ICR 667.

(a) The contract of employment distinguished from other personal work contracts

In *Montgomery v Johnson Underwood Ltd* [2001] IRLR 269, the Court of Appeal, in the context of deciding upon the employment status of an agency worker (as to which see further Supplement para 12.28) re-emphasized the two notions of a minimum amount of control over the worker and a minimum degree of mutual obligation between employer and worker as indispensable to the finding of a contract of employment, and therefore as more than simply factors to be considered among others in making that classification. **12.23**

n39: *Express & Echo Publications Ltd v Tanton* was distinguished in *Macfarlane v Glasgow City Council* [2001] IRLR 7, EAT.

(b) Intermittent work relationships

nn42, 43: the decisions in the *Carmichael* and the *Clark* cases have been followed and applied in *Stevedoring & Haulage Services Ltd v Fuller* [2001] IRLR 627, CA, where the employment of a casual dockworker was, equally, held to lack the continuing irreducible minimum of mutual obligation necessary to enable it to be regarded as taking place under a single continuing global or over-arching contract. **12.25**

(c) Work relationships involving intermediaries

In *Abbey Life Assurance Co Ltd v Tansell* [2000] ICR 789, the Court of Appeal held that the relationship of principal and contract worker could exist through two intermediaries, namely a service company and an employment agency. **12.27**

In *Montgomery v Johnson Underwood Ltd* [2001] ICR 819, the approach taken by Waite LJ in the earlier *McMeechan* case was expressly not followed. However, in *Dacas v Brook Street Bureau (UK) Ltd* [2003] IRLR 190, the EAT followed the *McMeechan* case in upholding the possibility of a contract of employment with the agency in respect of a single temporary placement with a client company, while in *Franks v Reuters Ltd* [2003] ICR 1166 the CA found that an implied contract of employment arose between the worker and the client company in the course of a prolonged assignment. **12.28**

(d) Conclusion

n48: the reference to *Clerk & Lindsell on Torts* should now be to the 18th edn (2000) ch 24. **12.30**

n49: the reference to S Deakin and GS Morris, *Labour Law* should now be to the 3rd edn (2000) ch 10.

B. The Formation and Content of Work Relationships

(2) Incapacity and Illegality in the Making of Personal Work Contracts

(a) Personal work contracts involving tax or social security fraud

12.35 The approach taken in *Leighton v Michael* was followed by the Court of Appeal in *Hall v Woolston Hall Leisure Ltd* [2001] ICR 99, and apparently regarded as generally applicable to discrimination claims where the employment arrangements in question involve fraud upon the Revenue, unless the worker actively participates in the unlawful scheme.

(3) Form and Formality in the Making of Personal Work Contracts; Statutory Particulars of the Terms of Contracts of Employment

12.37 Some significant changes to the law concerning statutory particulars will be made by ss 35–38 of the Employment Act 2002; at the time of writing it is expected that those provisions will come into effect in October 2004. Disciplinary and dismissal procedures will be required to be specified; particulars will be able to be given in the alternative form of a written contract of employment or letter of engagement; and employment tribunals will be able to award compensation for failure in respect of the provision of employment particulars.

12.38 **n69**: it is expected that with effect from October 2004, small firms will be included—s 38 of the Employment Act 2002.

(4) Control of Discrimination in the Formation and Content of Personal Work Contracts

12.39 **n71**: section 99, as elaborated by a series of subsequent measures detailed under n72 below, both gives effect to Council Directive (EEC) 92/85 on pregnant workers [1992] OJ L348/1 and protects employees taking leave for family reasons in the prescribed circumstances.

n72: as amended by s7 and Sch 4 of the Employment Relations Act 1999, by ss 1, 3 of the Employment Act 2002, and by SI 1999/3312, 2001/4010, 2002/2788, 2002/2789, 2002/3207, and 2002/3236, the provisions of ERA 1996, ss 71–80I now provide for maternity leave, adoption leave, parental leave, paternity leave, and a right to flexible working in connection with parenthood.

n75b: (Note to be added to concluding words of this para (12.39).) See Fixed-term Employees (Prevention of Less Favourable Treatment) Regulations 2002 SI 2002/2034.

12.40 The European Community acquired a new capacity to legislate about a wide range of types of discrimination, in relation to employment as well as to various other areas of activity, under the 1997 Treaty of Amsterdam which introduced what is now numbered Article 13 of the Treaty establishing the European Community. That power has been used to enact what is known as the Race Directive (Council Directive (EC) 2000/43 [2000] OJ L199/86) which concerns discrimination on the grounds of race or ethnic origin, and what is known as the Framework Directive (Council Directive (EC) 2000/78) [2001] OJ L002/42 which concerns discrimination in employment on the grounds of religion, disability, age, or sexual orientation. Measures to implement these Directives in English law and generally to revise the existing legislation concerned with discrimination have been enacted and are coming into effect in the course of 2003/04 (with the exception of age discrimination, with regard to which legislation is required and expected by 2006). The measures are SI 2003/1626 (race), SI 2003/1657 (sex), SI 2003/1660 (religion or belief), SI 2003/1661 (sexual orientation), SI 2003/1673 (disability). These measures make important changes not only to the scope of controls upon discrimination in employment, but also to the ways in which discrimination is defined, for example, by introducing at various points the notion that in order to be *justified*, indirect discrimination must be a *proportionate* response to the need for which it is effected. (There had also been a partial re-definition of discrimination under s1 of the Sex Discrimination Act 1975 by the Sex Discrimination (Indirect Discrimination and Burden of Proof) Regulations 2001 SI 2001/2660, and an extension of the Act to include gender reassignment by the Sex Discrimination (Gender Reassignment) Regulations 1999 SI 1999/1102.)

(5) The Construction and Implied Terms of Personal Work Contracts in General

(b) The construction of the terms of personal work contracts

In the important case of *Henry v London General Transport Services Ltd* [2002] ICR 910, the Court of Appeal held that a tradition of settling terms and conditions of employment by collective bargaining between the employer and a recognized trade union could itself operate as a custom which was sufficiently 'reasonable, certain, and notorious' to make a particular collective agreement binding upon workers affected by it even where it involved a worsening of their terms and conditions of employment, and even where all the workers concerned were not aware of that custom or its effect. **12.47**

n99: the reference to S Deakin and GS Morris, *Labour Law* should now be to the 3rd edn (2001) 262–3. **12.48**

(d) The implied term as to mutual trust and confidence

The decision of the House of Lords in the *Malik v BCCI* case was given on the basis of *assumed* facts, the issue being whether those facts disclosed a cause of action. In *Bank of Credit and Commerce International SA v Ali (No 3)* [2000] ICR **12.51**

1354, some test cases were tried to ascertain whether stigma damages for breach of the implied term as to mutual trust and confidence would be recoverable on the actual facts. These claims were dismissed on the ground that, although breach of the implied term could be shown, the employees concerned had failed to show an actual recoverable loss consisting in damage to their employment prospects demonstrably caused by their employer's wrongdoing. The decision was upheld by the Court of Appeal—[2002] ICR 1258.

In the leading case of *Johnson v Unisys Ltd* [2001] ICR 480, the House of Lords identified or imposed a significant restriction upon the scope of application of the implied term as to mutual trust and confidence, holding that it did not apply so as to give a remedy in damages in respect of the employer's way of exercising a contractual power or right of dismissal. The reason given for that restriction was that Parliament, when enacting the unfair dismissal legislation which provided for limited awards of statutory compensation in that respect, had thereby intended to exclude the possibility of unlimited awards of common law damages for the conduct in question. This was a rather unusual way of ascertaining the content and scope of an implied term of the contract of employment. Determining how far the restriction applies to *constructive* dismissal has proved difficult; the Court of Appeal provided guidance in *McCabe v Cornwall County Council* [2003] ICR 501.

(6) The Legal Regulation of Remuneration for Employment

(a) **Minimum rates of pay**

12.54 In *Edmonds v Lawson* [2000] ICR 567, the Court of Appeal held that a pupil barrister, although having a legally binding contract with the members of her chambers, was not employed by them under a contract of apprenticeship, and was not in any other sense a 'worker' within the meaning of the National Minimum Wage Act 1998.

(c) **Stability of income and the laying-off of workers by employers**

12.60 The decision in the *Carmichael* case has been followed and applied in *Stevedoring & Haulage Services Ltd v Fuller* [2001] IRLR 627, CA, see Supplement para 12.25.

(7) The Legal Regulation of Health, Safety and Welfare at Work

12.68 The principles governing the common law obligation described in this paragraph have been clarified by the Court of Appeal in *Hatton v Sutherland* [2002] ICR 613 and *Pratley v Surrey County Council* [2003] IRLR 794. The implied obligation as to mutual trust and confidence may possibly operate as a parallel or further source of protection of the employee against psychiatric injury caused by the employer's wrongful conduct towards him or her, as in the case of *Gogay v Hertfordshire County Council* [2000] IRLR 703, CA.

n69: the recent measures, specified in para 12.40 of this Supplement, which revise and extend the law of discrimination in employment, expressly include harassment in the category of proscribed conduct for all the other kinds of discrimination in employment. **12.69**

(9) The Implied Obligations of Workers Under Personal Work Contracts

(b) Implied terms as to co-operation, flexibility, and loyalty

The employer's duty of care to the worker in the giving of references to potential subsequent employers is further expounded by the Court of Appeal in the case of *Cox v Sun Alliance Life Ltd* [2001] IRLR 448, from which it appears that discharge of the duty of care to provide an accurate and fair reference will usually involve making reasonable inquiry into the factual basis of the statements in the reference. **12.78**

C. The Termination and Transfer of Work Relationships

(1) The Duration and Variation of Personal Work Contracts

(a) Duration, and terminability by notice, or by payment in lieu of notice

Under reg 8 of the Fixed-term Employees (Prevention of Less Favourable Treatment) Regulations 2002 SI 2002/2034, employees under successive fixed-term contracts of employment are converted into 'permanent employees' where they have been continuously employed for four years or more (time before 10 July 2002 not counting for this purpose), and where the employment for a fixed term was not justified on objective grounds at the specified time. **12.82**

(b) Termination, and variation of terms

n211: the reference to S Deakin and GS Morris, *Labour Law* should now be to the 3rd edn (2001) 273–4. **12.86**

(2) Dismissal and Its Alternatives

The concept of dismissal

n217: reg 11 and Sch 2 of the Fixed-term Employees (Prevention of Less Favourable Treatment) Regulations 2002 SI 2002/2034 have substituted the new terminology of 'limited-term contracts terminated by virtue of the limiting event'. **12.89**

(3) Wrongful Dismissal, and Other Common Law Regulation Based Upon Termination of the Contract of Employment

(b) Damages

12.97 The prediction of the alleviation of the restrictions on damages for wrongful dismissal associated with the *Addis* case has now been largely falsified by the decision of the House of Lords in the case of *Johnson v Unisys Ltd* [2001] ICR 480, see Supplement para 12.51.

(4) Unfair Dismissal, and Other Statutory Regulation Constructed on the Basis of It

(a) The concept of unfair dismissal

12.104 n259: *Foley v Post Office* is now reported at [2000] ICR 1283, CA.

12.104–7 Part 3 of the Employment Act 2002 provides for a new framework of statutory dispute resolution procedures; when those provisions are brought into effect, which at the time of writing is expected to take place in October 2004, employers and employees will be subject to mandatory minimum disciplinary, dismissal and grievance procedures. The law of unfair dismissal will be amended in significant respects so as to reflect the failure of employers or employees to follow the procedural requirements respectively placed upon them, but also so as partly to reverse the rule in *Polkey v Dayton Services Ltd* by providing that non-compliance by an employer with a procedural requirement over and above the statutory minimum requirements will not be regarded as by itself making the employer's action unreasonable 'if he shows that he would have decided to dismiss the employee if he had followed the procedure' (new ERA 1996, s 98A(2), to be added by Employment Act 2002, s 34).

(b) The right to remedies for unfair dismissal, and procedure

12.106 n271: this limit is reviewed, and usually increased, on an annual basis. By 2003 it had risen to £53,500.

(5) Redundancy and Transfer of Employment

(b) Transfer of employment

12.113 n298: Council Directive (EEC) 77/187 has since been amended and consolidated into Council Directive (EC) 2001/23 [2001] OJ L082/16.

13

BAILMENT

A. Definition and General Character

(1) Introduction

(a) Bailment as voluntary possession

n2: see now also *East West Corp v DKBS 1912* [2003] 1 Lloyd's Rep 239; *Sandeman Coprimar SA v Transitos y Integrales SL* [2003] EWCA Civ 113, [2003] 3 All ER 108, [2003] 2 Lloyd's Rep 172, CA; *Marcq v Christie Manson & Woods Ltd (t/a Christie's)* [2003] EWCA Civ 731, [2003] 3 WLR 980. In *East West Corp v DKBS 1912* [2003] 1 Lloyd's Rep 239 at 249 Mance LJ approved the statement in N Palmer, *Bailment* (2nd edn, 1991) 1285, that: 'The important question is not the literal meaning of bailment but the circle of relationships within which its characteristic duties will apply. For most practical purposes, any person who comes knowingly into the possession of another's goods is, prima facie, a bailee.' **13.01**

(b) Basic obligations common to all bailments

13.02 n7: see now also *East West Corp v DKBS 1912* [2003] 1 Lloyd's Rep 239.

(c) Bailment and delivery, contract, agreement

13.03 n18: see now also *East West Corp v DKBS 1912* [2003] 1 Lloyd's Rep 239.

n19: see now also *East West Corp v DKBS 1912* [2003] 1 Lloyd's Rep 239.

n22: see now also *East West Corp v DKBS 1912* [2003] 1 Lloyd's Rep 239; *Sandeman Coprimar SA v Transitos y Integrales SL* [2003] EWCA Civ 113, [2003] 3 All ER 108, [2003] 2 Lloyd's Rep 172, CA.

n30: see now also *Marcq v Christie Manson & Woods Ltd (t/a Christie's)* [2003] EWCA Civ 731, [2003] 3 WLR 980.

(d) Bailment and prior possession and ownership

13.05 n35: see now also *East West Corp v DKBS 1912* [2003] 1 Lloyd's Rep 239; *The Homburg Houtimport BV v Agrosin Private Ltd (The Starsin)* [2003] UKHL 12, [2003] 2 All ER 885.

n43: As to the sufficiency of a right of possession to cast the party thus entitled in the position of a bailor of the possessor, and so to ground a bailment between those parties, see *East West Corp v DKBS 1912* [2003] 1 Lloyd's Rep 239.

(2) The Essential Role of Possession

(b) Bailment and employment

13.07 n53: the rule does not apply to agents and independent contractors, who may get possession and be answerable as bailees: *Lotus Cars Ltd v Southampton Cargo Handling plc (The Rigoletto); Southampton Cargo Handling plc v Associated British Ports* [2000] 2 Lloyd's Rep 532, CA. And see Main Work para 13.20.

(d) Bailments and licences

13.10 n85: see now also *Lotus Cars Ltd v Southampton Cargo Handling plc (The Rigoletto); Southampton Cargo Handling plc v Associated British Ports* [2000] 2 Lloyd's Rep 532, CA.

(3) Consent to Possession

(a) Burden of proof

13.11 n87: in general terms, the alleged bailee must also consent to hold as bailee of the particular party interested in the goods, though such consent can be implied: see

KH Enterprise v Pioneer Container, The Pioneer Container [1994] AC 324, PC; *Marcq v Christie Manson & Woods Ltd (t/a Christie's)* [2003] EWCA Civ 731, [2003] 3 WLR 980, and paras 13.82, 13.83 below.

(4) Redelivery

(a) In general

n96: cf *Wincanton Ltd v P & O Trans European Ltd* [2001] EWCA Civ 227. **13.13**

(b) Mixtures and fungible goods

n103: see now also *Wincanton Ltd v P & O Trans European Ltd* [2001] EWCA Civ 227. **13.14**

n106: see further as to *mutuum*, *Wincanton Ltd v P & O Trans European Ltd* [2001] EWCA Civ 227.

n111: see now also *Glencore International AG v Metro Trading International Inc* [2001] 1 Lloyd's Rep 2000.

n114: see now also *Wincanton Ltd v P & O Trans European Ltd* [2001] EWCA Civ 227 (no bailment where pallets mixed with others of indistinguishable nature supplied from other sources).

(6) Bailment Distinguished from Other Transactions

(b) Bailment and sale of goods

n145: see now also *Wincanton Ltd v P & O Trans European Ltd* [2001] EWCA Civ 227. **13.18**

(d) Bailment and agency

n154: see now also *Lotus Cars Ltd v Southampton Cargo Handling plc (The Rigoletto); Southampton Cargo Handling plc v Associated British Ports* [2000] 2 Lloyd's Rep 532, CA. **13.20**

B. Principles Common to all Bailments

(1) The Bailee's Estoppel

(a) General

n158: see now also *East West Corp v DKBS 1912* [2003] 1 Lloyd's Rep 239; cf *Sandeman Coprimar SA v Transitos y Integrales SL* [2003] EWCA Civ 113, [2003] 3 All ER 108, [2003] 2 Lloyd's Rep 172, CA. **13.21**

(2) Possession as Title

(c) Mere right of possession

13.28 **n194**: see now also *East West Corp v DKBS 1912* [2003] 1 Lloyd's Rep 239.

(3) Insurance

13.31 **n208**: see now also *Ramco (UK) Ltd & Ors v International Insurance Company of Hannover Ltd & Anor* [2003] EWHC 2360 (Comm) (15 October 2003) [2003] EWHC.

n211: as to the obligation of the bailee to account to the bailor for an excess of any insurance proceeds see now *Ramco (UK) Ltd & Ors v International Insurance Company of Hannover Ltd & Anor* [2003] EWHC 2360 (Comm) (15 October 2003).

C. Gratuitous Bailments and Bailments for Reciprocal Advantage

(a) Reasons for making the distinction

13.33 **n215**: see now also *G Bosman (Transport) Ltd v LKW Walter International Transportorganisation AG* [2002] All ER (D) 13 (May), CA; cf *Khan v Grocutt* [2002] All ER (D) 154 (Dec), CA.

(b) Making the distinction[218]

13.34 **n218**: see now also *Wincanton Ltd v P & O Trans European Ltd* [2001] EWCA Civ 227.

n222: see now also *G Bosman (Transport) Ltd v LKW Walter International Transportorganisation AG* [2002] All ER (D) 13 (May), CA.

n223: cf *City Television v Conference and Training Office Ltd* (CA, 29 November 2001) (recipient of goods ordered by third party pursuant to deception treated, apparently without argument, as gratuitous bailee).

D. Gratuitous Bailments

(1) Gratuitous Custody

(b) Obligations of gratuitous custodian

13.36 **n228**: see now also *City Television v Conference and Training Office Ltd* (CA, 29

November 2001); *Khan v Grocutt* [2002] All ER (D) 154 (Dec), CA (bailment of insurance documents); cf *G Bosman (Transport) Ltd v LKW Walter International Transportorganisation AG* [2002] All ER (D) 13 (May), CA.

(3) Loan for Use

(a) Definition and character

n260: see now also *Wincanton Ltd v P & O Trans European Ltd* [2001] EWCA Civ 227 (reciprocally beneficial bailment of pallets not a gratuitous load). **13.45**

(b) Duties of the borrower

n262a: cf *Wincanton Ltd v P & O Trans European Ltd* [2001] EWCA Civ 227 (question whether borrower liable for even 'slight neglect' left open as not material to decision). **13.46**

(c) Duties of the lender

n271a: see now also *Flack v Hudson* [2001] 2 WLR 982, CA. **13.47**

E. Bailments for Reward and Reciprocal Advantage

(1) Custody for Reward

(b) Duties of the custodian for reward

n276: Where a bailee lawfully and with the express or implied consent of the bailor delegates to a third party the discharge of any part of his duty of care in respect of the goods (as, for example, where he engages a firm of security contractors to patrol the place where the goods are kept, or to install protective devices) he remains responsible for the manner in which the delegated task is performed, and is accordingly liable for the delegate's defaults: *G Bosman (Transport) Ltd v LKW Walter International Transportorganisation AG* [2002] All ER (D) 13 (May), CA, following *British Road Services v Arthur V Crutchley* [1968] 1 All ER 811, CA; cf *East West v DKBS* above. And see further paras 13.52 (bailee commiting deviation where delegation of possession unlawful), 13.83 (sub-bailment). **13.49**

(c) Burdens of proof

n291: see now also *AP(2)T v PS* [2004] EWHC 32, QB. **13.50**

n292: see now also *G Bosman (Transport) Ltd v LKW Walter International Transportorganisation AG* [2002] All ER (D) 13 (May), CA.

(2) Work and Labour for Reward

(c) Bailee's lien

(i) Particular lien

13.58 **n348**: applied in *Morris v Beaconsfield Motors* (2001) unreported 24 June, CA.

n349: cf *Morris v Beaconsfield Motors* (2001) unreported 24 June, CA.

(3) Hire[363]

(f) Relief for defaulting hirer

13.66 **n391**: as to chattel leasing generally see now *Michael Gerson v Wilkinson* [2001] QB 514, CA.

(4) Pledge

(a) Definition and character

13.67 **n399**: see now also *Marcq v Christie Manson & Woods Ltd (t/a Christie's)* [2003] EWCA Civ 731, [2003] 3 WLR 980 (delivery of chattel to auction house for sale, and acceptance by auction house, under contract giving auction house extensive powers of retention and sale designed to enforce obligations undertaken by the party delivering the chattel, held not to constitute a pledge of the chattel for purposes of the Torts (Interference with Goods) Act 1977, s 11(2)).

F. Attornment, Sub-bailment, and Other Ambulatory Bailments

(2) Sub-bailment

13.82 **n457**: see now also *Lotus Cars Ltd v Southampton Cargo Handling plc (The Rigoletto); Southampton Cargo Handling plc v Associated British Ports* [2000] 2 Lloyd's Rep 532, CA; *Wincanton Ltd v P & O Trans European Ltd* [2001] EWCA Civ 227 per Dyson LJ (no sub-bailment, but rather substitutional bailment as to which see Main Work para 13.84). see also *Marcq v Christie Manson & Woods Ltd (t/a Christie's)* [2003] EWCA Civ 731, [2003] 3 WLR 980; *East West Corp v DKBS 1912* [2003] 1 Lloyd's Rep 239; *Sandeman Coprimar SA v Transitos y Integrales SL* [2003] EWCA Civ 113, [2003] 3 All ER 108, [2003] 2 Lloyd's Rep 172, CA; *G Bosman (Transport) Ltd v LKW Walter International Transport-organisation AG* [2002] All ER (D) 13 (May), CA.

n458: as to the principles of sub-bailment generally, see the important recent decision in *East West Corp v DKBS 1912* [2003] 1 Lloyd's Rep 239, which confirms many of the propositions stated in the text of both this and the following paragraph, and indeed of the law of bailment generally. See also *Sandeman Coprimar*

SA v Transitos y Integrales SL [2003] EWCA Civ 113, [2003] 3 All ER 108, [2003] 2 Lloyd's Rep 172, CA; *G Bosman (Transport) Ltd v LKW Walter International Transportorganisation AG* [2002] All ER (D) 13 (May), CA.

n459: see now also *Marcq v Christie Manson & Woods Ltd (t/a Christie's)* [2003] EWCA Civ 731, [2003] 3 WLR 980.

n462: see now also *Marcq v Christie Manson & Woods Ltd (t/a Christie's)* [2003] EWCA Civ 731, [2003] 3 WLR 980 (auctioneer who accepts stolen painting for sale is not a bailee of the true owner where he has no notice (or, it appears, no means of acquiring notice) of the existence of the owner's interest. In this case the theft of the work was registered on a professional register on stolen art).

n465: see now also *G Bosman (Transport) Ltd v LKW Walter International* **13.83** *Transportorganisation AG* [2002] All ER (D) 13 (May), CA.

n469: and see also *City Television v Conference and Training Office Ltd* (CA, 29 November 2001) *per* Sedley LJ.

n470: see further *Lotus Cars Ltd v Southampton Cargo Handling plc (The Rigoletto); Southampton Cargo Handling plc v Associated British Ports* [2001] 2 Lloyd's Rep 532, CA.

n470: in exceptional cases the head bailor and the sub-bailee may occupy a direct contractual relationship, in which event the particular immunities and obligations arising under the terms of the sub-bailment might be directly enforced between those two parties: *Sandeman Coprimar SA v Transitos y Integrales SL* [2003] EWCA Civ 113, [2003] 3 All ER 108, [2003] 2 Lloyd's Rep 172, CA; and cf *The Homburg Houtimport BV v Agrosin Private Ltd (The Starsin)* [2003] UKHL 12, [2003] 2 All ER 885. But the head bailor's actual or ostensible consent to the terms of the sub-bailment can also (it appears) justify the direct enforcement of positive obligations between head bailor and sub-bailee, irrespective of whether they are contractually related: *Sandeman Coprimar SA v Transitos y Integrales SL* [2003] EWCA Civ 113, [2003] 3 All ER 108, [2003] 2 Lloyd's Rep 172, CA.

(3) Substitutional Bailment

n473: see now also *Wincanton Ltd v P & O Trans European Ltd* [2001] EWCA Civ **13.84** 227 *per* Dyson LJ.

n474: see now also generally *East West Corp v DKBS 1912* [2003] 1 Lloyd's Rep 239, *Sandeman Coprimar SA v Transitos y Integrales SL* [2003] EWCA Civ 113, [2003] 3 All ER 108, [2003] 2 Lloyd's Rep 172, CA, *G Bosman (Transport) Ltd v LKW Walter International Transportorganisation AG* [2002] All ER (D) 13 (May), CA.

G. Involuntary and Undisclosed Bailment

(1) Involuntary Bailment

13.87 **n495**: cf *City Television v Conference and Training Office Ltd* (CA, 29 November 2001). See now also *Marcq v Christie Manson & Woods Ltd (t/a Christie's)* [2003] EWCA Civ 731, [2003] 3 WLR 980.

(2) Undisclosed or Unconscious Bailment

13.91 **n516**: A further category of undisclosed bailment might arise where the possessor mistakenly believes that the party delivering the goods to him is the owner, whereas the goods are stolen and the true owner is someone other than the party making the delivery: cf *Marcq v Christie Manson & Woods Ltd (t/a Christie's)* [2003] EWCA Civ 731, [2003] 3 WLR 980 (no duty of care to verify title).

13.92 **n519**: distinguished in *Marcq v Christie Manson & Woods Ltd (t/a Christie's)* [2003] EWCA Civ 731, [2003] 3 WLR 980 (auctioneer not liable for redelivering unsold chattel to party who had delivered it for sale, where that party was believed to be the owner; auctioneer owed no duty of care to verify that party's ownership either on taking original delivery from him or on making redelivery to him).

14

TORT

A. Introduction

n4: as foreseen in this note *Clerk and Lindsell* does now include extended treatment of equitable wrongs: see D Alexander, 'Breach of Confidence' and, new in this edition, A Sprince, 'Breach of Fiduciary Duty' in A Dugdale (ed), *Clerk and Lindsell on Torts* (18th edn, 2000, 3rd Supplement 2003) [27-01]–[27-44] and [28-01]–[28-21] respectively. This example will now encourage the creation of a comprehensive law of civil wrongs. Cf 'there is no rational reason for having another category of wrongs, labelled equitable wrongs': AS Burrows, 'We Do This At Common Law But That in Equity' (2002) 22 OJLS 1, 9. That advance is long overdue. **14.01**

n9: but see Supplement paras 14.336–14.337. **14.06**

B. Negligence: Basic Concepts

(1) Duty of Care

(c) The onset of caution

14.32 The *Anns* test has now been significantly reinterpreted for Canada by the Supreme Court: *Cooper v Hobart* [2001] SCC 79 206 DLR (4th) 193, SCC, noted (2002) 118 LQR 221.

(d) The three-pronged inquiry

(ii) Proximity

14.40 **n58**: for a defence of proximity, A Kramer (2003) 11 Tort L Rev 30.

(iii) Fair, just and reasonable

14.43 **n63**: loose use of 'fair, just and reasonable' to deny any duty of care towards parents and children on the part of child protection authorities has had to be revised in the aftermath of *Osman v UK* (1998) 5 BHRC 293, ECHR and in the light of the incorporation of the Convention by the Human Rights Act 1998, so that it is now accepted that a common law duty of care is owed to the children but, on the argument that it would create a conflict of interest incompatible with the paramountcy of the interests of the children, not towards the parents whose lives stand in equal danger of being ruined when such interventions go wrong: *D v East Berkshire NHS Trust* [2003] EWCA Civ 1151, [2003] 4 All ER 796; cf *B v Attorney General of New Zealand* [2003] UKPC 61, [2003] 4 All ER 833. Further below Supplement para 14.106.

n65: the immunity of advocates from suits for professional negligence provided another example of the exclusion of a duty of care on grounds of public policy. A duty of care was thought to be inimical to the public interest in eliminating impediments to the smooth and reliable running of the process of litigation and adjudication. However, the House of Lords, sitting with seven judges, has now reviewed this immunity and has held, unanimously in relation to civil cases and by a majority for criminal cases, that in modern conditions the exclusion of a duty of care can no longer be justified: *Arthur JS Hall & Co v Simons* [2002] 1 AC 615, HL. The absolute immunity from the law of defamation of all that is said in court (see Main Work para 14.291) survives this decision and is very unlikely to be undercut by the law of negligence in the way that qualified privilege has been overthrown by *Spring v Guardian Assurance* [1995] 2 AC 296, HL.

14.44 **n67**: the exclusion of any duty of care towards the parents in relation to the expense of bringing up a healthy child extends to lost earnings on the part of the mother: *Greenfield v Irwin* [2001] EWCA Civ 113, [2001] 1 WLR 1279, CA. But that exclusion has now been held to stop short of preventing recovery of the expense of caring for a disabled child, so far as those costs are concerned which are encountered because of the disability: *Parkinson v St James and Seacroft University Hospital NHS Trust* [2001] EWCA Civ 530, [2002] QB 266, CA. In *Rees v Darlington Memorial Hospital NHS Trust* [2003] UKHL 52, [2003] 4 All ER 987 the Court of Appeal by a majority had added a further exception to cover the case in which the unwanted child was healthy but the mother was disabled. It had allowed the extra costs attributable to the mother's disability to be recovered, but the House of Lords, with seven Law Lords sitting, disagreed: there could be no recovery at all in respect of the upbringing of a healthy child. However, the House, by four to three, recognized that the negligent sterilization is an injury to the sexual and developmental autonomy of the parents and that that injury should attract a fixed conventional award of £15,000. Meanwhile in Australia a majority of the High Court has taken the entirely opposite view that where a sterilization goes wrong and negligence is proved the parents can recover full damages, that is, the whole cost of the upbringing of the unwanted child: *Cattanach v Melchior* [2003] HCA 38. See 120 LQR 23 (Care).

(2) Breach

(d) Costs and risks

n94: cf *Tomlinson v Congleton BC* [2003] UKHL 47, [2003] 3 WLR 705, introduced below, para 14.184. **14.59**

(3) Damage

(a) Causation

n102: where the medical evidence was that a single fibre of asbestos was just as likely to cause mesothelioma as multiple exposure, the Court of Appeal held, to the dismay of many, that claimants who have worked for a succession of employers must establish which employer's breach is responsible for the condition: *Fairchild v Glenhaven Funeral Services Ltd* [2001] EWCA Civ 1881, [2002] IRLR 129, CA. That meant in practice that such an employee would have no remedy at all. However, this was then reversed by the House of Lords: [2002] UKHL 22, [2003] 1 AC 32 which preferred to treat the several contributories as joint tortfeasors rather than defer to the strict logic of causation. In cases in which in the present state of scientific knowledge it is impossible to satisfy the threshold 'but for' test, in the interests of justice it will suffice to show that successive employers had materially increased the risk of injury. However, no doubt was thrown on the correctness on its facts of *Wilsher v Essex AHA*. On the limits of the *Fairchild* exception, see J Stapleton (2002) 10 Torts LJ 276 and, more generally, J Stapleton (2003) 119 LQR 388. **14.68**

(i) The balance of probabilities

14.70 The law on damages for the loss of a chance remains difficult. In *Gregg v Scott* [2002] EWCA Civ 1471, [2003] Lloyd's Rep Med 105 negligent medical advice caused a nine-month delay in the treatment of the claimant's cancer, reducing his chance of survival from 42% to 25%. Simon Brown LJ thought this was indistinguishable from *Hotson v East Berkshire AHA,* while Mance LJ thought it was a different case which merited the same decision on policy grounds: damages should not be recoverable for loss of a medical chance. The House of Lords gave leave to appeal.

(ii) The 'but for' test

14.71 **n106**: in *Chester v Afshar* [2002] EWCA Civ 724, [2003] QB 356 an operation entailed a slight but known risk, which in the event materialized. In an action for negligent failure to warn it was sufficient to show that, if the claimant had known of the risk, she would not have had the operation at that time, even though she might have had it in the end.

(iii) Successive unrelated events

14.73 In *Murrell v Healy* [2001] EWCA Civ 486, [2001] 4 All ER 345, CA the claimant had been injured in two successive car accidents over a period of six months. The Court of Appeal observed, abstaining from sorting out the confusion in the leading cases, that none had dealt with the liability of the second tortfeasor [19]. The court then took the opportunity to lay down very clearly that the latter could only be liable for the additional loss, if any, caused by the second event [22]. Faced again with successive torts, in *Rahman v Arearose Ltd* [2001] QB 351, CA, Laws LJ saw no inconsistency between *Baker v Willoughby* [1970] AC 467, HL, and *Jobling v United Dairies Ltd* [1982] AC 794, HL, and followed the former.

(b) Remoteness

(iv) The eggshell skull rule

14.85 **n125**: in *Lagden v O'Connor* [2003] UKHL 64, [2003] TLR 667, the House of Lords decided that *The Liesbosch* should no longer be followed, citing with approval B Coote, '*The Liesbosch* and Impecuniosity' (2001) 60 CLJ 511.

C. Negligence: Particular Cases

(1) Omissions

(b) Responsibility for other persons

14.91 A special case is *Watson v British Boxing Board of Control* [2001] 1 WLR 1256, CA, where Watson was a boxer who incurred serious brain damage when he suffered a cerebral haemorrhage and could not be expeditiously treated at the ringside. The Board had not organized the fight. The Board is merely the sport's self-regulator. Its regulations, under which all fights are organized, failed to require the immediate availability of suitable medical assistance. The Court of Appeal held that that failure was actionable negligence. The Board was under a duty to regulate with care. The court recognized that duty because, in a context in which physical injury was the object of the sport which the Board controlled, the Board had assumed and asserted responsibility in the very matter of keeping the degree of that injury within acceptable bounds and, further, because the boxing community was not so large as to open up the prospect of indeterminate liability and comprised individuals whose character and disposition rendered their protection from excesses especially necessary. The court was not impressed by the Board's counter-argument that it should be spared liability because it operated on a not-for-profit basis.

(e) **Liability of public bodies for failure to prevent damage**

n143: add D Fairgrieve, 'State Liability in Tort' (2003). **14.98**

*(ii) Return to the pre-*Anns *position?*

n154: a further step back from *Stovin v Wise* [1996] AC 923, HL was taken in *Kane v New Forest DC* [2001] EWCA Civ 878, [2002] 1 WLR 312, CA. There the claimant was seriously injured as he emerged from a New Forest footpath on to a road. The defendant planning authority had required the construction of the path as part of a development to which it had consented. It had been warned more than once that the path could not safely give on to the inside of a bend, but it had not seen that plans to open up the blind spot were carried through. The claimant's action was summarily dismissed by the judge and again on appeal as having no real chance of success in the light of *Stovin v Wise* and *Lam v Brennan and Borough of Torbay* [1997] PIQR P488, CA, but the Court of Appeal allowed it to proceed. The exclusion of a duty of care on the part of the authority in *Stovin v Wise* could not support the blanket immunity which the defendant had attempted to claim. In particular it could not cover the case in which the authority had itself created the hazard, rather than, as in *Stovin v Wise*, proved dilatory in dealing with a hazard not of its own making. **14.104**

(iii) Public law and human rights

The proposition with which this paragraph ends remains correct but the background has somewhat changed because the European Court of Human Rights has moderated its position in relation to the denial of a duty of care. That shift was facilitated by the House of Lords having itself responded to *Osman v United Kingdom* [1999] 1 FLR 193; (1998) 5 BHRC 293, ECHR by (a) being more cautious in striking out, (b) insisting that denial of a duty of care as not being 'fair, just and **14.106** reasonable' was not and was not to appear to be the dogmatic assertion of a blanket immunity but reflected a careful balancing of competing interests: *Barrett v Enfield LBC* [2001] 2 AC 550, HL; *W v Essex CC* [2001] 2 AC 592, HL, and (c) imposing liability on local education authorities in one important case: *Phelps v Hillingdon LBC* [1999] 1 WLR 500, HL.

Thus, when children who had been sexually abused in local authority homes appealed from *X (Minors) v Bedfordshire County Council* [1995] 2 AC 633, HL, the ECHR, although it found the United Kingdom in breach of Articles 3 (inhuman treatment) and 13 (inadequate local remedies), stepped back from *Osman v United Kingdom* in deciding that the exclusion of a duty of care did not amount to a breach of the right to a fair hearing under Article 6: *Z v United Kingdom* Application 29392/95, [2001] FLR 246, ECHR esp [99] and [100] and *TP and KM v United Kingdom* Application 28945/95, ECHR. For a lucid and balanced exposition: E McKendrick, 'Negligence and Human Rights: Reconsidering *Osman*' in D Friedmann and D Barak (eds), *Human Rights and Private Law* (Hart, 2002) 332. There is a certain danger that the English courts might read *Z v United Kingdom* as licensing a return to the old approach, which would be regrettable: A Davies, 'The European Convention and Negligence Actions: *Osman* "Reviewed" ' (2001) 117 LQR 521. For more recent cases in relation to sexual abuse, see Supplement para 14.43.

(a) The earliest instances of liability

14.109 n161: see Supplement paras 14.336–14.337.

(2) Psychiatric Injury

(c) The requirement of psychiatric illness

14.117 Damages for bereavement are now fixed at £10,000: Bereavement (Variation of Sum) (England and Wales) Order 2002 SI 2002/644.

14.118 Recent decisions have shown flexibility as to what counts as a single 'event'. In *North Glamorgan NHS Trust v Walters* [2003] PIQR P232 a period of 36 hours during which a mother saw her baby die was held to be a single horrifying event.

(d) Primary victims

14.119 The distinction between primary and secondary victims, derived from the model of traumatic catastrophes, does not comfortably cover situations where there is no single event. In *Hatton v Sutherland* [2002] EWCA Civ 76, [2002] 2 All ER 1, CA employees such as teachers had suffered breakdowns and continuing psychiatric injury because of years of overwork, exacerbated by innovations and efficiency gains such as are now commonplace. Such claimants count as primary victims.

There are no artificial inhibitions of their right to recover damages from their employer, as there are for secondary victims.

However, three of these four conjoined appeals nonetheless went against the employee. The Court of Appeal's instrument of restraint is an old-fashioned insistence on the standard of the reasonable person, endowed neither with special prescience nor limitless resources. The early signs of mental illness are often not visible and, if they are picked up, there is often not much that can be done. It is rarely reasonable to sack someone for his own good. Employers cannot be held to foresee more than was reasonably foreseeable in their situation, nor should they be expected to take extravagant precautions. The one victim who did get compensation had several times drawn attention to her workload and had asked for assistance which had been promised but not delivered, and her manager had treated her in an exploitative and unsympathetic manner.

(e) Secondary victims

(iii) Hearing and seeing

n184: now reported: [2000] 1 WLR 1970. A father who as a fireman was a rescuer of his own son from a car crash caused by the son's drunken and careless driving could not claim to be a primary victim, not having faced any physical danger himself. On the other hand he did satisfy the restrictive conditions which normally allow secondary victims to recover—relationship of affection, direct perception, immediate aftermath. He could not recover in respect of his post-traumatic disorder because on these facts it was not proper to recognize any duty of care: [2000] 1 WLR 1970, 1983–7. **14.129**

(iv) Other possible cases

The last sentence should be deleted, for it is now possible to say that this explanation is consistent with *Hatton v Sutherland*, discussed in Supplement para 14.119. **14.133**

(3) Economic Loss

(c) Disappointingly defective goods and houses

(iv) Rejection in other jurisdictions

For a comparison between English and Commonwealth approaches to problems of economic loss, see J Stapleton (2002) 50 UCLA L Rev 531. **14.163**

(d) The *Hedley Byrne* principle

(i) Words, acts, omissions

On misrepresentation in contract and tort, see J Cartwright, *Misrepresentation* (2002). **14.168**

(iii) Assumption of responsibility and reliance

14.172 Difficult questions can arise between corporate employer and employee as to which of them is to be deemed to have assumed responsibility for statements made by the employee in the course of his employment: *Merrett v Babb* [2001] EWCA Civ 214, [2001] 1 QB 1174, CA; *Standard Chartered Bank v Pakistan National Shipping Corporation (No 2)* [2000] 1 Lloyd's Rep 218, CA, noted E McKendrick and J Edelman (2002) 118 LQR 4.

14.173 NB: this paragraph is misnumbered in the Main Work as 17.173. The principle of *White v Jones* is not confined to the legal profession. On the same principle *Gorham v British Telecommunications plc* [2000] 1 WLR 2129, CA held an insurance company liable for negligent pensions advice. The *White v Jones* duty of care was recognized towards the dependants of a man who had made it clear that his main aim was to provide for his family.

14.178 n282: the authority of *X v Bedfordshire CC* is not at this point affected by the decision in *Z v United Kingdom* (cf Supplement para 14.106). The cases on *Hedley Byrne* liability of public bodies are hard to reconcile. Compare *Welton v North Cornwall DC* [1977] 1 WLR 570 and *Harris v Evans* [1998] 3 All ER 522.

(4) Statutory Negligence

14.179 On statutes in the law of tort: Stanton, Skidmore, Harris and Wright, *Statutory Torts* (2003).

(a) The Occupiers Liability Acts 1957 and 1984

(i) The duty to visitors

14.182 An occupier's responsibilities may, however, include making enquiries as to whether his independent contractor carries adequate insurance cover: *Gwilliam v West Hertfordshire Hospitals NHS Trust* [2002] EWCA Civ 1041, [2003]QB 443.

(iii) Trespassers and other uninvited entrants

14.184 *Tomlinson v Congleton BC* [2003] UKHL 47, [2003] 3 WLR 705 was decided under the 1984 Act but is of general importance in the law of negligence. The local authority had converted an old gravel pit and the surrounding land into a lake and park which attracted many visitors. Families went there to picnic and paddle, but swimming was known to be dangerous. The local authority put up notices prohibiting it but knew that teenagers and others often ignored them. Tomlinson, intending to swim, walked into the water and then, standing knee-deep, took a disastrous dive which broke his neck on a sandbank. Once he decided to swim he became a trespasser. His claim under the 1984 Act failed. The central reason, which would have been an answer to any action in negligence, was that, in the terms of s 1(3)(c) of the 1984 Act, it was not reasonable to expect the council to protect him from dangers manifestly inherent in his chosen activity. Even if there had been no notices the council would not have been liable. It was all the more unreasonable to expect protection given that effective measures to prevent swimming would have carried a high social cost, in that they would have reduced access and amenity for the thousands of visitors who used the site for the leisure activities for which it had been intended; cf the similar tragedy in *Donoghue v Folkestone Properties Ltd* [2003] EWCA Civ 231, [2003] QB 1008, where the claimant trespasser went for a midnight swim on Boxing Day. He dived from a slipway in the defendant's harbour and broke his neck on a concealed pile. There the central ground for denying his claim was s 1(3)(b) of the 1984 Act which makes it a condition of the duty that the occupier know or ought reasonably to know of the trespassers being in the vicinity of the danger. There was absolutely no reason to suspect swimmers in the middle of the night in the middle of winter.

(b) The Congenital Disabilities (Civil Liability) Act 1976

n297: add *Rees v Darlington Memorial Hospital NHS Trust* [2003] UKHL 52, [2003] 4 All ER 987, cf Supplement para 14.44. **14.191**

D. Negligence: Defences

(1) Contributory Negligence

(a) Fault

n306: confirmed by the House of Lords in *Standard Chartered Bank v Pakistan National Shipping Corp (No 2)* [2002] UKHL 43, [2003]1 All ER 173. **14.196**

(e) Contributory negligence and other torts

n319: cf Supplement para 14.196 n306. **14.205**

(2) Consent, Assumption of Risk

(c) Consent

n335: see also *Re B (Adult: Refusal of Treatment)* [2002] 2 All ER 449. **14.215**

(3) Illegality, Public Policy

(a) Theoretical and technical difficulties

Law Commission Consultation Paper No 160, *The Illegality Defence in Tort* (2001) suggests that the defence should be put on a statutory basis giving the **14.226** courts a structured discretion. In *Vellino v Chief Constable of Greater Manchester* [2002] 3 All ER 78 (CA) Sedley LJ, dissenting, argued for an apportionment solution based on the Law Reform (Contributory Neglence) Act 1945.

E. Concurrent Liability within Tort

(1) Trespass

(b) Trespass to the person: false imprisonment

14.243 n376: hence it is no defence to an action for false imprisonment that a prison governor acted in good faith in accordance with current case law, subsequently overruled: *R v Governor of Brockhill Prison, ex p Evans (No 2)* [2001] AC 19, HL. However, if a court makes a mistake and issues a judgment for a sentence longer than was intended, the error has to be corrected by due process of law. If it is not corrected and the prisoner serves longer than he should have done, there is no false imprisonment on the part of the governor: *Quinland v Governor of Swaleside Prison* [2002] EWCA Civ 174; [2003] QB 306. In the same case the Court of Appeal held that no action lay for negligence against the Criminal Appeal Office which had failed to act on a notification of the error. The reason was that, although the Crown Proceedings Act 1947 rendered the Crown liable in tort, s 2(5) expressly exempted acts of a judicial nature or done in execution of judicial process. The Court expressed the hope that compensation would be paid *ex gratia.*

(2) Nuisance

(a) Public nuisance

14.246 n382: and bridges: *Wandsworth LBC v Railtrack plc* [2002] QB 756 (CA).

(b) Private nuisance

(ii) Unreasonable user

14.250 n395: in *Dennis v Ministry of Defence* [2003] EWHC 793, (2003) 153 MLJ 364, [2003] TLR 270, Buckley J held that the public interest in training pilots was a factor relevant to his decision to award damages for noise rather than a declaration or injunction.

(iii) Delimiting the sphere of nuisance

14.251 The decision in *Hunter v Canary Wharf* may have to be modified in the light of the Human Rights Act 1998. In *McKenna v British Aluminium Ltd* [2002] Env L R 30, [2002] TLR 182 Neuburger J refused to strike out an action in nuisance and *Rylands v Fletcher* by claimants who had no proprietary interest. It is arguable that the Human Rights Act protects the homes and private lives of all citizens, not just as property owners. In *Pemberton v Southwark LBC* [2000] 1 WLR 1672 a 'tolerated trespasser' was held to have a sufficient interest to sue in nuisance.

(iv) The relation between nuisance and negligence

n407: in *Delaware Mansions Ltd v Westminster City Council* [2001] UKHL 55, [2002] 1 AC 321 it was held that reasonable remedial expenditure could be recovered in respect of damage done by a continuing natural nuisance of which the defendant knew or ought to have known, but the defendant must be given notice of the damage and a reasonable opportunity for abatement. The choice of label, nuisance or negligence, has little or no significance in this context. Following *Delaware Mansions Ltd v Westminster City Council*, above, *Abbahall Ltd v Smee* [2002] EWCA Civ 1831, [2003] 1 WLR 1472 held that, where the owner of a flying freehold allowed the roof to decay to the damage of the two floors in which that freehold subsisted and to the flat on the ground floor belonging to the claimant, the abatement of the nuisance would benefit both and that both should contribute equally. There was no principle which allowed the scale of the contributions to be adjusted to reflect differences in the parties' means. **14.254**

Failure to take reasonable steps to prevent hazards from damaging a neighbour's home may, however, be excluded by a statutory regime. In *Marcic v Thames Water Utilities Ltd* [2003] UKHL 66, [2004] 1 All ER 135 the House of Lords overruled the Court of Appeal decision that a water company with statutory powers and duties was liable for allowing its sewage system to flood the claimant's home. Liability for common law nuisance would be inconsistent with the procedures for controlling the water industry set up by the Water Industry Act 1991. The statutory scheme was a fair one, in accord with the European Convention on Human Rights. It left the oversight of the industry with the regulator and excluded actions by individuals until an undertaker had failed to comply with an enforcement order.

(3) The Liability in Rylands v Fletcher

(b) Reintegration into the general law

In *Transco plc v Stockport Metropolitan Borough Council* [2003] UKHL 61, an action brought to recover the costs of measures taken to protect a gas main from the escape of water from the water-supply of a tower block, the House of Lords was invited to consider following the example of the High Court of Australia and absorb *Rylands v Fletcher* into negligence. This invitation was declined. Their Lordships decided, with varying degrees of enthusiasm, that strict liability still had a part to play, limited though it now is by judicial interpretation and statutory regimes. Lord Bingham [10] and Lord Hoffmann [49] emphasized that it only applies where there is an exceptionally high risk of danger and mischief. As the test of cases excluded from the rule Lord Bingham [11] preferred 'ordinary user' to **14.259** 'reasonable' or 'natural' user. Use might not be 'ordinary' even when not unreasonable. Their Lordships followed *Cambridge Water Co v Eastern Counties Leather plc* [1994] 2 AC 264 in treating *Rylands v Fletcher* as a sub-species of nuisance, and three of them supposed that that in itself entailed the exclusion of liability for personal injury under this head.

In *McKenna v British Aluminium Ltd* [2002] Env L R 30, [2002] TLR 182 Neuburger J held that at common law a claimant in *Rylands v Fletcher* must, as in private nuisance generally, have a proprietary interest in land. But notice Supplement para 14.251 above.

(4) Liability for Animals

(b) Statutory reform

14.269 An animal may have more than one keeper. In such a case there is no reason why one keeper may not sue another: *Flack v Hudson* [2001] QB 698, CA.

The paragraph does not highlight the case in which a keeper may be strictly liable for an animal of a non-dangerous species under s 2(2) of the Act. In *Mirvahedy v Henley* [2003] UKHL 16, [2003] 2 AC 491 the House of Lords decided that a driver injured by a stampeding horse was entitled to the benefit of that section. The section says, inter alia, that the known likelihood of the damage must arise from abnormality or from characteristics only found in such an animal at particular times or in particular circumstances. A horse which is frightened is a horse in particular circumstances and to bolt uncontrollably is a normal response in those circumstances. With great difficulty the majority concluded that this kind of tragedy therefore fell within s 2(2). The minority would have said that a horse in a field which is 'frightened by something' is not 'in particular circumstances', making 'particular' mean something like 'special', as where a cow has a young calf with her.

(5) Product Liability

14.274 The standard of safety that persons generally are entitled to expect has been discussed in several cases. In *A v National Blood Authority* [2001] 3 All ER 289, where it was conceded that blood was a product for the purposes of the Act and the Directive and that its preparation was an industrial process, it was held that legitimate expectations were not limited by what was scientifically possible for the time being, at least unless the public be warned as to dangers not discoverable. Thus the public was entitled to rely on blood being uninfected, even though there was at the time no available test for Hepatitis C; cf *Richardson v LRC Products Ltd* [2000] Lloyd's Rep Med 280 (public aware of unreliability of condoms) and *Abouzaid v Mothercare (UK) Ltd* [2000] WP 1918530, The Times, 20 February 2001, CA, criticized (2001) 151 NLJ 424 (eye lost through defective elastic strap, irrelevant that producer unaware of the danger). That the concession in *A v*

National Blood Authority was rightly made can be inferred from Case C-203/99 *Veedfald v Arhus Amtskommune* [2001] ECR I-3569, The Times, 4 June 2001.

n442: *A v National Blood Authority* [2001] 3 All ER 289 emphasized that the s 4(1)(e) defence is directed only to whether there was actual or accessible knowledge of the risk. Whether it was possible to avoid the risk by taking reasonable care is irrelevant to a strict liability regime. **14.276**

The availability of punitive damages is no longer confined to particular causes of action: *Kuddus v Chief Constable of Leicestershire Constabulary* [2001] UKHL 29, [2002] 2 AC 122 overruling *AB v South West Water Services Ltd* [1993] QB 507, cf Main Work para 18.240. However, this is unlikely to produce an upsurge of punitive awards in product liability cases.

(6) Defamation

(d) Strict liability

n458: without ruling out strict liability altogether, the Court of Appeal in *Kerry O'Shea v MGN* [2001] EMLR 40, CA held that it would be a breach of Article 10 of the European Convention to impose strict liability where a pornographic photograph caused some people to think that the claimant was the woman depicted. **14.286**

n461: add *McManus v Beckham* [2002] EWCA Civ 939, [2002] 1 WLR 2982. **14.287**

(e) Defences

(i) Justification

The last two sentences should be read in the light of the new material on the protection of privacy which is discussed in Supplement para 14.335. **14.290**

(iii) Qualified privilege

In *Loutchansky v Times Newspapers (No 2)* [2001] EWCA Civ 1805, [2002] QB 783 the newspaper had sought to expose a Russian businessman as a gangster and money launderer. It made no attempt to justify, preferring to plead qualified privilege. It is clear from the judgment of the court, given by Lord Phillips MR, that the press privilege developed in *Reynolds v Times Newspapers* [2001] 2 AC 127, HL (see Main Work para 14.298) has diverged from other instances of qualified privilege and requires the formulation of its own questions. The judge had been wrong to ask whether the newspaper had been under a duty to publish in the sense of being open to legitimate criticism if it had not done so, for there certainly had to be cases in which publication would be privileged even though a decision not to publish would not have been open to criticism. The Court of Appeal sent this issue back for the judge to ask, bearing in mind the tensions between private and public interests, whether responsible journalists would have thought it right to **14.293** publish. This test could not but pre-empt the issue of malice, in that responsible journalists would not publish upon that motivation.

(h) Relationship with negligence and other torts

(i) Defamation and negligence

14.301 **n481**: there is a dictum of Lord Phillips in *D v East Berkshire NHS Trust* [2003] EWCA Civ 1151, [2003] 4 All ER 796, [102] which is flatly against allowing what was allowed in *Spring v Guardian Assurance*. He says there is no question of sidestepping the defence of qualified privilege by advancing a claim for defamation in the guise of a claim in negligence. The claims in *D v East Berkshire NHS Trust* were for psychiatric harm resulting from false accusations of child abuse which, as Lord Phillips remarked, have the elements of defamation. Perhaps the extreme sensitivity of investigations into child abuse suffices to distinguish the case from the commercial world of the *Spring* case.

F. Strict Liability: Interference with Property

(1) Common Law

(b) Parasitic protection at common law

(ii) Conversion

14.313 The most recent analysis of the nature of the tort is to be found in *Kuwait Airways Corp v Iraqi Airways Co (No 3)* [2002] UKHL 19; [2002] 2 AC 883, especially in the speech of Lord Nicholls [37]–[44] and [63]–[90]. The case concerned the civil liability of IAC in respect of ten civil aircraft of the KAC fleet captured by Iraq in the First Gulf War and assigned by the Iraqi government to IAC.

14.315 **Broad understanding of misappropriation. n506**: in *Marcq v Christie, Manson & Woods Ltd* [2003] EWCA Civ 731, [2003]3 WLR 980 this was applied to the auctioneers Christie's when in good faith they had received a painting from a non-owner, had tried to sell it in accordance with his instructions, and, having failed, returned it to him. Nothing the auctioneers had done had purported to alter the property in the painting as it lay when they received it. It would have been different if, having succeeded in a sale, they had delivered it to the new buyer.

14.316 **Claimant with a better right to possession.** Even a thief can sue. That there is almost no exception based on illegality on the part of the possessor is affirmed in a fine judgment of the Court of Appeal in *Costello v Chief Constable of Derbyshire Constabulary* [2001] EWCA Civ 381, [2001] 1 WLR 1437, CA, following and further explaining *Webb v Chief Constable of Merseyside Police* [2000] 2 QB 427, CA. Under s 19 of the Police and Criminal Evidence Act 1984 the police had seized from Costello a Ford Escort car. The temporary purpose of that seizure having been exhausted, they refused to return it on the ground that it had been stolen and Costello knew it. Although they were held to be correct in those beliefs [7] they were compelled to return the car to him. The wrongful possessor had a right to possession which could only be defeated by statute. Statute apart, the only exception was that the court would not order delivery up of something if it would be unlawful for him to receive it, as for instance prohibited drugs or a gun for which he held no licence [34].

14.317 In the *Costello* case (see Supplement para 14.316) the police were not in a position to resist Costello's claim by invoking s 8 of the Torts (Interference with Goods) Act 1977. In order to rely on a third party's better title under that section a defendant was required to identify that third party and to cause him to be joined as a party.

(2) Equity

(c) **Parasitic protection in equity**

14.330 In *Twinsectra Ltd v Yardley* [2002] UKHL 12, [2002] 2 AC 164, HL the House of Lords held that dishonesty in the context of dishonest assistance had both an objective and a subjective element. Objectively, the conduct in question must have been dishonest as judged by prevailing standards and, subjectively, the defendant must have known that it was so condemned (Lord Hutton [35] and [36], with the agreement of Lord Slynn, Lord Steyn, and Lord Hoffmann). Lord Millett would have dispensed with the subjective element altogether.

14.331 In the *Twinsectra* case (see Supplement para 14.330) there was no issue as to knowing receipt as opposed to knowing assistance but one paragraph in Lord Millett's speech gives a broad hint that he at least would accept it as an unjust enrichment liability, not requiring fault [105]. The best course may yet be to say that the one label has, impossibly, been trying to cover both a liability for a wrong and for an unjust enrichment, and that what the law requires is two separate packages, not one; cf Main Work paras 15.53 and 15.54 n83.

G. Intentional Torts

14.335 Although developments in the law of confidence have significantly improved protection of private information, the most recent cases have damped down the movement which appeared to be under way towards wider protection of the non-pecuniary interest in 'personhood', which entails mutual respect for autonomy, privacy, and equal dignity.

In relation to privacy account must now be taken of the Human Rights Act 1998 incorporating in particular Article 8 of the European Convention on Human Rights:

> (1) Everyone has the right to respect for his private and family life, his home and his correspondence.
> (2) There shall be no interference by a public authority with the exercise of this right except such as is in accordance with the law and is necessary in a democratic society in the interests of national security, public safety or the economic well-being of the country, for the prevention of disorder or crime, for the protection of health or morals, or for the protection of the rights or freedoms of others.

In *Douglas v Hello!* [2001] QB 967, CA, where film stars were trying to stop unauthorized publication of their wedding pictures, Sedley LJ favoured the view that they had 'a right of privacy' which was 'grounded in the equitable doctrine of breach of confidence, which accords recognition to the fact that the law has to protect not only those whose trust has been abused but those who find themselves subject to an unwanted intrusion into their personal lives' [126]. And in *Douglas v Hello! (No 6)* [2003] EWHC 786 (Ch), [2003] 3 All ER 996 Lindsay J found that OK magazine, in high-jacking the wedding photography was indeed in breach of confidence both in its role as a protector of privacy and as guardian of commercially sensitive information. Again in *Venables v News Group Newspapers Ltd* [2001] Fam 430 the murderers of a toddler obtained a stringent worldwide injunction to prevent disclosure of their post-release identities and location. Butler-Sloss P, having first noted that the right to respect for private life conferred by the European Convention could not be directly enforced against private persons or bodies such as newspapers, went on to adopt the view that the courts, as public bodies, were nevertheless bound to interpret the law so as to give effect to those rights [24]. She then turned to the interpretation and application of the law of confidence, engaging in the process of weighing and balancing which is necessary in taking account of other competing rights [30]–[50]. In *Campbell v Mirror Group* [2002] EWCA Civ 1373, [2003] QB 633, where the newspaper had published details of a super-model's drug addiction, the Court of Appeal thought that the necessary weighing and balancing had not been well done at first instance. It was not the case that every public figure forfeited the right to privacy [41] but full weight had to be given to freedom of expression in the public interest [64], [65], [71].

One key to the extension of the law of confidence is the rejection of the view that an obligation of confidence must be knowingly accepted by the person who gains access to the relevant matter or material. Some information is inherently confidential and carries the obligation of secrecy with it. Thus in *A v B plc* [2001] 1 WLR 2341, where a star footballer had sexual relationships with two women who then sold detailed accounts to newspapers, Jack J, reflecting the views of 'most people', held that facts concerning sexual relations, inside and outside marriage, should be regarded as inherently confidential [56]. On the facts the balancing exercise led the Court of Appeal to a different conclusion. It discharged the injunction on the ground that the freedom of the press should in this case prevail: *A v B plc* [2002] EWCA Civ 337, [2003] QB 195. The court gave detailed guidelines on the approach to be taken in such cases.

In *Wainwright v Home Office* [2003] UKHL 53, [2003] 3 WLR 1173 a woman and her son visiting a prisoner on remand to be tried for murder were strip searched for drugs in a callous manner which disregarded the code of practice for such searches. The House of Lords held that at common law there was no general wrong of infringement of privacy and, further, the European Convention did not require there to be such a general wrong. Lord Hoffmann, giving the leading speech, said that privacy was at most a value explaining particular liabilities and their modern dynamic. So in *Douglas v Hello!*, above, Sedley LJ should be understood as explaining the growth of abuse of confidence rather than as recognizing a new self-standing wrong [30]. That was not the way, in Lord Hoffmann's view, that the common law worked [31]. The incidents in the *Wainright* case occurred before the Human Rights Act 1998 came into force. Claims for invasion of privacy not covered by specific wrongs already known to the law will presumably be now advanced under the Act (cf *Peck v United Kingdom* [2003] TLR 49).

(1) Humiliation and Distress

14.336–14.337 There is now very little left of *Wilkinson v Downton*. In both *Wong v Parkside Health NHS Trust* [2001] EWCA Civ 1721, [2003] 3 All ER 932 and *Wainwright v Home Office* [2003] UKHL 53, [2003] 3 WLR 1173 it was said to go no further than claims for mental illness and, in effect, to add nothing to the law relating to negligently inflicted psychiatric injury, see Main Work from para 14.107. On the other hand, Lord Hoffman in the latter case said that what was wrong with the decision was that Wright J had been satisfied with 'imputed intent'. To escape the restrictive conditions which generally exclude liability for mere distress and humiliation short of psychiatric injury it would be necessary to show actual intention to produce those results or at the very least recklessness [44]–[45]. Lord Hoffmann reserved his position as to whether such an extension was desirable [46]. Both these cases say that there was no tort of humiliation or contempt of another's right to an equality of respect before the Protection from Harassment Act 1997. No account is taken of the argument that non-compensatory damages, now divided between exemplary and aggravated, were always concerned with the protection of that interest.

14.338 **n541**: *Thomas v News Group Newspapers* [2001] EWCA Civ 1233, [2002] EMLR 4 (harassment and freedom of the press). The Act protects individuals, not corporate persons: *Daiichi UK Ltd v Stop Huntingdon Animal Cruelty* [2003] TLR 570 (QBD).

14.339 Hence it has been held that mental illness is no defence to a charge of harassment: *R v Peter Sean C* [2001] EWCA Crim 1251; [2001] 2 FLR 757.

(3) Pure Economic Loss

(a) Deceit

14.348 **n 557**: confirmed by the House of Lords in *Standard Chartered Bank v Pakistan National Shipping Corp* [2003] 1 All ER 173.

(b) The economic torts

14.349 **n 558**: add H Carty, *An Analysis of the Economic Torts* (2001).

(i) Procuring breach of contract

14.350 **n559**: for an excellent historico-analytical study see S Waddams, 'Johanna Wagner and the Rival Opera Houses' (2001) 117 LQR 431.

14.355 **n574**: add *Michaels v Taylor Woodrow Developments Ltd* [2001] Ch 493.

H. Vicarious Liability

(1) Personal Liability and Vicarious Liability Distinguished

(b) Vicarious liability properly so-called

14.365 **n589**: meanwhile see *Merrett v Babb* [2001] QB 1174 (employee sued personally, employer having gone into liquidation).

(4) The 'Course of Employment'

14.377 **n600**: the 'close connection' test proposed by the Supreme Court of Canada in *Bazley v Currey* was approved and substantially adopted for cases of intentional wrongdoing by employees in *Lister v Hesley Hall Ltd* [2001] UKHL 22, [2002] 1 AC 215, HL. There a school was held liable for sexual abuse of boys at the school, the abuser being the warden of a residential annexe. This decision is of great importance for schools, hospitals and residential institutions for the vulnerable. In *Dubai Aluminium Ltd v Salaam* [2002] UKHL 48, [2002] 3 WLR 1913 the House of Lords used the 'close connection' test to determine the range of the vicarious liability of partners one for another under s 10 of the Partnership Act 1890. The High Court of Australia has chosen to stick to the traditional Salmond test of 'course of employment': *New South Wales v Lepore* [2003] HCA 4, cf N McBride (2003) 62 CLJ 255.

15

UNJUST ENRICHMENT

A. Introduction

(1) A Change of Name

n1: the sixth edition of *Goff and Jones on Restitution* was published in 2002. **15.01**

n4: add the hybrid RB Grantham and CEF Rickett, *Enrichment and Restitution in*

New Zealand (2000). It appears that the new *Restatement*, the reporter for which is Professor Andrew Kull, will adopt the hybrid form *Restatement of Restitution and Unjust Enrichment*: 'Symposium on Restitution and Unjust Enrichment' 79 Texas Law Review 1763, 1765 (2001). There is now P Birks, *Unjust Enrichment* (2003), which not only changes the name but also takes a new perspective on 'unjust' (Supplement paras 15.46–15.48).

n5: add P Jaffey *The Nature and Scope of Restitution* (2000). A second edition of *Burrows on Restitution* was published in 2002.

(3) Unjust Enrichment and Acquisitive Wrongdoing

15.04 **n9**: the contrast between gain-based recovery for wrongs as such and unjust enrichment, which is definitively not a wrong, should have been more emphasized: 'Symposium on Restitution and Unjust Enrichment' 79 Texas Law Review 1767 (P Birks), 1869 (J Edelman), 1879 (D Friedmann) (2001). The gap in the literature has been filled by J Edelman, *Gain-Based Damages* (2002). In *Attorney-General v Blake* [2001] 1 AC 268 (HL) the House of Lords accepted that a spy who as a member of the secret service had promised not to write unauthorized books was accountable for the profits of a book written in breach of that contract. That is a paradigmatic example of restitution for a wrong, here the wrong of breach of contract. It has nothing to do with unjust enrichment; cf Supplement paras 18.21 and 18.238. However, *Experience Hendrix v PPX Enterprises Inc* [2003] EWCA Civ 323, [2003] 1 All ER (Comm) 830 now shows that that case will rarely be applied. After the early death of Jimi Hendrix his father established the claimant company to preserve and market his work. A contractual settlement conceded to PPX, run by Hendrix's former manager, limited rights in some master tapes. PPX, dissatisfied, deliberately broke that contract. The claimant would never have agreed any terms enlarging PPX's rights. It was not possible to calculate the loss which the breach had inflicted on the claimant. The CA agreed that the defendant should surrender the benefit which it had acquired by its breach. However, in its view the relevant benefit was not its profits, as in the *Blake* case, but only the wrongful user of the tapes, for which the proper award was a royalty. This was the perfect case for a *Blake* account of profits, which had been given a fair wind by Sir Andrew Morritt V-C in *Esso Petroleum Co Ltd v Niad Ltd* [2001] All ER (D) 324 (Ch), 2001 WL 146190. The CA preferred the sceptical and restrictive tone of the reported arbitration in *AB Corporation v CD Company (The 'Sine Nomine')* [2002] 1 Lloyd's Rep 805. This attitude made the law a collaborator in the forced sale of an asset which the claimant company thought it had made safe.

B. Enrichment at the Expense of the Claimant

(1) Enrichment Immediately at the Expense of the Claimant

(b) Corresponding impoverishment

n 23: in *Roxborough v Rothmans of Pall Mall (Australia) Ltd* [2001] HCA 68, 208 CLR 516 the High Court of Australia once more held, Kirby J dissenting, that the impoverishment or continuing impoverishment of the claimant was not an element of, and did not impose a ceiling upon, the cause of action. The context was again the denial of any defence of passing on. It is, of course, commonly the case that the claimant has suffered a loss corresponding to the defendant's gain. The range of liability in unjust enrichment turns largely on whether or not that corresponding loss is a requirement. It is so held in some systems. The contrary view of English law maintained in the text (cf Birks 2003, n4 above, 64–6, 70–1) has been vigorously contested by Professor Mitchell McInnes: M McInnes, 'Interceptive Subtraction, Unjust Enrichment and Wrongs' [2003] CLJ 697–716. **15.17**

(3) Enrichment

(b) Benefits in kind

(ii) Guidelines for establishing enrichment

To the cases cited in n58 add *R on the application of Rowe v Vale of White Horse DC* [2003] 1 Lloyd's Rep 418 (QBD Admin Ct). The District Council had for many years supplied sewage services to householders without charging. Lightman J denied the Council's claim on the ground that the enrichment was not in the circumstances unjust. Even though they had not been freely accepted within Main Work para 15.43, yet these necessary services were incontrovertibly enriching, in the sense that the defendant would have had to acquire them anyhow if the claimant had not supplied them. **15.42**

C. Unjust: Deficient Intent

In laying out the method for determining whether an enrichment is unjust, these paragraphs assume that the alternative method discussed in Main Work paras 15.121–15.123 will not prevail, that is to say that English law will not go over to the civilian method in which the judge has to ask whether the enrichment at the expense of the claimant has a recognized explanation: does it have or does it lack a sufficient basis (*causa* or 'consideration')? In Birks 2003 (para 15.01 n4 above), 87–143 the author takes the view that, since the interest swaps cases (Main Work paras 15.98 and 15.121) did adopt that method and because English practice does in other ways tacitly accord with it, resistance to that change of method should be **15.46–15.48** abandoned. As is said in the text here, the 'no basis' approach and the 'unjust factors' approach are different methods. The one cannot be tacked on to the other. On the other hand both can be used, separately, on any set of facts. This Supplement endeavours to follow that policy.

(1) No Intent

(b) Equity

15.54 **n83**: add J Payne 'Unjust Enrichment, Trusts and Recipient Liability for Unlawful Dividends' (2003) 119 LQR 583, especially 602–4. In *Bank of Credit and Commerce International (Overseas) Ltd v Akindele* [2001] Ch 437, [2000] 4 All ER 221 (CA), where money had passed without the company's authority to Chief Akindele, who was not found to have been at fault and had anyhow given value, an opportunity presented itself for the Court of Appeal to review this area of the law in the light of Lord Nicholls' paper. But Nourse LJ, with whom Ward and Sedley LJJ agreed, regarded the matter as better left to the House of Lords. He registered a distaste for any strict liability on the ground that it would make for commercial uncertainty and preferred to insist that the receipt must be 'unconscionable', which might mean almost anything. Since liability in unjust enrichment is strict, albeit subject to defences, Nourse LJ's anxieties would carry away even the recovery of mistaken payments (cf Main Work para 15.58). In due course the House of Lords will no doubt have an opportunity to disentangle the fault-based liability for the wrong of misappropriating trust assets and the strict but fragile liability for unjust enrichment arising from the receipt of trust assets. The latter once recognized, it may well be that the former should be made to require dishonesty, with the subjective element on which the majority insisted for dishonest assistance in a breach of trust in *Twinsectra Ltd v Yardley* [2002] UKHL 12, [2002] 2 AC 164. In *Twinsectra* there was no live issue in the House of Lords as to a receipt-based liability, but Lord Millett did say, obiter but firmly, that a receipt-based liability 'does not depend on fault' [105]. This must be welcomed. The disapplication of the law of unjust enrichment in the case of recipients of trust money is not defensible.

(2) Impaired Intent

(a) Two recurrent problems

(ii) Requirements of fault and other inhibitions of the right to restitution

15.59 *Scottish Equitable plc v Derby* [2001] EWCA Civ 369, [2001] 3 All ER 818 (CA) shows once again that even a very careless claimant can recover from an innocent defendant, save so far as the defendant has changed his position (cf Main Work para 15.237). Although momentarily counter-intuitive, strict liability is both correct and necessary against one who has not changed his position and still holds surplus assets. Carelessness on the part of the mistaken payer gives the recipient no better claim to hold on to what he was never intended to have, cf Robert Goff J in his radical review of the cases in *Barclays Bank Ltd v WJ Simms Son & Cooke (Southern) Ltd* [1980] QB 677, 686. The same point is restated in *Dextra Bank and Trust Company Ltd v Bank of Jamaica* [2001]1 All ER Comm 193 (PC Jam) [45]. Liability in unjust enrichment is strict until disenrichment. A line is crossed when it can be seen that the claimant knowingly took the risk, waiving all inquiry.

(b) Five species of impairment

(i) Mistake

A new case on mistake of law raises an issue of first importance. *Deutsche Morgan Grenfell Group plc v IRC* [2003] EWHC 1779 (Ch), [2003] 4 All ER 645 arose in the aftermath of *Metallgesellschaft Ltd v IRC* and *Hoechst AG v IRC* C-397/98 and C-410/98, [2001] Ch 620 (ECJ) concerning the operation of the exemption from advance corporation tax under the Income and Corporation Taxes Act 1988, s 247. Companies within a group could give notice of a 'group income election' which would become an effective exemption after a lapse of three months unless an inspector of taxes rejected it within that time. A rejection by an inspector was subject to appeal. Having the exemption, companies within the group could pay dividends without having to pay advance corporation tax. The ECJ held that the exemption was unlawfully restricted to companies resident in the United Kingdom. The claimants constituted one group which would have made such an election but for that supposedly valid restriction. Had they made the election and obtained the exemption they would not have had to pay advance corporation tax, only mainstream corporation tax later. The effect was that they had paid millions of pounds earlier than necessary. They successfully sought restitution of the value of that money over time, measured in interest. 15.67

The case was squarely covered by *Kleinwort Benson Ltd v Lincoln CC* [1999] 2 AC 1 (HL) except, crucially, that the group had paid under a valid obligation. Every company is bound to pay advance corporation tax unless it does the things necessary to earn an exemption. The claimants had not. Money mistakenly paid to discharge a contractual obligation cannot be recovered unless there was no obligation to discharge. Similarly, there can be no restitution of money paid to discharge a mistaken judgment unless the judgment is quashed. Yet in *Deutsche Morgan Grenfell* the claimants succeeded, without any attempt being made to allow an election and exemption out of time. Park J does not ignore this peculiarity ([21]–[22]) but he minimizes its effect. At one point, again downplaying the fact the payments were due, he says that the claimants could have fallen back on *Woolwich Equitable Building Society v Inland Revenue Commissioners* [1993] AC

70 (HL) to recover the payments as 'money paid pursuant to an unlawful taxation measure' [37]. See further Supplement paras 15.161–15.167. On all views, the outcome must be suspect. Its anomalous nature becomes doubly apparent if the 'no basis' approach is taken seriously (Supplement paras 15.46–15.48). There was a recognized basis for the payment, namely the discharge of a valid obligation and seemingly no way that that obligation could be invalidated.

15.69 In *Dextra Bank and Trust Company Ltd v Bank of Jamaica* [2002] 1 All ER Com 193 (PC Jam) the importance of the line between mistakes and mispredictions was underlined. Indeed one reason why the claimant bank was said to have no restitutionary right was precisely that it had merely mispredicted the future consequences of its payment [29]. The *Dextra* distinction highlights the flaw in the mistake analysis in *Deutsche Morgan Grenfell* which was in turn derived directly from the majority in the *Lincoln* case itself. In both cases the best evidence was taken into account and a belief was formed which could not be falsified other than by reference to a case decided subsequently. There was no impairment but only an exercise of judgment which, later, turned out to be incorrect. However, essential as the *Dextra* distinction is to the analysis of mistakes, whether it led to a correct decision on its own facts is not clear. The denial of any cause of action is best tested on the counter-factual hypothesis that there had been no disenrichment. Had the Bank of Jamaica still had the $3 million, the claimant would almost certainly have been entitled to recover. The facts are very little different from *RE Jones v Waring & Gillow Ltd* [1926] AC 670 (HL). If such cases are approached using the 'no basis' method used in the void interest swaps cases, it is evident in both that the basis of the payment was the making of a contract, which was not made because the parties were irredeemably at cross-purposes. Nor was either payer a conscious risk-taker, cf Main Work para 15.72. There was no basis for the payments.

(ii) Pressure

15.80 **n126**: more recent cases leave this problem unresolved, save in suggesting that a basket of factors has to be taken into consideration in deciding whether withholding a contractual right amounts to illegitimate pressure. Two important decisions of Dyson J represent current judicial thinking: *DSND Subsea Ltd v Petroleum Geo-Services ASA* [2000] BLR 530 (TCC), noted R Bigwood (2001) 117 LQR 376; *Carillion Construction Ltd v Felix (UK) Ltd* [2001] BLR 1 (TCC).

(iii) Relational dependence

15.81 There is now a considerable tension between cases which treat undue influence as too much influence, impairing the autonomy of the weak party, and cases which view it as abusive exploitation of that weakness. The language of *Royal Bank of Scotland v Etridge (No 2)* [2001] UKHL 44, [2002] 2 AC 773 would make it an equitable wrong. The effect is to narrow its range to pressure, bullying and abuse.

Undue influence has not historically been understood as a wrong. As in 'undue anxiety', the word is better taken as indicating too much rather than improper: too much influence on one side, hence crippled autonomy on the other. A woman taught never to contradict her husband in business matters, as in the *Aboody* case (Main Work para 15.82 and n127), lacks autonomy but it is not necessary to characterize her husband, no less the victim of their culture, as a wrongdoer. Moreover, undue influence is commonly established by presumption (Main Work para 15.83). A presumed want of autonomy is not objectionable, but the same cannot be said of presumed wrongdoing. The Court of Appeal in *Hammond v Osborn* [2002] EWCA Civ 885, [2002] WTLR 1125 is true to *Allcard v Skinner* (1887) 36 Ch D 145 (CA), which certainly did not turn on wrongdoing. In *Hammond* the defendant, locked in a marriage at best dreary, devoted herself to the care of a retired schoolmaster in very poor health. They had met when he was having difficulty walking home. She had stopped to help him. She more than once refused gifts. Undeterred he finally succeeded in pressing her, with no inducement on her part, to accept a very large sum of money. The gift took no account of his own possible needs for the future nor of his liability to tax. Then, much sooner than anyone had expected, he died. The next of kin emerged from the shadows. In the Court of Appeal they succeeded in recovering the money. The schoolmaster's gratitude and affection for Mrs Osborn could not alter the fact that his dependence on her shut out other advice. As with the young nun who gave her property to her order, his autonomy was impaired. Nothing had been done to bring in an independent adviser to enable him to 'exercise an independent will about it'. The gift was voidable because it was not 'the product of full, free and independent volition' (Ward LJ [60]). This approach was approved and followed in *Niersmans v Perticcio* [2004] EWCA Civ 372, esp [1]–[2] and [20].

In contrast, two recent cases in the Privy Council look for wrongdoing. In *R v Attorney-General for England and Wales* [2003] UKPC 22, [2003] EMLR 24 (PCNZ) R was a soldier who relied on undue influence to resist the enforcement of a confidentiality contract against publication of matters relating to his service in the SAS. He lost because their Lordships insisted that wrongful exploitation was the essence of undue influence. The majority accepted that the Army exercised influence over R but in making signature of the contract a condition of continued service in the special forces it had not unfairly exploited the influence which it had. 'Undue' meant, for them, 'improper' or 'unconscionable', not 'too much'. The parallel in misrepresentation would be to insist that the prefix 'mis-' supposed bad behaviour, as it does where insurance is 'missold'. That would spell the end of relief for innocent misrepresentation. Lord Scott of Foscote dissented. Rescission for undue influence in his view still flowed from lack of autonomy, not from fault in the party benefiting. No allegation of impropriety had been made against the Mother Superior in *Allcard v Skinner*.

Taking a similar stance three months later, *National Commercial Bank (Jamaica) Ltd v Hew* [2002] UKPC 65, [2003] All ER (D) 404 (June) excluded undue influence by a bank on the ground that there had been no wicked exploitation, no abuse of the customer who had incurred huge debts because he was set on developing an unpromising site.

15.82 In *Royal Bank of Scotland v Etridge (No 2)* [2001] UKHL 44, [2002] 2 AC 773 their Lordships in effect laid down a code of conduct which in all ordinary cases will insulate lenders from undue influence or other vitiating factors arising between a principal borrower and a person giving security, usually the wife of the borrower. The lender who fails to follow the code will not be protected in any case in which security is given by a person in a non-commercial relationship to the borrower. The person giving security, very frequently but not always the wife of the principal borrower, must receive independent legal advice from a person acting in this matter for her and in her interest; that adviser must be armed with sufficient information about the nature and purpose of lending to make the advice useful and realistic; the advice must not be given in the presence of the borrower; and the adviser must certify to the lender that the advice was given and understood.

15.83 The text observes that in a number of special relationships a presumption of undue influence extends to both the want of autonomy and its having caused the particular transfer, while in other cases the party seeking relief can lead evidence to show the want of autonomy within the relationship and then rely on a presumption as to the causation. In the *Etridge* case the House of Lords takes the view that the second and weaker of these presumptions hardly merits the name, since the same conclusion would be expected to flow from the ordinary operation of the rules as to onus of proof. The 'presumption' merely resembles an evidential rule such as '*res ipsa loquitur*'([14]–[18] Lord Nicholls, [105]–[107] Lord Hobhouse, [161] Lord Scott).

15.84 **n132**: in the *Etridge* case their Lordships declined the invitation to eliminate altogether the requirement of 'manifest disadvantage' which had been implicit in the sceptical judgment of the Court of Appeal in *Barclays Bank plc v Coleman* [2000] 1 All ER 385 (CA) 399 (itself one of the appeals heard in the *Etridge* case). They preferred instead to rephrase the requirement and reorient it in relation to the weakened second presumption. In effect the law is now that, unless the transaction is of such a character as 'not to be accounted for on the ground of ... ordinary motives on which ordinary men act', very positive evidence of actual undue influence will be needed before a transfer is to be rescinded [2001] 4 All ER 449 [21]–[31] Lord Nicholls, adopting the words of Lindley LJ in *Allcard v Skinner* (1887) 36 Ch D 145 (CA) 185. The story of Naboth's vineyard, coveted by Ahab and Jezebel (1 Kings 21), shows that external explicability of that kind cannot always be the end of the story. Naboth did not want to part with his ancestral vineyard at any price at all. Extreme means were used to part him from it.

(v) Transactional disadvantage

The *Etridge* code of practice will not be triggered by undue influence or misrepresentation but, prophylactically, by a particular kind of transaction: security for business borrowing given by a person in a non-commercial relationship with the borrower. If such cases were handled here, as instances of transactional inequality, the effect would be to cut out the troublesome digression through undue influence. The giving of security in such circumstances would simply be voidable unless the code of practice were complied with, the reason being that, as can be seen in the opening scenes of *The Merchant of Venice*, optimism and the ties of affection routinely combine to impair the judgment. The 'special equity' in *Yerkey v Jones* (1939) 63 CLR 649 (HCA) could have been, and could still be, modernized on these lines. **15.88**

D. Unjust: Qualified Intent

(1) Conditional Qualifications: Terminology

n161: an extreme example of the inveterate error identified in the text can be seen in *Roxborough v Rothmans of Pall Mall (Australia) Ltd* [2001] HCA 68, 208 CLR 516 in the dissenting judgment of Kirby J [165]–[169], notwithstanding that the other judgments go out of their way to repudiate the notion that failure of consideration must be a failure of contractual reciprocation: esp the judgment of Gleeson, Gaudron, and Hayne JJ [16]. **15.98**

n166: *Roxborough v Rothmans of Pall Mall (Australia) Ltd* [2001] HCA 68, 208 CLR 516 would appear on its face to support the unorthodox proposition that there can be a failure of basis within a valid contract. The claimant-appellants had bought tobacco goods at prices fixed to include payments in respect of tax which the sellers would have to pay to the NSW government. When that tax was held to be unconstitutional and void, the HCA allowed recovery by the retailers on the ground that that part of the price had been paid on a basis which subsequently failed to sustain itself. The contract had indeed been discharged, though only by full performance. No attempt was made to say that it had been rescinded or terminated. The best explanation of this may be analogy to many cases of which *Norwich Union v Price* [1934] AC 455 (PC Aus) is the type. Under a valid contract the insurer paid an insured loss, which had not in fact happened. So here under a valid contract the claimants were obliged to pay a severable sum referable to tax, and there was no tax. The 'no basis' approach sees both as cases in which the putative basis was discharge of an obligation, and the obligation had not been triggered. There was no obligation. This reasoning does not in any way derogate from the proposition that a payment made in performance of a valid contractual obligation cannot be recovered. **15.100**

(2) The Requirement of Total Failure

15.101 **n 168**: if and so far as a partial failure of consideration is one in which the claimant has received part of the expected contractual reciprocation, there is no longer any requirement of 'total failure' beyond counter-restitution in kind or money (Main Work paras 15.313–15.321). But, when 'total failure' means 'total failure of the basis of the transfer' it is still true that the basis must fail and that failure cannot easily bear any meaning other than total failure. *Roxborough v Rothmans of Pall Mall (Australia) Ltd* [2001] HCA 68, 208 CLR 516 is not a case in which there was no total failure. The basis was an obligation to pay tax, and there was no such obligation.

(3) Three Types of Failure of Basis

(b) Failure of basis: the coming about of some state of affairs

15.127 In *R on the application of Rowe v Vale of White Horse DC* [2003] 1 Lloyd's Rep 418 (QBD Admin Ct), introduced above in connection with Supplement para 15.42, the District Council supplied sewage services in the expectation that the householders would later agree to pay. The outcome which it wanted was payment in return. Lightman J denied recovery, despite the undoubted enrichment at the authority's expense. The reason which he gave turned directly on his finding that the householder had not freely accepted the benefit, but few people nowadays think that free acceptance is relevant as such to 'unjust', as opposed to enrichment: A Burrows, *The Law of Restitution* (2nd edn 2002) 402–7. The better explanation is that the supply was a voluntary transfer which could not be said to have been made on the basis that the householders would pay because the District Council for reasons of its own knowingly took the risk that the householders would accept a fait accompli. A risk-taker is a grudging gift-giver. The basis of the enrichment was, grudgingly, gift. The facts of free acceptance would certainly have been relevant to negativing risk-taking, for one who knows the intended basis is payment and nonetheless holds back when he could have spoken out can no longer say that the other should bear the risk of his later choosing not to do so. Mistake would have served the same purpose. Had the District Council mistakenly believed that it had contracted to supply the services, it would not have been a knowing risk-taker.

(c) Failure of basis: application

15.130–15.131 In *Twinsectra Ltd v Yardley* [2002] UKHL 12, [2002] 2 AC 164 the House of Lords imposed a construction on '*Quistclose* trusts' which, where it applies, means that there is no role for the law of unjust enrichment. Money tied to a particular purpose is to be understood as held on an express or genuinely implied trust for the settlor himself with power to apply the fund to the purpose. If the purpose cannot be pursued or is repudiated, the settlor as the beneficiary of the express trust can demand the fund. It is difficult to see how this could apply to any case in which the fund-holder is under a positive obligation to pursue the purpose as well as a negative obligation not to use the money for any other. There is no obvious justification for downgrading an obligation to fight vivisection to a power to do so. In such cases, it seems probable and right that what is said in Main Work para 15.131 will remain true, that the obligation will be contractual and that on the failure of the purpose there will be a restitutionary trust for the settlor. It will not escape notice, however, that, if that is correct, it is a construction which could also apply even in cases in which *Twinsectra* could apply, rendering the latter superfluous.

E. Unjust: Policies Requiring Restitution

(1) Payments Pursuant to a Common Liability

The material considered in this section has now been analysed at greater length in C Mitchell, *The Law of Contribution and Reimbursement* (2003). It is argued there that the policy reason for restitution in contribution and reimbursement cases is the need to reconcile the conflicting objectives pursued by the law in various situations where a claimant and a defendant are both legally liable to a third party who is forbidden to recover from both of them in full. On the one hand, the law aims to give the third party the fullest possible means of recovering what is due to him, by allowing him to sue either the claimant or the defendant for the full amount; on the other hand, the law also aims to make the defendant bear an appropriate share of the burden of paying the third party. These twin goals are achieved by allowing the third party to recover from the claimant in full, and then, if the third party exercises this right, by making a contribution or reimbursement award against the defendant in cases where the claimant has been obliged to pay more than his fair share of their common liability. **15.150–15.155**

In *Dubai Aluminium Co Ltd v Salaam* [2002] UKHL 48, [2003] 2 AC 366 [72] and [76], Lord Hobhouse confirmed that all contribution and reimbursement claims lie in unjust enrichment and are governed by a common set of principles, notwithstanding the fact that for historical reasons such claims are currently governed by a number of different statutory, common law, and equitable regimes.

(2) Benefits Conferred in an Emergency

(b) Exceptional cases

It may well be that non-contractual general average awards are also made pursuant **15.158**
to a policy of encouraging rescuers. See FD Rose, 'General Average as Restitution'

(1997) 113 LQR 569, citing JF Donaldson, CT Ellis, and CS Staughton (eds), *Lowndes and Rudolf on the Law of General Average and the York-Antwerp Rules* (9th edn, 1964), para 11.

(3) Payments to Public Authorities

15.161–15.167 The scope of the *Woolwich* principle has been considered in several cases. In *R (on the application of British Sky Broadcasting Group plc) v Customs & Excise Commissioners* [2001] EWHC Admin 127, [2001] STC 437 [33]–[36], Elias J held that in principle a *Woolwich* claim would lie to recover VAT payments even though these had been lawfully demanded, if the taxpayer had been treated unfairly by the C & E Commissioners. The alleged unfairness in the case (which was not established on the facts) was that similar VAT payments had not been demanded of comparator taxpayers. It was relevant to Elias J's finding vis-à-vis the *Woolwich* claim that the inconsistency of treatment suffered by the claimant could not have been remedied by backdating the comparator taxpayers' VAT liability because of the Sheldon principle (an extra-statutory concession that a VAT demand cannot be backdated once a taxpayer has received a written reassurance from the Commissioners that the taxpayer owes no VAT). In *Norwich CC v Stringer* [2001] 33 HLR 15 (CA), the defendant local authority overpaid housing benefit to a landlord, the landlord repaid the overpayment, but then sought to recover his repayment when he realized that the defendant had not followed the procedure laid down by the statutory scheme under which it had been entitled to the repayment. This unmeritorious claim was quite rightly rejected by Buxton LJ on the basis that it would be wholly artificial to equiparate this case, where the reality was that the council was repaid money to which the claimant had never been entitled with a case where a public authority is demanding a citizen's own money from him under powers it does not have. It would also have been possible to say that the procedural failure left intact a natural obligation to repay.

In *Waikato Regional Airport v Attorney General* [2003] UKPC 50, [2003] All ER (D) 399 (Jun), the Privy Council was clearly troubled by the line which the *Woolwich* principle required to be drawn around taxes and levies. The case arose out of a dispute about the legality of the New Zealand government's scheme for covering the cost of biosecurity procedures at airports. Statute required that biosecurity costs be recovered from end-users under a scheme which took into consideration the principles of equity and efficiency. The scheme as implemented was such that public money was concentrated on the big international airports, while the small regional airports had to pay high charges which they then had to try to collect from the airlines and passengers which flew from them. The Privy Council concluded, agreeing with Wild J at first instance but reversing the New Zealand Court of Appeal, that these levies were ultra vires and void as having flagrantly neglected the statutory requirement of equity between all entry points. Wild J had allowed recovery not of the whole sum paid but only of the excess over what it would have been fair to ask the regional airports to bear. The Privy Council did not disturb his decision in that respect. These charges fell within the *Woolwich* line because they were governmental levies; they were not exacted simply as the price payable for a commercial service ([79]–[80]). At the same time their Lordships did not avert their eyes from the fact that at least one of the cases on which *Woolwich* relied did concern a statutorily controlled commercial contract, namely *South of Scotland Electricity Board v British Oxygen Company Ltd* [1959] 1 WLR 587 (HL Sc). This adds an extra dimension to the difficulty of drawing the line.

The relationships between statutory regimes for the recovery of undue payments of tax, common law actions for judicial review, and common law actions for the recovery of overpaid taxes on the grounds of mistake of law or in line with the *Woolwich* principle, have been discussed in two cases. In *Eagerpath Ltd v Edwards (Inspector of Taxes)* [2001] STC 26 (CA), their Lordships draw no very clear conclusions, save for the fact that the Taxes Management Act 1970, s 33, is 'well past pensionable age in a new rights-based legal culture' ([40] Henry LJ).

In *Deutsche Morgan Grenfell Group plc v Inland Revenue Commissioners* [2003] EWHC 1779 (Ch), [2003] STC 1017 (noted S Hedley [2003] 5 Web JCLI), Park J held that a claimant which made a mistake of law when paying tax that was not due was free to choose whether to claim the money back under the *Woolwich* principle or on the ground of mistake of law. Hence the claimant was free to take advantage of the special limitation rule in the Limitation Act 1980, s 32(1)(c), governing claims to recover mistaken payments. The government intends to reverse this decision by legislation in 2004: 'Tax Overpaid in Earlier Years', Inland Revenue Press Release, 20 November 2003, available online at: www.gnn.gov.uk/gnn/national.nsf. The difficulty with the *Deutsche Morgan Grenfell* case, in that the tax was in fact due all along since no election for exemption had been made, is discussed above in connection with paras 15.67–15.68. The problem of drawing the boundaries of the *Woolwich* principle disappear if it is synthesized with the 'absence of consideration' of the cases on void interest swaps, especially *Guinness Mahon & Co Ltd v Kensington and Chelsea Royal London BC* [1999] QB 215 (CA). *Woolwich* and the swaps cases are, then, saying the same rather simple thing: a supposedly obligatory payment made where in fact there was no obligation is recoverable. The basis of the payment being the discharge of the supposed obligation, the absence of the obligation produces a failure of consideration (= basis). Resistance to 'no consideration' or 'no basis' has been misplaced.

(4) Withdrawal from an Illegal Transaction

The Law Commission's criticisms of the law in this area won the strong sympathy **15.168–**
of Mance LJ in *Collier v Collier* [2002] EWCA Civ 1095, [2002] BPIR 1057, **15.172**
[105]–[106], where his Lordship favoured legislative intervention to abandon the

'reliance' principle in *Tinsley v Milligan* in favour of a discretionary approach. At [108] he confirmed that a claimant seeking to rely on the withdrawal rule in *Tribe v Tribe* need not sincerely repent of his fraudulent intentions, but at [111] he also held that 'however generous an attitude is taken' towards the question whether a claimant might recover under this rule even though some part of his purpose has been carried through, recovery could not be permitted 'where creditors have successfully been deceived over a number of years'. In the same case, at [46], Aldous LJ held that the claimant (who was still alive) had had the additional benefit of a second 'illegal purpose for a number of years, namely to defraud the Inland Revenue if he died'. It is hard to understand what this benefit can have entailed, except perhaps the personal satisfaction to him of knowing that death duties would have been avoided in the event of his death.

(5) Insolvency Policies

15.173 n341: see too S Degeling, 'Restitution for Vulnerable Transactions' in J Armour and H Bennett (eds), *Vulnerable Transactions in Corporate Insolvency* (2003) 385.

In *Re Tain Construction Ltd, Rose v AIB Group (UK) plc* [2003] EWHC 1737 (Ch), [2003] 1 WLR 2791, Nicholas Warren QC, sitting as a deputy High Court judge, held that in principle a change of position defence might be raised against a claim to recover benefits transferred pursuant to a transaction that is void by operation of the Insolvency Act 1986, s 127.

F. Rights to Restitution

(3) Proprietary Restitutionary Rights Arising from Unjust Enrichment

When will the claimant in unjust enrichment have a proprietary interest?

(i) Three general doctrines

15.191 n358: for a powerful argument that the House of Lords in *Foskett v McKeown* [2001] AC 102 (HL) fell into error in not attributing the claimants' proprietary right to unjust enrichment, see now Professor Andrew Burrows, 'Proprietary Restitution: Unmasking Unjust Enrichment' (2001) 117 LQR 412. On similar lines P Birks, 'Property, Unjust Enrichment, and Tracing' [2001] CLP 231.

15.199 n374: in *Clark v Cutland* [2003] EWCA Civ 810, [2003] 4 All ER 743 (CA) where money had been syphoned from company accounts by a director without authority and in part paid to the trustees of his pension, the Court of Appeal spoke of an equitable lien as 'remedy' granted by the court [31]. This relapse into the language of discretionary 'remedy' is unwelcome, but the case is not reliable, distorted as it is by curious concessions.

(5) Subrogation

In the *Banque Financière* case Lord Hoffmann made it crystal clear that the reason why a claimant is entitled to be subrogated to a third party's extinguished rights of action against a defendant is to reverse the defendant's unjust enrichment at the claimant's expense. At the same time he consigned to the dustbin of history the explanation of this entitlement that had previously been offered in a series of old cases, that a claimant whose money has been used to discharge a mortgage over a defendant's property is entitled to a presumption that the mortgage should be kept alive and transferred to the claimant: in his Lordship's view this was a legal fiction that lacked explanatory force and should be discarded forever. These were powerful dicta that greatly assisted our understanding of this tricky area. It was therefore particularly disappointing to see Jonathan Parker LJ take the fictional presumption out of the dustbin, brush it down, and set it back on its feet again in *Halifax plc v Omar* [2002] EWCA Civ 121, blithely distinguishing the *Banque Financière* case on the ground that it was concerned with extinguished personal rights rather than with extinguished secured rights, as though that can possibly have made a difference to the underlying reason for the claimant's entitlement to the remedy. Worse swiftly followed in *Eagle Star Insurance v Karasiewicz* [2002] EWCA Civ 940, where Arden LJ drew on the misconceptions of *Halifax* and *Foskett v McKeown* [2001] AC 102 (HL) (criticized in Supplement para 15.191) to hold that where money has been lent to pay off a secured claim 'the creditor who seeks to be subrogated is given the remedy by way of satisfaction of a pre-existing equitable proprietary right which is vindicated by the order for subrogation'. 15.225

A different sort of misconception marred *Niru Battery Manufacturing Co v Milestone Trading Ltd (No 2)* [2003] EWHC 1032 (Comm), where Moore-Bick J held that the claimant could not recover the value of its payment to a third party from the defendant by suing the defendant directly in an action for contribution or reimbursement, but that the claimant could recover by acquiring the third party's extinguished rights of action against the defendant via (reviving) subrogation. This was incoherent because in principle reviving subrogation claims only have a supplementary role to play: if the facts do not support recovery via a direct personal claim, then they cannot support recovery via a subrogated action either.

(a) Two kinds of subrogation

(i) Reviving subrogation

n429: the account given here of *Caledonia North Sea Ltd v London Bridge Engineering Ltd* 2000 SLT 1123 (Ct of Session, Inner House) is misleading. Lord President Rodger did hold that if the insurer's payment had extinguished the insured's rights of action, it could have acquired the right to sue in the insured's 15.229

name via reviving subrogation; but he and the other three judges also held that in fact the insurer's payments had not extinguished the insured's rights of action, with the result that the insurer had been entitled to acquire the right to sue in the insured's name via simple subrogation. The House of Lords dismissed an appeal on the ground that the Inner House had been correct to hold that the insurer's payments had left the insured's rights of action intact, and their Lordships made no reference to the remainder of the Lord President's analysis: *Caledonia North Sea Ltd v British Telecommunications plc* [2002] 1 Lloyd's Rep 553, HL. To reach this conclusion their Lordships had to distinguish a long line of double insurance cases saying that payment by one insurer extinguishes the insured's right against the other insurer, but they were unable to offer convincing grounds for this distinction. Further discussion can be found in C Mitchell, *The Law of Contribution and Reimbursement* (2003) paras 9.07–9.15.

G. Defences

(1) Enrichment-Related Defences

(a) Change of position

15.240 n439: in *Scottish Equitable plc v Derby* [2001] 3 All ER 818 (CA) the Court of Appeal affirmed the decision of Harrison J. Mr Derby's pension had been massively and carelessly overpaid. He could be allowed the £9,662 which had marginally raised the family's standard of living. That being a loss caused by the enrichment. The court would not in that regard put the defendant to rigorous proof of specific items of expenditure, nor charge him with too heavy an onus. But the onset of old age, the dearth of job opportunities, and his other personal problems had not been caused by the payment. The defence conferred no general discretion to express sympathy through reduced liability. The discharge of his mortgage and the purchase of an annuity from the Norwich Union had been caused by the overpayment, but, given the willingness of the Norwich Union to unwind the annuity contract, neither were detriments which disenriched him: [2001] All ER 818 [30]–[36] (Robert Walker LJ), [53]–[54] (Simon Brown LJ).

(i) Anticipatory disenrichment

15.244 n444: in *Dextra Bank and Trust Company Ltd v Bank of Jamaica* [2001] 1 All ER (Comm) 193 (PC Jam) came down firmly against the requirement that a change of position must come after the receipt. An anticipatory disenrichment can suffice [36]–[38]. The decision of Clarke J in the *South Tyneside* case was described as based on 'exceptional facts' and note was taken of critical comment upon his conclusion [39]. This position had earlier been firmly and lucidly taken, with the support of comparative law, by M Jewell, 'Change of Position' in P Birks and F Rose (eds), *Lessons of the Swaps Litigation* (2000) 273–90. *Commerzbank AG v Gareth Price-Jones* [2003] EWCA Civ 1663, [2003] All ER (D) 303 (Nov) then confirmed that an anticipatory disenrichment would suffice. An investment banker had received a second notification of his bonus, raising it from £250,000 to £265,000. He understood that he would receive both sums and therefore decided to stay on with the claimant bank. In due course the bank did mistakenly pay both the original and higher sum. Mummery LJ's judgment, with which Sedley LJ agreed, is notable for consistently using language which allows a distinction to be drawn within the generic defence between a change of position which consists in an elimination of the enrichment—a disenrichment—and other changes of position which do not. He held that the defendant had not succeeded in showing that his staying on with the bank amounted to a disenrichment and that, in the absence of any disenrichment, his decision not to seek employment elsewhere had not been 'sufficiently significant, precise, or substantial in extent to be treated as a change of position, which would make full restitution inequitable [40]. The court's treatment of non-disenriching changes of position is further discussed in Supplement para 15.309.

(ii) Disqualification

In the *Dextra* case the Privy Council noted that, if the fault of one side were taken into account it would be necessary to take into account the fault of both sides [42]. Having reviewed the grave difficulties inherent in deciding issues of relative fault in relation to mistaken payments and other unjust enrichments, it firmly rejected any exercise of that kind [43]–[46]. It follows from this that the only relevance of fault is in deciding whether or not the defendant should be allowed to rely on the defence of change of position in the first place. In principle all those who have changed their position in good faith are qualified to rely on the defence [42]. It is clearly intended and logically implied that the careless but honest recipient should be allowed to set off his disenrichment. The case does not explore the rare facts, as in Main Work para 15.248, in which a recipient is both honest and aware of not being entitled to the money. **15.245**

n446: in *Niru Battery v Milestone Trading (No 1)* [2002] EWHC 1425 (Comm), [2002] 2 All ER (Comm) 705 Moore-Bick J declined to restrict disqualification from the defence of disenrichment to the kind of subjective dishonesty required by *Twinsectra Ltd v Yardley* [2002] UKHL 12, [2002] 2 AC 164 for dishonest assistance in a breach of trust. Bad faith would disqualify, and bad faith did not require subjective awareness of disapprobation [45]. An Iranian bank paid nearly US$6 million to the credit of a customer of the CAI bank under a letter of credit covering a shipment of lead to Iran. The recipient bank CAI knew that the shipment had never been made but it allowed itself to be persuaded by the customer that, in the light of the troubled history of the contract and assurances that a substitute shipment was being arranged, it made sense to release the money. The question was whether, having paid out the money in these circumstances, the CAI bank was disqualified from relying on the defence of change of position. Moore-Bick J remained true to the *Dextra* case. Negligence did not disqualify [125], but the bank was nonetheless disqualified. Its conduct was discreditable according to prevailing professional standards, so that it could not be said to have acted in good faith. In the Court of Appeal [2003] EWCA Civ 1446 the CAI bank remained disqualified, but the court's approach is difficult to reconcile with the *Dextra* case. It softened the test for disqualification. Deliberately invoking the language of cases on liability for knowing receipt, it held that an enrichee would be disqualified from pleading the defence wherever it would be inequitable or unconscionable for it not to remain liable. These words offer no guidance and invite an inscrutable exercise in judicial evaluation. In *National Bank of Egypt v Oman Housing Bank* [2002] EWHC 1760 (Comm), [2003] 1 All ER (Comm) 246, 251–2 David Steele J specifically endorsed the need for a bulwark against inquiries into comparative fault. But the soft vocabulary of the *Niru* Court of Appeal will make it difficult to hold that line, *Dextra* having seen that disqualification for anything less than bad faith would lead straight to the undesirable exercise in comparative fault. *Commerzbank AG v Gareth Price-Jones* [2003] EWCA Civ 1663, [2003] All ER (D) 303 (Nov), discussed in Supplement para 15.244, shows the same tendency to revert to soft language, especially the judgment of Munby J which is marked by extreme antipathy to analysis of words such as 'equitable' and 'fair'.

(2) An Expense-Related Defence: Passing On

15.269 n473: in *Roxborough v Rothmans of Pall Mall (Australia) Ltd* [2001] HCA 68, 208 CLR 516 the High Court of Australia again denied the viability of a defence of passing on. Kirby J, dissenting, thought that as between private parties the defence should be admitted. In *Waikato Regional Airport v Attorney General* [2003] UKPC 50 (30 June 2003), [2003] All ER (D) 399 (Jun), which is discussed above, one question was whether the government might have a defence to the extent that the regional airports had passed on the ultra vires charges to the airlines and thus made good the loss which consisted in their having paid them. The Privy Council noted these repudiations of the defence but did not find it necessary to express a view on the matter because the factual basis for such a defence had not been made out.

15.270 n474: the *Air Canada* majority also thought that the threat of disruption of public finances should in itself be a defence. In the *Waikato* case (previous note) the Privy Council was sceptical, indicating that, if there were such a defence, it would not be triggered unless the disruption and disproportion were extreme [82].Cf *Deutsche Morgan Grenfell Group plc v IRC* [2003] 4 All ER 645 (Ch D) 655–6.

(3) *Unjust-Related Defences*

(a) Finality

(iii) Contract for finality

n489: the footnote implies a warning that *Bell v Lever Bros Ltd* [1932] AC 161 (HL) might be about to be undermined, but on appeal *BCCI v Ali* [2001] 1 All ER 961 (HL) decided no more than that a release is likely to be construed in a manner hostile to the person seeking to rely on it, so that only the clearest of clear words will be taken to have released claims of which the releasing party knew nothing. **15.278**

(iv) Estoppel

The Court of Appeal has twice shown itself unwilling to apply the logic of the **15.280–** *Avon* case to create a total defence regardless of the scale of the recipient's reliance. **15.282** In each case the court invoked an exception to cover, and prevent, gross disproportion: *Scottish Equitable plc v Derby* [2001] 3 All ER 818 (CA) [44]; *National Westminster Bank Plc v Somer* [2001] EWCA Civ 970, [2002] 1 All ER 198 [46]–[48], [62], [67]. 'Gross' will soon mean 'any'. Under such a regime it will be impossible to effect a permanent, binding estoppel which will be stronger than the defence of change of position. The better way forward may be through construction. Where the facts make it reasonable to rely on the payer's representation, there will be a prima facie estoppel, but a representation that a given sum was due or that all relevant calculations have been checked need not in normal circumstances be given effect as though it were a perpetual undertaking never to reopen the matter. If the representation is construed as accepting responsibility until further notice, the representee will be safe in making reliance expenditure until the representation is retracted. It would be consonant with ordinary expectations if a mistaken representor were in general allowed to retract his representation so long as and to the extent that restitution will not leave the defendant to bear the ill consequences of any detrimental reliance. In highly exceptional circumstances a permanent estoppel may still be found, perfected by less that 100% reliance expenditure.

(b) Stultification

(i) Bona fide purchase (understood as protecting exceptions to nemo dat*)*

n510: in *Royal Bank of Scotland v Etridge (No 2)* [2001] UKHL 44, [2001] 3 All ER 449 (HL) the House of Lords finally drew a clear distinction between this defence and the role of notice and the absence of notice in the cases in which homes have been made security for business borrowing. In these security cases the reason why the lender has to be shown to have had some degree of knowledge of the undue influence or other vitiation is not that he would otherwise have the defence of bona fide purchase. The lender never claims to be a bona fide purchaser from a **15.292**

third party. It is an element of the cause of action of the party giving security, albeit in this context much watered down, that the lender be shown to have known of the vitiating factor. The security-giver, having been under undue influence or misrepresentation, has a prima facie right to restitution. The competing interest in protecting the process of contracting from an inordinate need to make inquiries explains why it must be shown that the lender knew or ought to have known of the vitiation: [2001] 4 All ER 449 [38]–[43] (Lord Nicholls). This valuable correction, a considerable improvement on that attempted in *Barclays Bank v Boulter* [1999] 1 WLR 1919, [1999] 4 All ER 513 (HL) will be better secured if the short name of the defence is slightly lengthened by the habitual addition of the words 'from a third party'; cf *Dextra Bank and Trust Company Ltd v Bank of Jamaica* [2001] 1 All ER (Comm) 193 (PC Jam) [47].

(iii) Illegality

15.299 **n516**: the other side of the penny is that the policy of the protective illegality may allow the other party no recourse at all, however disproportionate the outcome. In *Wilson v First County Trust Ltd* [2003] UKHL 40, [2003] 2 All ER (Comm) 491 Mrs Wilson had pledged her BMW car for a loan of £5,000. The written contract failed to comply with the requirements of the Consumer Credit Act. The House of Lords reaffirmed that the disciplinary policy of the Act required the non-compliant lender have no recourse at all in relation to the money lent ([49], [121]–[123], [172]). The borrower could not be sued on the contract. She was entitled to recover the car pledged as security, and she was immune to any claim in unjust enrichment: cf *Dimond v Lovell* [2002] 1 AC 384 (HL).

(c) Other unjust-related defences

(i) Non-disenriching changes of position

15.309 **n535**: in *Commerzbank AG v Gareth Price-Jones* [2003] EWCA Civ 1663, [2003] All ER (D) 303 (Nov), discussed in Supplement paras 15.244 and 15.125, all three judges must be to taken to have affirmed the possibility of non-disenriching changes of position capable of founding a defence. Munby J was highly critical of writers who had suggested the contrary. Such matters as getting married or starting a family would have satisfied him (without analysing them as disenrichments). However, he alone makes no distinction between disenrichment and other cases and thus fails to see the great difficulty of explaining why one should retain an extant enrichment to which one was not entitled. A customer who still has the surplus £30 will struggle in vain to avoid returning change accidentally given for £50 rather than £20, however innocently received and however careless the shop. Disenrichment entirely changes the picture. A question of relocating an extant gain suddenly turns into the familiar task of allocating a loss.

A non-disenriching change of position, if one is ultimately found, will pose a problem of quantification. Supposing the enrichee still to have all the enrichment as in the *Commerzbank* case, it is not obvious how one would know by how much to reduce the liability. Munby J offers no suggestions.

16

INSOLVENCY

A. Introduction: Structure and Process

(c) The bankruptcy and liquidation process

(i) Bankruptcy

In extreme cases, a bankrupt may be committed to prison for contempt of court, as when, for example, the bankrupt refuses to comply with a possession order (*Tuohy v Bell* [2003] BPIR 749 (CA)). **16.10**

n23: on the court's unfettered power to dismiss or adjourn a bankruptcy petition, see *Re Micklethwait* [2003] BPIR 101.

n30: where the prosecution proves that a debt has been concealed, the burden of showing the absence of an intention to conceal shifts to the bankrupt (*R v Daniel* [2002] BPIR 1193).

The discharge of a bankrupt does not release him from debts arising out of his 'fraud or fraudulent breach of trust' (s 281(3) of the Insolvency Act 1986). In *Mander v Evans* [2001] 3 All ER 811), the court held that this phrase does not extend to a claim for undue influence or other form of constructive fraud. **16.11**

In accordance with the policy of giving bankrupts a 'second chance', which infused the White Paper that led to the Enterprise Act 2002 (*Insolvency—A Second Chance* (Cm 5234, July 2001)), the period before discharge, formerly usually three years, has now been reduced to a normal maximum of one year after the making of the bankruptcy order (s 279 of the Insolvency Act 1986 as added by s 256 of the Enterprise Act; see also Sch 19 to the latter). In addition, the Act contains a number of provisions that diminish post-bankruptcy restrictions on an individual's activities and that reduce the number of bankruptcy offences (s 281A of the Insolvency Act as added by s 257 of the Enterprise Act, ss 265–68 of the Enterprise Act, s 31 of the Insolvency Act as added by Sch 21 to the Enterprise Act, and Sch 4A to the Insolvency Act as added by Sch 20 to the Enterprise Act). The use of bankruptcy restrictions, however, should serve to prevent rogue directors from opting instead for sole trader status since, consistently with the Company Directors Disqualification Act 1986, they can be restricted for up to 15 years (Sch 4A, para 4(2)(b) to the Insolvency Act, as added by Sch 20 to the Enterprise Act). The Enterprise Act has already been amended by the Secretary of State under rule-making powers (see s 248(4) of the Enterprise Act). The Insolvency Rules 1986 have been amended in consequence of the legislative changes (see the Insolvency Amendment Rules 2003 (SI 2003/1730). Some provisions of the Enterprise Act came into force on 15 September 2003; others will come into effect on 1 April 2004 (see the Enterprise Act 2002 (Commencement No 4 and Transitional Provisions and Savings) Order 2003 (SI 2003/2093).

n32: since bankruptcy is a class remedy, a court may not revoke a bankruptcy order by consent and without investigation, even if the petitioning creditor does not oppose annulment of the order (see *Housiaux v HM Commissioners of Customs and Excise* [2003] BPIR 858).

(d) Voluntary arrangements

(i) CVAs

16.17 A CVA does not have to involve a composition of claims against the company but may give rise only to a moratorium. Hence, in *Commissioners of Inland Revenue v Adam & Partners* [2001] 1 BCLC 222 (CA), the court approved an arrangement the purpose of which was to give the chargee bank a cost-effective way of enforcing its security, even though preference and unsecured creditors had no prospect at all of any dividend ensuing from the CVA. The moratorium did not as such confiscate the rights of those other creditors to any dividend that might be declared.

Unlike other insolvency procedures, namely, administration, liquidation and bankruptcy, a CVA does not place an embargo as such on the bringing of legal proceedings against the company. Hence a claimant, seeking unliquidated damages for wrongful dismissal by the company and for the unlawful detention of his chattels, was at liberty to pursue his claim in *Alman v Approach Housing Ltd* [2001] 1 BCLC 530. Since CVAs and IVAs operate as contracts binding affected creditors (see *Johnson v Davies* [1999] Ch 117, CA), such as the claimant in this case, the arrangement as a matter of construction may be apt to exclude such claims being made, but no term to that effect will be implied as a matter of business efficacy.

Re TBL Realisations plc [2001] All ER (D) 229 makes the point that a creditor whose claim is rejected by the supervisor of the CVA, or upon whose claim the supervisor declines to put a value, may not vote at the meeting. Consequently, that external creditor is not bound by the CVA. A court may direct that moneys be retained outside the CVA to satisfy the claim but, once moneys received under the CVA have by its terms been impressed with a trust for the CVA creditors, they may not be paid over to the external creditor.

The existence of a trust over CVA moneys appears to be a matter of construction of the CVA (see *Re Kudos Glass Ltd* [2001] 1 BCLC 390). The trust will not be determined if a liquidation petition is presented by the directors or by a creditor external to the CVA, but it will be determined if a CVA creditor or the supervisor presents the petition (ibid, citing *Re Excalibur Airways Ltd* [1998] 1 BCLC 436). Since the CVA takes effect as a matter of contract, the range of assets caught by the CVA (such as uncollected post-liquidation book debts) is a matter of construction of the CVA (*Re Kudos Glass*).

The Insolvency Bill referred to has become the Insolvency Act 2000 and is now fully in force (see the Insolvency Act 2000 (Commencement No 3 and Transitional Provisions) Order 2002 (SI 2002/2711, bringing all provisions into force not already in force).

In *Re Pan Atlantic Insurance Co Ltd* [2003] EWHC 1696 (Ch), provisional liquidators determined that a scheme of arrangement under s 425 of the Companies Act 1985 was preferable to a compulsory winding-up. The limited availability of access to the courts under s 425 was proportionate and there had been no infringement of Article 6 of the European Convention on Human Rights.

n60: members and unsecured creditors may mount such a challenge but not secured creditors: *Swindon Town Properties Ltd v Swindon Town Football Co Ltd* (High Ct, 4 July 2002).

Although the rules on CVAs do not expressly state that they give rise to trusts of **16.18**
the assets in the hands of the supervisors of the arrangement, the Court of Appeal in *NT Gallagher & Son Ltd v Tomlinson* [2002] EWCA 404 was of the view (at [29]) that the appellants had rightly conceded the existence of a trust over CVA assets (see also *Re Leisure Study Group Ltd* [1994] 2 BCLC 65).

(ii) IVAs

16.19 The rules concerning IVAs have been modified by Sch 3 to the Insolvency Act 2000.

An IVA will not be revoked on the basis of the debtor's bad faith behaviour in arriving at a secret arrangement with selected creditors. The proper sanction in such a case is for the court to make a bankruptcy order against the debtor under s 276 of the Insolvency Act 1986 (see *Cadbury Schweppes plc v Somji* [2001] 1 WLR 615 (CA)).

Before an IVA order can be made, it must relate to a proposal that is serious and viable and worthy of consideration by the creditors (see *Shah v Cooper* [2003] BPIR 1018).

In *Cooper v Official Receiver* [2003] BPIR 55, the father of a debtor made a payment to the supervisor of his son's IVA. When a creditor successfully challenged the IVA on the ground of a failure to disclose all details of the son's indebtedness, the son was declared bankrupt. Jacob J held that the money paid by the father was not impressed with a trust so as to be returned to the father if the trust failed, with the result that the money could be claimed by the Official Receiver as the son's trustee in bankruptcy. However, in *Welburn v Dibb Lupton Broomhead* [2003] BPIR 768, the debtor's claim for breach of contract against a building firm formed part of the debtor's assets included in the IVA and was impressed with a trust in favour of the participating IVA creditors. Since the debtor only had the bare legal title to the claim, it fell to the supervisor of the IVA to give instructions to the firm of solicitors appointed by the debtor to handle the claim. In the *Welburn* case, the question related to the nature of the debtor's interest in property the subject of the IVA; in the *Cooper* case, the question was whether property transferred by a third party to the supervisor had been transferred outright or on trust terms.

In *Lombard Natwest Factors Ltd v Koutrouzas* [2003] BPIR 1084, one of two co-sureties entered into an IVA. The IVA having a suspensive effect on creditors' rights against the debtor pending the implementation of its terms, the court held that it did not on its construction release the other co-surety. According to *Lloyds Bank plc v Ellicott* [2003] BPIR 632, where one of two co-debtors enters into an IVA, the effect of the IVA should be dealt with in proceedings to which both co-debtors are parties. Where a creditor brings proceedings against the solvent co-debtor, the latter should bring a Part 20 claim which should be heard at the same time as the creditor's claim for summary judgment (see also *Johnson v Davies* [1999] Ch 117).

The Enterprise Act 2002 (s 264) introduces changes to IVAs in those cases, rare at present, where the IVA operates post-bankruptcy. By amendment to the Insolvency Act 1986 (adding ss 261, 263A–G and 389B), it allows for the appointment of the Official Receiver as the supervisor of a voluntary arrangement. Where the Official Receiver is the proposed nominee, a fast-track scheme is introduced which dispenses with the need for a creditors' meeting to sanction the appointment of the Official Receiver as supervisor and allows creditors only to deal with the Official Receiver's proposal on a 'take it or leave it' basis (see Sch 22 to the Enterprise Act).

n75: a nominee, who has previously given advice to a debtor prior to acting as an IVA nominee, may owe a duty of care to the debtor in respect of that advice (see *Prosser v Castle Sanderson Solicitors* [2003] BCC 440).

n76: see further *Re N (A Debtor)* [2002] BPIR 1024.

(e) Other insolvency procedures: receivership and administration

(i) Receivers

In accordance with a policy of transparency and properly aligned incentives, announced in the White Paper *Insolvency—A Second Chance* (Cm 5234, July 2001), the Enterprise Act 2002 restricts the extent to which a creditor may exercise a power to appoint in the name of the company debtor an administrative receiver. The starting point is that administrative receivers will be superseded by administrators, but two important categories of exception will be suffered to continue after the implementation of the Enterprise Act. The first exception concerns rights of a chargee already in existence ('grandfather rights') prior to a date to be appointed by the Secretary of State (s 250 of the Enterprise Act, adding a new s 72A(4)(a) of the Insolvency Act 1986). The appointed day is 15 September 2003 (the Insolvency Act 1986, Section 72A (Appointed Date) Order 2003 (SI 2003/2095)). It is possible, though perhaps unlikely, that a chargee with an all moneys clause could allow a loan agreement to roll over indefinitely without its ever being fully paid off, so avoiding the effect of the new legislation. Another possibility, more fanciful still, would be for major lenders to create a series of special corporate vehicles which would then create the usual range of fixed and floating charges under an all moneys debenture, with loans to future borrowers being channelled through such companies and borrowers' assets vested in them. All of this supposes that the regime of administration, as amended by the Enterprise Act, will prove unpalatable to major lenders, which may prove to be far from the case. **16.20**

The second exception consists of a series of 'carve-outs', exempting from the new legislation a series of transactions in specialized markets (s 249 of the Enterprise Act, adding new ss 72B–G of the Insolvency Act). The exceptions in question consist of: capital market transactions where the expected debt is at least £50 million; public-private partnership projects with creditor step-in rights (that is, rights to assume sole or principal contractual responsibility for the project); utility projects designed for the purposes of a regulated business and including step-in rights; financed projects with step-in rights where the expected debt is at least £50 million; and financial market transactions giving rise to market and similar charges under Part VII of the Companies Act 1989 and related provisions. Changes have already been made concerning the carve-out list by the Secretary of State (see the Insolvency Act 1986 (Amendment) (Administrative Receivership and Urban Regeneration etc.) Order 2003 (SI 2003/1832) and the Insolvency Act 1986 (Amendment) (Administrative Receivership and Capital Market Arrangements) Order 2003 (SI 2003/1468)).

(ii) Administrators

16.22 In *Re TXU UK Ltd* [2002] EWHC 2784 (Ch), the court, following *Denny v Yeldon* [1995] 1 BCLC 560) held that the statutory purposes for which an administrator might be appointed went only to what administrators, as officers of the court, were trying to achieve. They did not prevent administrators from exercising their powers for the benefit of creditors of the company, even when such exercise was not directed towards the fulfilment of a statutory purpose.

The court's power to appoint an administrator, which requires the company to be unable to pay its debts (see now para 11(a) of Sch B1 to the Insolvency Act 1986 as added by s 248(2) of the Enterprise Act 2002), may be exercised only if the petitioner shows on a balance of probabilities the company's inability to pay its debts (*Re Colt Telecom Group plc* [2002] EWCH 2815 (Ch)).

The inability of a company to pay its debts may be based either on a balance sheet insolvency test or on the failure of the company to pay its debts as they fall due. The company in *Re Far East Abrasives Ltd* [2003] BPIR 375 was insolvent on a balance sheet but was able to pay all of its creditors on time with the exception of the petitioner. The court made the administration order.

Although administrators do not make distributions to unsecured creditors, this was exceptionally permitted (under s 8 of the Insolvency Act 1986, before the changes wrought by the Enterprise Act 2002 came into force) in one case where the distribution advanced the purposes for which the administrator had been appointed and the creditor was being treated no more favourably than fellow creditors in the event of the purpose failing and the company going into liquidation (*Rolph v AY Bank Ltd* [2002] BPIR 1231).

Administration is not a winding-up procedure. Indeed, in *Re Henry Charles Ltd* [2003] All ER (D) 432, a company that had been struck off was restored to the register so that an administration order might be made.

The Enterprise Act 2002 makes major changes to the law governing administration. No longer will one or more of four purposes of an administration have to be specified in an application to the court. Instead, there are three clear purposes specified for all administrations in descending order of importance (s 248 of the Enterprise Act introducing an amended s 8 of the Insolvency Act 1986 and a new Sch B1 to the Act (see para 3(1)).

First of all, there is the rescue of the 'company' as a going concern. If this were to be amended to 'business', one could well imagine the administrator tarrying a while longer over this first purpose. As it is, it will only be in the rarest of cases that the company itself can be saved. Secondly, where this is 'not reasonably practicable', the administrator must strive for 'a better result for the company's creditors as a whole' than would be likely on a liquidation. No doubt case law will clarify what is meant by 'reasonably practicable'. How the administrator takes account of the welfare of the company's creditors as a whole is not obvious, given the incurable optimism of some unsecured creditors and the professional pessimism of a floating chargee seeing the disintegration of its security as the company carries on trading under the administrator. It is, however, unlikely that the administrator will have to deal with creditors in their various classes.

Only in the event of this second purpose proving not to be reasonably practicable will the administrator turn to the third purpose of realizing property so as to make a distribution to one or more secured or preferential creditors. Under the new legislation, the administrator is firmly fixed with the task of making distributions to (usually preferential and secured) creditors. The priority rules remain unchanged (Sch B1, paras 65, 70–73). It may be that the changes will do little to alter the outcome of an out-of-court administration, relative to an out-of-court receivership, except that the administrator's scrupulous adherence to the statutorily prescribed forms and deliberations may result in a slower and more defensive process than was formerly the case with receivership.

Over and above these three purposes and the guidance of reasonable practicability, the administrator must exercise his functions in the interests of creditors of the company as a whole (which seems to add little to what has gone before) (Sch B1, para 3(2)). More interestingly, when making distributions to preferential and secured creditors, he must not unnecessarily harm the interests of creditors of the company as a whole (Sch B1, para 3(4)(b)). It may be that the preservation of goodwill, as occurred in the court-appointed receivership case of *Re Newdigate Colliery Ltd* [1912] Ch 468, may make its presence felt. In *Ash and Newman Ltd v Creative Devices Research Ltd* [1991] BCLC 403, the court remarked that a receiver might be restrained by injunction from disregarding a contract entered into by the company if he could not be said thereby to be preferring the interests of a secured creditor. Going further, Vinelott J in *Astor Chemical Ltd v Synthetic Technology Ltd* [1990] BCC 97 stated that a receiver could not always disregard contractual obligations binding on the company. He might not do so, for example, if 'there is a doubt whether there will be a surplus of assets available to the company and the other creditors after meeting the debt due' *and* 'if the breach would seriously damage the reputation of the company and impair its goodwill', or, if the charge did not extend to all assets, where the breach of contract might prevent the company trading with its other assets.

The Enterprise Act 2002 contains complex new provisions dealing with the conduct of administration and with creditors' meetings (Sch B1; see also the Insolvency Amendment Rules 2003 (SI 2003/1730)). These provisions prompt the question whether unsecured creditors will exercise too much influence on the conduct of an administration. At the very least, the preparation and presentation of proposals to a creditors' meeting is likely to delay the realization of any security. The administrator's proposals may not include any action that would affect a secured creditor's rights of enforcement or a preferential creditor's preference (Sch B1, para 73) and, in the conduct of the administration, the administrator is amenable to a court application based on unfair conduct at the behest of secured creditors or other aggrieved persons (Sch B1, para 74). Nevertheless, if the company's prospects are dismal, in that the first two of the administrator's purposes cannot be accomplished, or the only assets for distribution to unsecured creditors are the moneys set aside for unsecured creditors (see Supplement para 16.98), the administrator is dispensed from having to convene a creditors' meeting (Sch B1, para 52(1)). There yet remains some potential for making the life of the administrator difficult: unsecured creditors whose claims amount to at least 10% of the debts of the company can insist on a meeting (para 52(2)). The attitude of the Inland Revenue and Customs and Excise, whose preferential status is taken away under the Act (see Supplement para 16.114), may prove important.

The loss of a floating chargee's contractual power to procure the appointment of an administrative receiver is compensated to a substantial extent by a new power granted to the holder of a qualifying floating charge to appoint an administrator without making a court application (Sch B1, para 14). (A qualifying floating charge is one that passes a test (see Sch B1, para 14(3)) that accords with the test of an administrative receiver in s 29(2) of the Insolvency Act 1986.) This will obviously dispense with any *de facto* need to produce an independent report on the company's affairs. The cost of administration, and therefore the size of the inroad made into floating charge assets, ought therefore to be diminished. A qualifying floating charge must either contain a power to appoint an administrative receiver or an administrator—which would permit a chargee with grandfather rights to opt for the new procedure instead—or must make specific reference to the appointment provision in the new Sch B1 (para 14(2)(a)). The only notice requirement is that the chargee notify a prior floating chargee (not fixed chargee) of an intention to appoint. That may stimulate the prior chargee to choose its own administrator. There is also a procedure for a later chargee to give notice to a prior floating chargee of an intention to appoint an out-of-court administrator (para 15(1)). This gives the prior chargee time to make an appointment and prevents the later chargee from appointing (para 7).

In the case of a court appointment, the court must be satisfied that the company is unable to pay its debts (Sch B1, para 11). No such requirement is imposed in the case of appointment by a floating chargee. This is perhaps curious: since the floating chargee has a statutory power of appointment, and since no reference is made to default or to inability to pay, what becomes of case law (*Bank of Baroda v Panessar* [1987] Ch 335) dealing with the making of a prior demand for payment? Contractual limits on the appointment of an administrative receiver are likely to be carried over to the new statutory power to appoint an administrator. There is provision, however, for the court to make an appointment, whether or not the company is unable to pay its debts, at the behest of a floating chargee that could instead have appointed directly out of court (Sch B1, para 35). The significance of and need for this procedure is unclear.

The floating chargee's power of appointment fosters the sort of continuing relationship that already exists between a chargee bank and insolvency accountants: will the conduct of an administrator appointed by the bank therefore be so very different from the conduct of an administrative receiver? It is noteworthy that, if another person makes a court application for the appointment of an administrator, the court is obliged instead to appoint a person specified by the holder of a qualifying floating charge in the absence of special considerations (Sch B1, para 36). It may well be that the process of appointment of insolvency professionals continues largely as before, only they will now be called administrators instead of administrative receivers and will need to show a paper trail to establish that they considered other interests prior to making distributions to the bank. Transparency, after all, is not about outcomes but about the visibility of procedures. If this is the case, the floating charge will remain alive and well and will serve the cause of those creditors who desire the power to appoint an administrator directly without going to court. A creditor with a floating charge, using the new appointment procedure, will also get the benefit of the administrator's power to restrict the enforcement of title retention rights enjoyed by unpaid sellers, hire purchase finance companies and the like (para 43).

The floating chargee's power of appointment may not, however, be exercised if the company is in the course of a winding-up (Sch B1, para 8). Nevertheless, that chargee may apply for the appointment of an administrator in the case of a compulsory (but not a voluntary) winding-up (Sch B1, para 37). Confining the application to compulsory winding-up appears odd to say the least. Where it can act, the court has a wide range of powers including the power to discharge the winding-up order (para 37(3)). Where a company is in administration, no winding-up resolution may be passed or winding-up order made (paras 40, 42).

B. The Estate of the Insolvent and Its Distribution

(1) The Estate of the Insolvent in the Insolvency Process

(a) The content of the insolvent's estate

16.25 The distribution of the estate is made to those creditors who have submitted a proof under s 322 of the Insolvency Act 1986 (bankruptcy) or r 4.73 of the Insolvency Rules (winding-up). A debt admitted to proof may yet be expunged if it is shown on the balance of probabilities that it ought not to have been admitted to proof in the first place: *Re Globe Legal Services Ltd* (High Ct, 13 September 2000).

In *Smith (Administrator of Cosslett (Contractors) Ltd) v Bridgend County Council* [2002] 1 AC 336, Lord Hoffmann notes that the property of a company does not vest in the liquidator upon a winding-up but observes that the liquidator has the power to gather in the company's assets. Hence, when s 395 of the Companies Act 1985 provides that an unregistered charge is void against a liquidator, it means that it is void against a company acting through its liquidator.

A liquidator, in deciding whether to accept or reject a creditor's proof in whole or in part, acts in a quasi-judicial capacity. Hence, a court making a winding-up order may, in appropriate circumstances, in the case of a judgment debt, go behind the judgment to see if the debt was truly due (see *Re Menastar Finance Ltd* [2003] BCC 404).

Under the Enterprise Act 2002, the bankrupt's home is no longer part of his estate at the end of a three-year period commencing with the date of the bankruptcy if, in the meantime, the trustee has not sold the home or other prescribed events occur (s 261 adding a new s 283A of the Insolvency Act 1986). If the trustee applies to the court for an order to sell the bankrupt's home, this application will be dismissed in the case of a low value home (s 261 of the Enterprise Act adding a new s 313A of the Insolvency Act).

(ii) Examples of property

16.30 n117: the judge's order for the transfer of the quota in *Swift v Dairywise Farms Ltd* was later upheld by the Court of Appeal (1 February 2001).

16.31 In *Dear v Reeves* [2002] Ch 1, the Court of Appeal held that a right of pre-emption concerning land amounted to property under s 436 and therefore vested in the holder's trustee-in-bankruptcy. Under s 436, it was both a 'thing in action' and an 'interest' that was 'future or . . . contingent'.

(iii) Trusts

n126: for the requirement of certainty of beneficiaries, see *OT Computers v First National Tricity Finance* [2003] EWCH 1010 (Ch). **16.33**

(iv) Divesting clauses

A company may not enter into a contract by which, in the event of its insolvency, it divests itself of patent rights (see *Fraser v Oystertec plc* (High Ct, 8 September 2003)). **16.34**

(v) Bankrupts, pensions, and after-acquired property

The sums that a bankrupt may retain for the 'reasonable domestic needs of the bankrupt and his family' (s 310(2) of the Insolvency Act 1986) include a sum sufficient to pay private school fees (see *Scott v Davis* [2003] BPIR 1009). **16.35**

n144: the appeal in *Patel v Jones* [2001] EWCA Civ 779 was dismissed. **16.37**

n148: see now also *Patel v Jones* [2001] EWCA Civ 779.

Where a bankrupt has both a proprietary and a personal claim, so that the trustee in whom the cause of action has vested is bound to account to the bankrupt for recoveries representing the personal cause of action, it is incorrect to regard the trustee as the bare trustee of the bankrupt's cause of action so that the bankrupt may bring proceedings in his own name after joining the trustee: *Mulkerrins v Pricewaterhouse Coopers* [2001] BPIR 106 (CA). **16.38**

A new income payments scheme is introduced in the Enterprise Act 2002 in order to reduce the involvement of the court in non-contentious schemes (ss 259–260). This involves the recognition of binding income payments agreements made between the bankrupt and the Official Receiver or trustee-in-bankruptcy. These agreements, enforceable as though they were made by court order, are limited to a three-year term and can operate after the discharge of the bankrupt (which occurs one year after the making of the bankruptcy order under new provisions in the Act: see Supplement para 16.11).

(vi) Bankrupts and litigation

In *Cork v Rawlins* [2001] 4 All ER 50, CA the bankrupt, a landscape gardener, had taken out policies to ensure that certain loans, obtained for the construction of a bungalow, would be repaid in the event of his becoming 'permanently disabled'. He sustained serious physical injury, which prevented him from working. This led to his transferring the business to his son and selling the bungalow to his son and daughter. The loans were repaid from the proceeds of that sale, which took place prior to the bankruptcy, itself occurring before the moneys due under the policies were paid. The bankrupt was certainly affected by pain and suffering consequent **16.39** upon the accident, but the policy moneys were paid on the occasion of his disablement, not his pain and suffering. Consequently, they formed part of his estate available for distribution. The policies, moreover, had been paid for out of assets that would otherwise have been available for the bankrupt's creditors.

In *Mulkerrins v Pricewaterhouse Coopers* [2003] UKHL 41, a case dealing with estoppel *per rem adjudicatam*, Lord Millett (at [17]), supported by the other members of the court, was of the view that a bankrupt's action against financial advisers, for financial loss arising from negligent advice that led to her bankruptcy, was a personal claim that was not to be made available to her creditors in bankruptcy. She was 'claiming damages for the very making of the bankruptcy order under which [the creditors' claim] arose'. Lord Millett seems also to have been of the view that the claim was not after-acquired property (see Main Work para 16.35).

n161: where it was thought on the law as it stood at the time that the bankrupt could initiate proceedings himself for medical negligence, it was not negligent for his legal advisers to fail to mention the possibility that he might take an assignment from his trustee in bankruptcy of the medical negligence claim (see *Kaberry v Freethcartwright* [2003] BPIR 606).

(c) Disclaimer of onerous property

(ii) Disclaimer and leases

16.50 **n207**: for this reason, a surety's covenant to accept a reversion of a lease continues notwithstanding a disclaimer of the lease by the lessee's liquidator. Moreover, a sale of the premises by the lessor transfers the benefit of the surety's covenant to the purchaser: *Scottish Widows plc v Tripipatkul* [2003] EWHC 1874 (Ch).

(iii) Disclaimer and waste management licences

16.53 In *Environmental Agency v Hillridge Ltd* [2003] EWHC 3023 (Ch), Blackburne J followed the Court of Appeal in *Re Celtic Extraction Ltd* [1999] 4 All ER 684 and went on to hold that the effect of a licensee's disclaimer was also to disclaim its interest in a trust fund that it had set up to make financial provision to meet its obligations under the licence. The fund reverted to the Crown as *bona vacantia*.

(d) Assignment of causes of action

(iii) Causes of action as property

16.57 The assignment of a cause of action may be set aside if it is for an inadequate consideration, as was done by the Court of Appeal in *Faryab v Smith* (CA, 13 December 2000). In that case, a bankrupt's cause of action for £2 million against a firm of solicitors was assigned by his trustee to the solicitors themselves, for a sum (£17,000) equivalent to the trustee's estimate of his own fees and expenses.

The action was speculative but the bankrupt was a skilled litigant in person and the amount received by the trustee small in relation to the possible outcome of successful litigation. Consequently, as explained by Lord Hoffmann in *Stein v Blake* [1996] AC 243, 260, a more appropriate course for the trustee would have been for him to have assigned the cause of action to the bankrupt in return for a share of any recoveries.

(e) Embargo on proceedings against the insolvent

(iii) Executions

The sheriff's duty to retain moneys for 14 days applies in all cases where he has sold goods taken in execution and thus the words 'to avoid the sale of others' in Main Work para 16.64 text to n277 are to be deleted. **16.64**

(f) Dispositions of the insolvent's property

(i) General

In an important judgment, the Court of Appeal in *Hollicourt (Contracts) Ltd v Bank of Ireland* [2001] 1 All ER 289, reversing the court below and disapproving on this point *Re Gray's Inn Construction Ltd* [1980] 1 All ER 814, held that s 127 only invalidated the dispositions of company property to payees of cheques. A bank acting as agent for the company in accordance with its mandate was not at risk of a restitutionary liability: there was no disposition of company money in its favour. Section 127 did not invalidate the bank's mandate. In the words of Mummery LJ delivering the judgment of the court (at 295): 'The beneficial ownership of the property represented by the cheque was never transferred to the bank, to which no alienation of the company's property was made.' **16.74**

In *Re Dewrun Ltd* (High Ct, 28 July 2000), Neuburger J emphasized the need to interpret flexibly, in the interests of justice, the jurisdiction in s 127 to uphold a transaction. The company transferred certain land to another company, which in turn granted a charge by way of legal mortgage over the land in favour of a bank. The bank was successful in its application to have the transaction in favour of the transferee company validated but only to the extent of the bank's charge, even though '[t]he concept of a transaction which is void for some purposes but not for others, or which is void to some extent only, is somewhat quaint, but . . . not . . . legally or conceptually impossible'.

(iii) Bank accounts

Much of the discussion in the Main Work in this paragraph and in para 16.84 seems now to have been rendered redundant in view of the decision of the Court of Appeal in *Hollicourt (Contracts) Ltd v Bank of Ireland* [2001] 1 All ER 289, a case dealing with payments out of an account in credit. In the judgment of the **16.83** court (at 295), s 127 does not 'impinge on the legal validity of intermediate steps, such as banking transactions, which are merely part of the process by which dispositions of the company's property are made'. Instead, 'it impinges on the end result of the process of payment initiated by the company, ie the point of ultimate receipt of the company's property in consequence of a disposition by the company'. There is therefore no need to analyse traffic through a bank account to determine how far and to what extent a bank obtains company property in those cases where it is carrying out a mandate to make payment to a third party.

In *Re Tain Construction Ltd, Rose v AIB Group (UK) plc* [2003] All ER (D) 91, Ch, payments into an overdrawn bank account were held by Nicholas Warren QC, following *Re Gray's Inn Construction Co Ltd* [1980] 1 WLR 711, CA, to be dispositions of property under s 127 of the Insolvency Act 1986 and not a mere adjustment of entries in an account between a bank and its customer. The bank had acted in good faith (more than six months passed before the winding-up petition was advertised) but the grant of a validation order would have allowed the bank to be paid in full in breach of the *pari passu* principle and the bank had not acted so as to benefit other creditors of the company. The discretion to grant a validation order was not to be exercised so as to provide a remedy for the mistakes of a liquidator or creditors of a company. A further point in the case was this. In the belief that it had been paid in full, the bank had released a charge that it had over the house of the company's director and sole shareholder. The judge was not prepared to rule out a change of position as a defence to a claim for repayment by the liquidator but held that such a defence was unavailable on the facts of the case.

(2) Secured Creditors in the Insolvency Process

(b) Dealing with secured assets

(ii) Administration

16.91 In a recent White Paper, *Insolvency—A Second Chance* (Cm 5234, July 2001), the government signalled its intention of introducing legislation to prevent a debenture holder from procuring the appointment of administrative receivers in order to block the appointment of an administrator. An exception would be made for capital market transactions. In a later press release, the government indicated that this would be without prejudice to existing powers of appointment.

In *Re Carter Commercial Developments Ltd* [2002] BCC 803, solicitors with a lien over a company's title deeds and documents were given leave under s 11(3)(d) of the Insolvency Act 1986 (see now para 43(2) of Sch B1 to that Act as added by s 248(2) of the Enterprise Act 2002) were given leave to enforce their lien. It was not appropriate to force a dilution of their legal position on solicitors in circumstances where no bank was prepared to advance funds to the company on the faith of security offered by the administrators.

(iii) Administrative receivership

In *UCA France Champignon v Fisher Foods Ltd* [2002] EWHC 1906 (QB), administrative receivers were unsuccessful in seeking to discharge an injunction granted in favour of French suppliers of mushrooms on reservation of title terms; the undertaking given by the receivers, to account to the French suppliers if the reservation of title clause was valid, was not extensive enough to protect the interests of the French suppliers. It did not cover a claim in the French courts in respect of mushrooms supplied prior to the appointment of the receivers. **16.97**

(3) Distributing the Insolvent's Assets

(a) The *pari passu* rule

(i) General

It has always been axiomatic in English law that secured creditors rank ahead of unsecured creditors, the latter being entitled to a dividend only out of the unencumbered assets of the insolvent. The creation by statute of classes of named preferential creditors, ranking ahead of a floating chargee (see Main Work para 16.114), was at the expense of this principle. A further erosion of the principle, this time in favour of unsecured creditors as a class, is to be found in the Enterprise Act 2002, which creates a modest 'lifeboat' for unsecured creditors (s 252, introducing new s 176A of the Insolvency Act 1986). The new provision, which applies in the case of receivership, administration and liquidation, requires the office holder to make available for unsecured creditors 'a prescribed part of the company's net property', the net property being the property that would otherwise be available for distribution to the holders of a floating charge. A ceiling of £600,000 is placed on the prescribed part available for distribution under s 176A. No special distribution will take place thereunder if the company's net property is less than £10,000 and 'the liquidator, administrator or receiver thinks that the cost of making a distribution to secured creditors would be disproportionate to the benefits' (s 176A(4)(b)). Trivial, uneconomic distributions are thus avoided. Where a prescribed part is distributable, the unsecured creditors receive 50% of the first £10,000 and 20% of the remaining net property of the company (subject to the £600,000 ceiling). (See the Insolvency Act 1986 (Prescribed Part) Order 2003 (SI 2003/2097).) **16.98**

Since the company's net property is defined as that which would be available to floating chargees, the unsecured creditors' new rights are therefore not at the expense of preferential creditors or other secured creditors or title retainers. In quantifying the company's net property, the cost of realizing that property and unspecified 'other matters' are taken into account. No reference is made to the costs of distribution to unsecured creditors, though these may come in later under 'other matters'. The rights of unsecured creditors under the new provision, however, are not at the expense of voluntary arrangements and schemes of arrangement if these exclude the new rights. For practical purposes, therefore, some of the lost Crown preferential claim would appear to be transformed into the new unsecured creditors' lifeboat rights. The remainder (so far as there are no other preferential creditors to claim it) appears to have gone to the floating chargee.

16.99 In *Money Markets International Stockbrokers Ltd v London Stock Exchange Ltd* [2001] 4 All ER 223, Neuberger J disapproved of the reasoning in *Re Garrud* to the extent that it upheld a forfeiture of property taking effect in an insolvency when it could also take effect outside insolvency. The judge considered this line of reasoning to be inconsistent with the decision of the House of Lords in *British Eagle International Airlines Ltd v Cie Nationale Air France* [1975] 2 All ER 390. The *Money Markets* case makes the further point that the forfeiture of unassignable property rights (in this case, a share in the London Stock Exchange shortly before it demutualized) or other property without value will not be struck down. Considering at length the authorities in this area, Neuberger J was moved to say that 'it is not possible to discern a coherent rule, or even an entirely coherent set of rules, to enable one to assess in any particular case whether such a provision . . . falls foul of the principle [that forfeiture clauses taking effect in insolvency are void]'.

In this vein, Lord Scott's speech in *Smith (Administrator of Cosslett (Contractors) Ltd) v Bridgend County Council* [2002] 1 AC 336 is notable for the subtle way in which he treats a local authority's seizure of an insolvent construction company's assets, pursuant to a contractual entitlement, as not amounting to a forfeiture: the seizure was not in satisfaction of the local authority's claim but merely on account of it.

(iii) Settlement systems

16.103 **n434**: see also *North Atlantic Insurance Co Ltd v Nationwide General Insurance Co Ltd* [2003] EWHC 449 (reinsurance pools and agency agreements).

(b) Expenses of the insolvency process

16.108 The decision of Rimer J in *Re Leyland Daf Ltd* [2000] All ER (D) 1867 (following on this point *Re Portbase Clothing Ltd* [1993] Ch 388) confirmed that the expenses of the winding-up rank ahead of the secured claim of a floating chargee, regardless of whether or when the floating charge crystallizes. This followed from the clear language of s 175. The decision of Rimer J was affirmed by the Court of Appeal *sub nom Buchler v Talbot* [2002] EWCA Civ 228. The court, in the process, followed its earlier decision in *Re Barleycorn Enterprises Ltd* [1970] 2 All ER 155 at the expense of its own supposedly inconsistent decision in *Re Regent's Canal Ironworks Co* (1875) 3 Ch D 411. After a meticulous examination of the antecedents of s 175 of the Insolvency Act 1986 and related provisions, Chadwick LJ concluded that legislation enacted after *Re Regent's Canal Ironworks Co* had altered the meaning of the 'assets' of the company. These now included property the subject of a floating charge, so that the effect of advancing preference creditors ahead of a floating chargee, since the expenses of the liquidation ranked ahead of the claims of preference creditors, was to place expenses of the liquidation creditors ahead of the floating chargee in respect of property covered by a floating charge.

An interesting feature of Rimer J's judgment in *Re Leyland Daf Ltd* is the light it throws on the subordinated character of the floating chargee's claim where an administrative receivership is succeeded by a liquidation. Receivership preference creditors are not necessarily the same as liquidation preference creditors (the types of creditor are the same but the dates of their entitlement are different). Furthermore, s 40 lays a duty on the administrative receiver first to pay preference creditors, whereas s 175 does not lay a similar duty on the liquidator but rather states that the claims of preference creditors rank after the expenses of the winding-up but ahead of the claim of a floating chargee. In *Re Leyland Daf Ltd*, the liquidator, seeking to recover expenses of the winding-up, claimed assets still in the hands of joint administrative receivers and not yet distributed to the floating chargee. Rimer J, applying s 175, found for the liquidator on this point. He noted, however, the liquidator's concession that he could not retrieve assets already distributed by the administrative receivers, and observed the curious conclusion that the rights of the liquidator depended upon the speed with which an administrative receiver performed his functions. On this point, the liquidator showed commendable restraint but the language of s 175 does give some comfort to more ambitious liquidators, or even liquidation preference creditors, seeking to unravel disbursements previously made by an administrative receiver. This is plainly undesirable. One response is to say that winding-up expenses and preference claims rank ahead, as s 175 states, of the *claims* of a floating chargee. A chargee already paid is to that extent no longer making a claim.

The decision of the House of Lords in *Kahn v Commissioners of Inland Revenue* [2002] UKHL 6 (cited also as *Re Toshoku Finance plc* [2002] 1 WLR 671) throws light upon the rules relating to the expenses of the liquidation. The case concerned an insolvent company's liability to pay corporation tax on interest owed to it by another member of the same corporate group as a result of a loan facility opened between the two companies. The debtor company was also insolvent; no interest had been or therefore would be paid to the creditor company. The liquidators disputed their liability to pay corporation tax and also sought directions in the present proceedings whether the tax claim was an expense of the liquidation enjoying priority over other unsecured claims against the company.

The House of Lords held, first, that the payment of corporation tax was a 'necessary disbursement' by the liquidators under r 4.218(1)(m) despite the reference to corporation tax payable in different circumstances in r 4.218(1)(p). More importantly, for present purposes, the court also held that the list in r 4.218 was with certain qualifications 'a definitive statement of what counted as an expense of the liquidation' (Lord Hoffmann at [13]). The court did not have a discretion to add expenses to or subtract expenses from the list in a given case (though a statutory discretion existed under ss 115 and 156 of the Insolvency Act 1986 to rearrange priority among the expenses listed in r 4.218). Counsel for the liquidators had unsuccessfully contended that there was an enveloping discretion which permitted the court to except the application of the expenses rule in a case where it was not fair to impose a burden on the persons for whose benefit the estate was being administered.

The *Kahn* case is also important for the explanation it gives concerning the distinction between pre-liquidation expenses and expenses of the liquidation. In principle, debts arising out of pre-liquidation contracts but accruing due after the liquidation can be proved in the winding-up since there exists machinery for valuing contingent claims against the company. Nevertheless, where, for example, a liquidator continued to occupy premises rented by the company without paying rent, a court might under a statutory discretion (see now s 130(2) of the Insolvency Act 1986) permit distress or execution against the company's assets (see *Re Lundy Granite Co* (1871) LR 6 Ch App 462). From that discretionary position the law had moved to treat debts of this kind as expenses of the liquidation so that under r 4.218 they acquired a formal priority over other unsecured claims against the company.

Further questions concerning the interaction between floating charge realizations and expenses of the liquidation arose before Anthony Mann QC in *Re Demaglass Ltd* [2002] All ER (D) 155. The liquidators in that case sought to have all floating charge realizations in the hands of the receivers turned over to them so that they could be applied to the liquidators' future activities generating expenses not yet quantifiable. The court rejected the claim, first, because expenses referred to in r 4.218 referred to actual disbursements, and secondly, because there was no statutory justification for the claim to have all floating charge realizations turned over.

The costs awarded to a successful litigant in proceedings against a company in liquidation (see r 4.220(2)) have priority over other expenses of the liquidation. The powers of the court in ss 115 and 156 of the Insolvency Act 1986 to rearrange priority are confined to expenses claims listed in r 4.218 (*Re MT Realisations Ltd* [2003] EWHC 2895 (Ch)).

(c) Priority: expenses, preference creditors, unsecured creditors and members

(i) Floating charges

The Court of Appeal, reversing the court below on this point, has held that the costs of litigation (in this case for unlawful preferences and for wrongful trading) are not recoverable under r 4.218 (whether as costs incurred in getting in the assets or as necessary disbursements by the liquidator), regardless of whether the liquidator's action is successful or unsuccessful: *Re Floor Fourteen Ltd* (*sub nom Lewis v Commissioner of Inland Revenue*) [2001] 3 All ER 499. The fruits of a successful action were not assets of the company but were to be held on trust for those creditors entitled to the assets of the company. Nevertheless, the decision of the Court of Appeal on this point has now been reversed by legislative means. The Insolvency (Amendment) (No 2) Rules 2002 (SI 2002/2712), in r 4 and Part 2, para 23, have inserted as expenses of the liquidation in r 4.218(1)(a) of the Insolvency Rules 1986 the words '[expenses] . . . otherwise relating to the conduct of any legal proceedings which [the liquidator] has power to bring or defend whether in his own name or in the name of the company'. The Enterprise Act 2002, however, in s 253, counterbalances this new rule by subjecting the conduct of the liquidator in initiating proceedings to new controls: the liquidator must first obtain the approval of the creditors' committee or of the court to do so. **16.112**

n457: *Re Floor Fourteen Ltd (sub nom Lewis v Commissioner of Inland Revenue)* was reversed by the Court of Appeal on other grounds, The Times, 15 November 2000.

In *Re Floor Fourteen Ltd* (*sub nom Lewis v Commissioner of Inland Revenue*), The Times, 15 November 2000, the Court of Appeal once again approved Millett J's analysis of ss 115 and 175 in *Re MC Bacon Ltd* [1991] Ch 127. It considered itself bound on this point by its own earlier decision in *Re RS & M Engineering Co Ltd* [2000] BCC 445 (cited as *Mond v Hammond Suddards* [2000] Ch 40) and declined to follow the contrary dicta of Chadwick and Phillips LJJ in *Re Exchange Travel Holdings Ltd (No 3)* [1997] 2 BCLC 579 (a case that regrettably had not been brought to the attention of the court in *Mond v Hammond Suddards*). **16.113**

(ii) Preferential claims

The Enterprise Act 2002 abolishes Crown preference (s 251). The claims affected are debts due to the Inland Revenue and to Customs and Excise and social security contributions. **16.114**

(d) Set-off (insolvency and receivership)

(ii) Scope of set-off

In *Smith (Administrator of Cosslett (Contractors) Ltd) v Bridgend County Council* **16.125**

[2002] 1 AC 336, however, the House of Lords held that mutuality was absent as between a local authority's claim for breach of contract and the company's claim against the council for conversion of its plant left on site. Just like the case of a misappropriation of company assets, a conversion of the plant was not a 'dealing' with the company.

(iv) Contingent claims and set-off

16.130 n518: *Re a Debtor (No 66 of 1955)* [1956] 1 WLR 1226 was followed in *Secretary of State for Trade and Industry v Frid* [2002] All ER (D) 76, where David Mackie QC stated that the injustice of the case could be redressed only by a higher court.

C. Powers and Liabilities of Insolvency Officers, Administrators and Administrative Receivers

(1) Dealing with the Estate

(a) Business, assets and creditors

(i) Powers of the liquidator

16.139 n553: for the power of a liquidator to waive privilege and make documents available to the Inland Revenue bringing a s 212 misfeasance action, see *Re Loquitur Ltd* [2002] EWHC 430, where the directors did not have standing to seek a discharge of the order permitting the liquidator to do so.

(iii) Powers of the administrator and the administrative receiver

16.142 The powers of the administrator under Sch 1 to gather in the company's property and to take proceedings in the name of the company were considered at length by the House of Lords in *Smith (Administrator of Cosslett (Contractors) Ltd) v Bridgend County Council* [2002] 1 AC 336. The administrator had 'ample power' to cause the company to bring an action against a local authority for converting its plant and equipment pursuant to a charge that was void for want of registration under s 395 of the Companies Act 1985.

(b) Rights of those dealing with the insolvent

(ii) Receivership: general

16.146 The indemnity afforded to administrators extends not only to net salaries and wages paid to employees but also to PAYE and National Insurance contributions. In a test case, the Court of Appeal in *Commissioners of Inland Revenue v Lawrence* [2001] 1 BCLC 204 (CA) held that these amounts represented 'sums payable in respect of liabilities incurred . . . under contracts of employment' within s 19(6).

(iii) Receivers and contracts of employment

In *Re Antal International Ltd* [2003] EWHC 1339, administrators of a company were held not to have adopted contracts of employment with French employees of the company, despite the lapse of more than 14 days after they took office before they terminated the contracts, since they had mistakenly believed the employees to be under contract to a French subsidiary of the company in administration. **16.148**

(iv) Receivers and rates

The entry of a company into liquidation puts an end to an administrative receiver's deemed agency to act for the company (under s 44(1)(a)). Nevertheless, the court in *Rees v Boston Borough Council* (High Ct, 21 December 2000) held that administrative receivers were not personally liable for non-domestic rates arising after the liquidator's appointment. Section 44(1)(a) did not as such prevent that receiver from acting for the company and did not prevent the company, for example, through the person of the liquidator, from appointing administrative receivers to act for it. The administrative receivers, on the facts, occupied the land on behalf of the company and not as principals. Consequently, they were not personally liable for rates. **16.151**

(2) Bringing Proceedings

(a) Vulnerable transactions and fraudulent conveyances

(i) Distributable assets

A liquidator or trustee-in-bankruptcy bringing proceedings in respect of undervalue transactions, unlawful preferences, and fraudulent conveyances is required under new provisions contained in the Enterprise Act 2002 to obtain the sanction of the court (ss 253 and 262). **16.152**

(ii) Undervalue transactions

The decision of the House of Lords in *Phillips v Brewin Dolphin Lawrie* [2001] UKHL 2 is important for the way that it defines 'transaction' under s 238(4)(b). In that case, liquidators unsuccessfully sought to have a share sale set aside on the ground of undervalue by isolating one part of the transactional scheme and having that assessed for undervalue, a form of inverted cherry-picking. A stockbroking business was sold by the seller transferring its business assets to a subsidiary for a nominal sum and then transferring the shares in that subsidiary to the buyer for a consideration equivalent to about one-third of their value. Further consideration, however, was provided to the seller by the buyer's parent company, which accepted a sub-lease of computer equipment leased to the seller. The House of Lords held that the consideration for the share sale included the entry by the parent into the sub-lease, even though this was not mentioned in the share sale **16.154** agreement as part of the consideration. This accords with the spirit of commercial transactions. (Another way of reaching the same conclusion, if supported by the evidence, might have been to treat the buyer's procurement of its parent's entry into the sub-lease as part of the consideration for the shares.) Nevertheless, since the sub-lease was in breach of a no-assignment clause in the head lease, the parent's undertaking to pay sub-rentals was worthless so that in fact the consideration for the share sale was confined to the undervalue sum paid by the buyer itself.

Following the decision of the House of Lords in the *Phillips v Brewin Dolphin Lawrie* case, Morritt V-C in *Re Thoars* [2002] EWHC 2416 (Ch) looked at subsequent events in determining whether an undervalue transaction had occurred. A life insurance policy with a surrender value of £71.96 was assigned shortly before his death by the insolvent deceased in return for the transferee paying a cash sum of £1,900 and the annual premium of £1,176 and undertaking to pay future annual premiums. The deceased had been suffering from cirrhosis of the liver and was on the active list for a liver transplant. The court concluded that the transaction had taken place at an undervalue: the sum payable on death was £185,568.

n591: natural love and affection between transferor and transferee does not cure an undervalue transaction (*Simms v Oakes* [2002] BPIR 1244).

n593: the transfer of property can take place at an undervalue when its earlier acquisition by the transferor was financed by a third party: *Re Pozzuto* [2003] EWHC 431 (Ch).

16.157 In *Whalley v Doney* [2003] EWHC 227 (Ch), the court could not in an undervalue case make an order under s 238(4) of the Insolvency Act 1986 restoring the company to the position it was in before the transaction because, if the company had not entered into the transaction, it would have been worse off and would have had to close down its business.

(iv) Fraudulent conveyances

16.160 A useful review of the s 423 authorities is given by Hart J in *Law Society v Southall* (High Ct, 11 December 2000), noting that a transaction may be set aside where a solvent donor at the time of the gift is contemplating a risky transaction. The judge declined to express a view on whether the section requires the creditor ultimately prejudiced by the conveyance to have been of the type foreseeably at risk at the time of the transfer. In that case, the donee wife's application for summary judgment in her favour was dismissed by Hart J on the ground that the Law Society, challenging the gift, had a real prospect of showing that it was made for the purpose of putting the assets beyond the reach of the donor's creditors. The Court of Appeal ([2001] EWCA 2001), however, upheld the donee wife's appeal because there was no evidence at the time of the gift that the donor was in financial difficulties or was conducting a risky business. The memoranda of gift executed by the donor were strange and obsessive but there was clear evidence that their purpose was to avoid tax.

n616: but see now *Law Society v Southall* (High Ct, 11 December 2000), where Hart J thought that the possible requirement of a dominant intention was 'capable of serious argument'. According to *Kubiangha v Ekpenyong* [2002] 2 BCLC 597, however, the substantial purpose required for a transaction to be set aside under s 423(3) need not be the sole or a dominant purpose.

The decision of the Court of Appeal in *Jones v National Westminster Bank plc* [2001] EWCA Civ 1541 is somewhat at variance with the decision of the House of Lords in *Phillips v Brewin Dolphin Lawrie* (see Supplement para 16.154), on undervalue transactions and s 238, in defining the scope of transactions that taken together should be considered as giving rise to a fraudulent conveyance. The case concerned a farming couple who had granted to a bank an agricultural charge over their farm and farming assets. In financial difficulties, they incorporated a company in which they were the sole shareholders and then granted the company a 20-year lease of the farm, selling to the company the farming assets, the price of which was to be paid in 20 annual instalments. The trial judge, upheld by the Court of Appeal, held that the lease of land was at a sufficient undervalue ('significantly less') because the grant of the lease diminished the value of the freehold and commensurately gave the company lessee a surrender value for the lease over and above the useful value of the land for which it paid rent. The sale of the farming assets was also at an undervalue because the instalments were deferred and were unsecured. Finally, no account should be taken of the value to the farming couple of the shares in the company. The company had prospered at the bank's expense. An overall assessment of the value remaining in the hands of the farming couple would of course have ignored the effect of the scheme. This was to rob the bank of its effective security by postponing the bank to the company as purchasers for value in respect of the farm and its assets while, at the same time, transferring assets to the farming couple, shares and an income stream, that were not the subject of the agricultural charge. It is questionable whether such a fragmented approach to defining the transaction would have been appropriate if the complainant had been an unsecured creditor. **16.161**

(v) Unlawful preferences

In the case of property sold by a company to its directors and leased back from them, part of the consideration supplied by the directors under the sale was the release of a debt owed to them by the company. The directors failed to discharge the burden of proof in s 239(6) of the Insolvency Act 1986: there was no compelling reason for the transaction that could have benefited the company as opposed to the directors. **16.166**

(b) Misfeasance and wrongful and fraudulent trading

(i) Misfeasance

16.172 There is a developing case law to the effect that directors of a company that becomes insolvent owe a fiduciary duty to creditors of the company to consider their interests as paramount (see *Colin Gwyer and Associates Ltd v London Wharf (Limehouse) Ltd* [2002] EWHC 2748 (Ch); *Re Pantone 485 Ltd* [2002] 1 BCLC 266). Thus a board resolution would be open to challenge if it were passed without proper consideration being given to the interests of creditors.

(ii) Fraudulent trading

16.173 The Court of Appeal in *Morris v Bank of America & National Savings Trust Association* [2002] EWCA Civ 425, in an appeal dealing with a case management decision, reiterated at [11] what it had said in an earlier case of the same name ([2000] 1 All ER 954, 963), that for liability for fraudulent trading under s 213 of the Insolvency Act 1986 there had to be knowledge (which embraced wilful blindness and reckless indifference) that the company's business was being carried on with intent to defraud creditors or with some other fraudulent purpose. See also to the same effect *Morris v Bank of India* [2003] EWHC 1868 (Ch).

For there to be fraudulent trading, it is necessary to show that the business itself has been carried on with an intention to defraud, and not merely that individual creditors were defrauded in the course of the business (*Morphitis v Bernasconi*, The Times, 12 March 2003).

A liquidator bringing proceedings for fraudulent or wrongful trading must first obtain the sanction of the court under a new provision in the Enterprise Act 2002 (s 253).

(iii) Wrongful trading

16.174 For a wrongful trading claim to succeed, there must have arisen a net deficiency in the company's estate from the time when the directors should have perceived that liquidation was inevitable to the time when in fact liquidation took place (*Re Marini Ltd* [2003] EWHC 334).

(c) Powers of investigation and examination

16.177 The court in *Re Trading Partners Ltd* [2001] All ER (D) 68) (cited also as *Akers v Lomas*) has held that working papers and litigation documents, held by administrative receivers of another company, are 'books, papers and other records' for the purpose of a liquidator's application under s 236. The section formed part of a composite code designed to secure information for office holders. It should be given a wide meaning on a case-by-case basis unless the production was unnecessary or oppressive. Office holders were entitled to information concerning the dealings of the company with another company with a view to giving them a comprehensive understanding of the company in respect of which they were acting. Section 236 was therefore capable of extending to documents brought into existence as a result of the conduct of a liquidation, administration or receivership of another company.

Where provisional liquidators, having already commenced fraud proceedings against directors, were then appointed liquidators and sought orders under s 236 of the Insolvency Act 1986, the Court of Appeal in *Shierson v Rastogi* [2002] EWCA Civ 1624 held that they were entitled to the examination orders sought. The legitimate requirements of the liquidators to obtain speedy information (the company's files lacked documentation in respect of transactions concluded in the months prior to corporate collapse) outweighed the oppressive effect of requiring the directors to provide what amounted to pre-trial depositions and to prove the case against themselves under oath. It was a 'paradigm case for the exercise of powers under s.236' (Mance LJ at [63]). The questions to be put to the directors would be only such questions as the court would allow and the directors would have legal representation (r 4.9(1)). The directors conceded that they could not mount a challenge under Article 6 (fair trial) of the European Convention on Human Rights. Following on from the decision of the European Court of Human Rights in *Saunders v United Kingdom* [1996] EHRR 313, s 433 of the Insolvency Act had been amended to prohibit the use in criminal proceedings of statements obtained under s 236 of the Insolvency Act against persons making those statements. Section 433, however, did not give the directors 'derivative use immunity', so as to protect them if the police or the Serious Fraud Office used transcripts of the examination to construct a criminal case against them.

The House of Lords in *Official Receiver v Wadge Rapps & Hunt* [2003] UKHL 49 held that the court's powers in s 236 of the Insolvency Act 1986 to order a director to provide information to an office holder, on the latter's application, could be lawfully exercised even if the sole or principal purpose behind the application was to gather evidence for use in disqualification proceedings under the Company Directors Disqualification Act 1986. Applications under s 236 are not confined to the purposes of winding-up. Indeed, s 236 permits the official receiver to apply whether or not he is the liquidator.

(3) The Conduct of Insolvency Officers, Administrators and Receivers

(a) Personal liability

In *Oldham v Kyrris* [2003] EWCA Civ 1506, the Court of Appeal held that, in the absence of a special relationship, an administrator owes no common law duty of care to unsecured creditors in the conduct of the administration. It was assisted in **16.178** reaching this conclusion by the existence of the summary misfeasance remedy in s 212 of the Insolvency Act 1986. The issue of a liquidator's common law duty of care to creditors had earlier been left open in *A & J Fabrications Ltd v Grant Thornton* [1998] BCLC 227, Ch.

16.180 **n687**: see now also *Cohen v TSB Bank plc* [2002] 2 BCLC 32.

16.181 The Court of Appeal has on two recent occasions reaffirmed the duties owed by receivers and mortgagees regarding property the subject of a security. A mortgagee is entitled to remain 'totally passive' or may instead decide to sell without waiting even a short time for the market to rise. He is not a trustee of the power of sale of the property. Similarly, the mortgagee is not bound to improve or increase the value of the property. If he sets out to do this, he is not bound by any election to delay selling the property. The mortgagee's duty to take care in the conduct of the sale is an equitable duty and not a duty in tort. See *Silven Properties Ltd v Royal Bank of Scotland plc* [2003] EWCA Civ 1409 and *Raja v Austin Gray* [2002] EWCA Civ 1965. The receiver acting as agent of the mortgagor, moreover, is in the same position as the mortgagee except that he cannot remain passive. In determining the extent of any exceptions, regard had first to be had to 'the wider management duties imposed on a receiver (but not on a mortgagee)' to see if these might 'require a receiver (and in particular a receiver appointed the agent of the mortgagor) to postpone a sale until after steps have been taken . . . calculated to increase the price obtainable' from a sale of the property (*Silven Properties Ltd v Royal Bank of Scotland plc* at [24]). The 'scope or content of the duty must depend on and reflect the special nature of the relationship between the Bank, the [Mortgagor] and the Receivers arising under the terms of the mortgages and the appointments of the Receivers, and in particular the role of the Receivers in securing repayment of the secured debt and the primacy of their obligations in this regard to the Bank' (ibid at [29]). Accordingly, the receivers in *Silven* were under no duty to take 'pre-marketing steps'. The fiduciary duty is owed to all those known to the mortgagee or receiver as having an interest in the equity of redemption (*Raja v Austin Gray*).

In the case of a receiver appointed by the court in a partnership action, no duty is owed by the receiver to a disappointed purchaser of the property, in this case one of the partners (see *McGowan v Chadwick* [2002] EWCA Civ 1758).

The breach of a mortgagee's duty, under New Zealand legislation, 'to take reasonable care to obtain the best price reasonably obtainable at the time of sale', is dependent upon all the circumstances, including the taking of an account of all benefits accruing to the mortgagor (see *Newport Farms Ltd v Damesh Holdings Ltd* (The Times, 15 July 2003 (PC)).

n690: see *Lloyds Bank plc v Cassidy* [2002] EWCA Civ 1427 where Mance LJ states at [41] that 'there may be some scope for further examination of the borderline between the supposed area of freedom, which exists when a mortgagee or receiver decides not to sell, and the area of duty, which exists in relation to the exercise of the power to sell. Once a mortgagee or receiver has decided to sell, he or she cannot, presumably, avoid liability if he or she fails to accept or follow up an obviously favourable proposal. It cannot be an answer to any claim to say that a decision was taken not to sell pursuant to that particular proposal.' But see also *Den Norske Bank ASA v Acemex Management Co Ltd* (The Independent, 11 November 2003), where the Court of Appeal reiterates that the mortgagee's freedom to determine when to sell is not to be undermined by the application of the mortgagee's duty to obtain a proper price.

(b) Officers of the court and *ex p James*

The rule in *ex p James* was applied by the Court of Appeal in *Patel v Jones* [2001] EWCA Civ 779, where a bankrupt made further pension contributions in the mistaken belief that his pension had not vested in his trustee-in-bankruptcy. The trustee was not entitled to so much of the pension as was attributable to the bankrupt's post-bankruptcy service and contributions. **16.182**

17

PRIVATE INTERNATIONAL LAW

A. Introduction and Principles

(1) The Nature of the Subject

See *Damberg v Damberg* (2001) 52 NSWLR 492, NSW CA (refusal to accept that unproved foreign law is the same as the *lex fori*); and to broadly similar effect, see **17.03** also *Shaker v Al Bedrawi* [2002] EWCA Civ 1452, [2003] Ch 350, CA. If foreign law is so offensive as make its recognition contrary to public policy, it will not be allowed to be proved: *Kuwait Airways Corp v Iraq Airways Co* [2002] UKHL 19, [2002] 2 AC 883.

(3) Connecting Factors

(a) Personal connecting factors

(i) Domicile

17.08 n15: see now also *Reddington v Riach's Executor* 2002 SLT 537 (Ct Sess).

(4) The Exclusive Domain of the Lex Fori

(a) Procedural matters

(ii) Interim procedure

17.15 n26: for assessment of the competing issues, see *Motorola Credit Corp v Uzan* [2003] EWCA Civ 752, [2004] 1 WLR 113 CA.

For developments in relation to the Brussels Convention, see Supplement paras 17.31–17.84.

(b) Penal laws and revenue claims

17.19 See *Kuwait Airways Corp v Iraqi Airways Co (Nos 4 and 5)* [2002] UKHL 19, [2002] 2 AC 883 (non-recognition of Iraqi decree in flagrant breach of international law).

17.20 In *Damberg v Damberg* (2001) 52 NSWLR 492, NSW CA, the court refused to make an order which risked enforcement of foreign revenue law.

(c) Public policy

(i) Foreign rules

17.23 See now also *Kuwait Airways Corp v Iraq Airways Co (Nos 4 and 5)* [2002] UKHL 19, [2002] 2 AC 883 (non-recognition of Iraqi decree).

B. The Jurisdiction of English Courts

(1) Jurisdictional Schemes and Rules

(a) Subject matter jurisdiction

17.28 For developments in relation to the Brussels Convention, see Supplement paras 17.31–17.84. The common law blanket exclusion of jurisdiction may be open to challenge under Article 6 of the European Convention on Human Rights: cf *Prince Hans-Adam II of Liechtenstein v Germany*, 12 July 2001.

n44: *Pearce v Ove Arup Partnership Ltd* is reported at [2000] Ch 403, CA.

(b) Personal jurisdiction

For proceedings instituted on or after 1 March 2002, the Brussels Convention is superseded by Council Regulation (EC) 44/2001 (2001 OJ L12/1) for all contracting states except Denmark (for which the Brussels Convention remains in effect, as it does for proceedings instituted before 1 March 2002). The Lugano Convention is unaffected. Gibraltar is part of the United Kingdom for the purposes of the Regulation. Where the Regulation departs from the corresponding provisions of the Brussels Convention, this is pointed out; otherwise the substance of the law is unaltered apart from the numbering. References to jurisdiction under the Conventions are references to jurisdiction under the Conventions or the Regulation, as the case may be, unless the contrary is stated. **17.31–17.84**

(2) The Brussels and Lugano Conventions

(a) The Conventions: scheme and domain

(i) Scheme

See the entry under Supplement paras 17.31–17.84. References to the European Court on the interpretation of Council Regulation (EC) 44/2001 will by made under Article 234 EC (ex 177) as modified by Article 68 EC (ex 73p). **17.34**

The Brussels Convention was amended on the accession of Austria, Finland and Sweden; Poland has acceded to the Lugano Convention: Civil Jurisdiction and Judgments Act 1982 (Amendment) Order 2000, SI 2000/1824.

n53: for the declaration required to be made, now see paras 1.3A–3C of the Practice Direction.

(ii) Internal United Kingdom jurisdiction

The intra-UK jurisdictional rules in Sch 4 to the 1982 Act are amended by Civil Jurisdiction and Judgments Order 2001, SI 2001/3929, Sch 2, para 4, to reflect (but not exactly copy) the provisions of Council Regulation (EC) 44/2001. **17.35**

n58: *Agnew v Länsförsäkringsbolagens AB* is now reported at [2001] 1 AC 223.

(iii) Interpretation

On the meaning of being sued, see *The Ikarian Reefer* [2000] 1 WLR 603, CA (claim under Supreme Court Act 1981, s 51 against non-party for costs order). **17.36**

(iv) Material scope: civil or commercial matters

17.37 Proceedings by a consumers' representative body to prevent use of unfair contract terms by trader are within Article 1: Case C-167/00 *VfK v Henkel* [2002] ECR I-8111.

17.38 On customs, see Case C-266/01 *Preservatrice Foncière TIARD SA v Staat der Nederlanden* [2003] ECR I-4867; on bankruptcy, see *Ashurst v Pollard* [2001] Ch 595, CA; on social security, see Case C-271/00 *Gemeente Steenbergen v Baten* [2002] ECR I-10489, [2003] 1 WLR 1916.

(b) **Domicile**

(i) United Kingdom domicile

17.39 For the purposes of Council Regulation (EC) 44/2001, ss 41 and 45 of the 1982 Act are reproduced as Civil Jurisdiction and Judgments Order 2001, SI 2001/3929, Sch 1, paras 9 and 12. Section 42 is not reproduced: *apart from* Article 22.2 (which corresponds to Article 16.2 of the Convention, and for which Sch 1, para 10 of the Order provides a special definition of domicile) a uniform definition of a company's domicile is provided by Article 60.1: the place where it has its statutory seat, central administration, or principal place of business (and on which, see *King v Crown Energy Trading AG* [2003] EWHC 133 (Comm), 11 February 2003).

(ii) Domicile elsewhere

17.40 On the domicile of companies, see Supplement para 17.39.

(c) **Jurisdictional rules of the Brussels Convention**

(i) Exclusive jurisdiction, regardless of domicile

17.41–17.47 Articles 22 and 29 of Council Regulation (EC) 44/2001 correspond to Articles 16 and 23 of the Convention.

17.42 Article 22.1 of Council Regulation (EC) 44/2001 has the same effect as Article 16.1(b) of the Convention only if the tenant is a natural person.

n71: *Dansommer A/S v Götz* is reported at [2000] ECR I-393.

n74: see now also Case C-518/98 *Gaillard v Chekili* [2001] ECR I-2771 (action for rescission of contract for sale of land not within Article); *Ashurst v Pollard* [2001] Ch 595, CA (action by trustee in bankruptcy to force sale of foreign land not within Article).

17.43 In relation to partnerships, see *Phillips v Symes* [2002] 1 WLR 853.

17.44 **n80**: cf *Ashurst v Pollard* [2001] Ch 595, CA.

Proceedings to enforce a French judgment by garnishing a debt situated in Switzerland are within the exclusive jurisdiction of the Swiss courts: *Kuwait Oil Tanker Co SAK v UBS AG* [2003] UKHL 31, [2004] 1 AC 300. **17.46**

(ii) Jurisdiction by appearance

Article 24 of Council Regulation (EC) 44/2001 corresponds to Article 18 of the Convention. For application, see *Harada v Turner* [2003] EWCA Civ 1695. **17.47**

(iii) Insurance and consumer contracts

The insurance provisions (Articles 7–12A) are largely reproduced as Articles 8–14 of Council Regulation (EC) 44/2001; the consumer contract provisions are reproduced in altered form in Articles 15–17 of Council Regulation (EC) 44/2001; and a new section for jurisdiction over contracts of employment is created by Articles 18–21. **17.48**

The insurance contract provisions are inapplicable to reinsurance: Case C-412/98 *Universal General Insurance Co v Groupe Josi Reinsurance Co SA* [2000] ECR I-5925. **17.49**

n88: *Agnew v Länsförsäkringsbolagens AB* is reported at [2001] 1 AC 223.

The definition of a consumer contract in Council Regulation (EC) 44/2001 departs from that in Article 13 of the Convention: the third hypothesis (contracts preceded by advertising or invitation) now refers to contracts concluded with a person who pursues commercial activities in the consumer's state, or who by any means directs such activities to that state or to states including that one. This will apply to contracts preceded by website advertising and made by consumers over the internet. On the Brussels Convention version of contracts preceded by advertising, see Case C-96/00 *Gabriel v Schlank & Schick GmbH* [2002] ECR I-6367; and *Rayner v Davies* [2002] EWCA Civ 1880, [2003] 1 All ER (Comm) 394. **17.50**

Articles 18–21 of Council Regulation (EC) 44/2001, based in part on Articles 5.1 and 17 of the Convention, deal with jurisdiction over individual contracts of employment. Where the employer or employee is not domiciled in a member state, Article 4 will apply to claims against him. Otherwise the employer may be sued where he is domiciled, or in another member state in which the employee habitually carries out his work. The employee may only be sued in the member state in which he is domiciled. Jurisdiction agreements are effective only if entered into after the dispute has arisen or if they widen the employee's choice of court. On employees whose duties lack a clear geographical centre, see C-37/00 *Weber v Universal Ogden Services Ltd* [2002] ECR I-2013, [2002] QB 1189, ECJ. On employees seconded to another employer, see Case C-437/00 *Pugliese v Finmeccanica SpA* [2003] ECR I-3573. **17.50A**

(iv) Agreements on jurisdiction

17.51–17.54 Article 23 of Council Regulation (EC) 44/2001 corresponds to Article 17 of the Convention, but also diverges from it.

17.52 Article 23.2 of Council Regulation (EC) 44/2001 defines 'writing' to include any communication by electronic means which provides a durable record in writing.

n95: see now also Case C-387/98 *Coreck Maritime GmbH v Handelsveem BV* [2000] ECR I-9337 (formal consent of third parties not needed if they succeed to rights and obligations of contracting party).

n97: see now also Case C-387/98 *Coreck Maritime GmbH v Handelsveem BV* [2000] ECR I-9337.

17.53 On the respective roles of national and European law, see now *Provimi Ltd v Aventis Animal Nutrition Ltd*, 6 May 2003. On the invalidation of agreements on arbitration or jurisdiction by the Unfair Terms in Consumer Contracts Regulations 1999, SI 1999/2083 (enacting Council Directive 93/13 on Unfair Terms in Consumer Contracts ([1993] OJ L95/29) see Case C-240/98 *Océano Grupo Editorial SA v Quintero* [2000] ECR I-4941.

17.54 Article 23.1 of Council Regulation (EC) 44/2001 expressly validates non-exclusive jurisdiction agreements. On the validity of non-exclusive jurisdiction agreements under the Lugano Convention, see *Insured Financial Structures Ltd v Elektrocieplownia Tychy SA* [2003] QB 1260, CA.

17.55 For the provisions of Council Regulation (EC) 44/2001 dealing with jurisdiction agreements in contracts of employment, see Supplement para 17.50A.

(vi) Special jurisdiction over defendants domiciled in another contracting state

17.58 Article 5.1 of Council Regulation (EC) 44/2001 departs from the corresponding provision of the Convention. The place for performance of the obligation in question is defined as (for sales of goods) the place in a member state where the goods were to be delivered, and (for provision of services) the place in a member state where the services should have been provided; only outside these will the general rule in Article 5.1 of the Convention continue to apply.

A claim for damages for failing to negotiate a contract in good faith is not within Article 5.1: Case C-334/00 *Fonderie Officine Meccaniche Tacconi SpA v HWS Maschinenfabrik GmbH* [2002] ECR I-7357 (because the obligation was imposed by law and not freely assumed by the parties), and neither are proceedings brought against a trader by a public authority to prevent the use of unfair terms in consumer contracts: Case C-167/00 *VfK v Henkel* [2002] ECR I-8111 (because the claimant is not party to a contract with the defendant).

n112: *Agnew v Länsförsäkringsbolagens AB* is reported at [2001] 1 AC 223.

Where a negative obligation has a specified place for performance, Article 5.1 may apply (*Kenburn Waste Management v Bergmann* [2002] EWCA Civ 98, [2002] CLC 644, but where the negative obligation has no specific place where its observance is required, Article 5.1 has no application: Case C-256/00 *Besix SA v WAB AG* [2002] ECR I-1699. On obligations required to be performed in many states over time, see C-37/00 *Weber v Universal Ogden Services Ltd* [2002] ECR I-2013, [2002] QB 1189, ECJ (a case on contracts of employment). **17.59**

The view in the Main Work is to be questioned in the light of Case C-334/00 *Fonderie Officine Meccaniche Tacconi SpA v HWS Maschinenfabrik GmbH* [2002] I-7357, where a claim based on breach of the obligation to negotiate a contract in good faith, which was imposed by law and not freely assumed by the parties, was not within Article 5.1. It may be that this case has no proper application to a case in which a contract, albeit a voidable one, is concluded. For earlier authority in relation to misrepresentation, see *Alfred Dunhill Ltd v Diffusion Internationale de Maroquinerie de Prestige SARL* [2001] CLC 949. **17.61**

n123: *Agnew v Länsförsäkringsbolagens AB* is reported at [2001] 1 AC 223.

Jurisdiction is determined by the original injury, not any subsequent worsening of it, even if this gives rise to a further claim: *Henderson v Jaouen* [2002] EWCA Civ 75, [2002] 1 WLR 2971, CA. **17.62**

Article 5.3 covers claims alleging dishonest assistance of breach of trust: *Casio Computer Co Ltd v Sayo* [2001] EWCA Civ 661, [2001] Intl Litigation Procedure 594. It also applies to claims for damages resulting from the failure to negotiate a contract in good faith (Case C-334/00 *Fonderie Officine Meccaniche Tacconi SpA v HWS Maschinenfabrik GmbH* [2002] ECR I-7357), and to proceedings brought to prevent the use of unfair contract terms by a trader (Case C-167/00 *VfK v Henkel* [2002] ECR I-8111), as the liability sought to be enforced was not contractual. **17.63**

Article 5.3 of Council Regulation (EC) 44/2001 gives special jurisdiction to the courts for the place where the harmful event *may* occur.

n126: see now also *Alfred Dunhill Ltd v Diffusion Internationale de Maroquinerie de Prestige SARL* [2001] CLC 949.

See now also *Anton Durbeck GmbH v Den Norske Bank ASA* [2003] QB 1160, CA. **17.64**

The date on which the anchor defendant must be domiciled in the forum is the issue of process, not of service: *Canada Trust Co v Stolzenberg (No 2)* [2002] 1 AC 1. **17.70**

n138: case C-51/97 states that a contract claim against A is not connected to a tort claim against B, even when the single loss was caused by either A or B. This was questioned in *Watson v First Choice Holidays* [2001] EWCA Civ 972, [2001] 2 Lloyd's Rep 339 (reference to European Court of Justice withdrawn).

(viii) Removal of jurisdiction: lis pendens *and related actions*

17.74 Articles 27–30 of Council Regulation (EC) 44/2001 diverge from Articles 21 and 22 of the Convention. The Regulation will apply when the proceedings are commenced after 1 March 2002 in two member states; otherwise Articles 21 and 22 of the Convention govern.

17.75 Article 27 of Council Regulation (EC) 44/2001 reproduces Article 21 of the Convention.

n146: the court seised second has no right to proceed in a case where it is persuaded that it has exclusive jurisdiction under Article 23, even if it distrusts the motives of the party who has commenced proceedings elsewhere in breach of contract: Case C-116/02 *Erich Gasser GmbH v MISAT Srl*, [2004] 1 Lloyd's Rep 222, ECJ.

17.76 The identity of cause is, in principle, assessed only by reference to claims, and not to defences which have been or may be raised: Case C-111/01 *Gantner Electronic GmbH v Basch Exploitatie Maatschappij BV* [2003] ECR I-4207.

17.77 Article 30 of Council Regulation (EC) 44/2001 makes uniform provision for the date of seisin as that on which the claim form is lodged with the court if this precedes service; and as the date of service if this precedes lodging with the court. Under English procedure, the first rule will apply.

A court which has only appointed an expert to look into the possible causes of an accident is not seised: *Miles Platt Ltd v Townroe Ltd* [2003] EWCA Civ 154, [2003] 1 All ER (Comm) 561, CA.

(ix) Procedural modification of Convention jurisdiction

17.80 **n155**: see now also to this effect: *Canada Trust Co v Stolzenberg (No 2)* [2002] 1 AC 1.

17.81 The question of whether a court with jurisdiction under Article 2 may stay proceedings when the natural forum lies in a non-contracting state has been referred to the Court of Justice in *Owusu v Jackson* [2002] EWCA Civ 877, [2002] Intl Litigation Procedure 813, and in *American Motorists Insurance Co v Cellstar Corp* [2003] EWCA Civ 206, [2003] Intl Litigation Procedure 370.

On the final sentence of the Main Work para 17.81, see *International Credit and Investment (Overseas) Ltd v Adham* [1999] Intl Litigation Procedure 302, CA.

n156: see now also *Ace Insurance SA-NV v Zurich Insurance Co* [2001] EWCA Civ 173, [2001] 1 Lloyd's Rep 618.

n158: see also *Turner v Grovit* [2001] UKHL 65, [2002] 1 WLR 107 (referred to the ECJ by the House of Lords). See now also *The Ivan Zagubanski* [2002] 1 Lloyd's Rep 106; *OT Africa Line Ltd v Hijazy* [2001] 1 Lloyd's Rep 76, CA. However, the decision of the European Court in Case C-159/02 *Turner*, 27 April 2004, means that the power to grant anti-suit injunctions against the courts of another member state is inconsistent with the Regulation. **17.83**

n160: *Turner v Grovit* was appealed to the House of Lords, who referred it to the European Court: [2001] UKHL 65, [2002] 1 WLR 107, HL: see above.

n161: but the automatic refusal to recognize a judgment obtained in defiance of an injunction and in contempt of the court may violate the European Convention on Human Rights, Article 6: cf *Krombach v France*, 13 February 2001 (ECHR).

(x) Applications for provisional or protective measures

Article 31 of Council Regulation (EC) 44/2001 reproduces Article 24 of the Convention. On maintenance pending suit, see *Wermuth v Wermuth* [2003] EWCA Civ 50, [2003] 1 WLR 942, CA (not a provisional or protective measure). **17.84**

(3) Common Law and Rules of Court

(b) Jurisdiction based on service of process within England

(ii) Contesting jurisdiction

The period for contesting the jurisdiction in now 14 days (but in the Commercial Court, 28 days: CPR 58.7(2)) from filing the acknowledgment of service: CPR 11(4). **17.88**

n167: see now also *Lubbe v Cape plc* [2000] 1 WLR 1545, HL. **17.90**

The House of Lords in *Lubbe v Cape plc* [2000] 1 WLR 1545 disapproved the view of the courts below: no significance attaches to the fact that the foreign court was available only because the defendant undertook to submit to it. **17.91**

n170: see now also *Lubbe v Cape plc* [2000] 1 WLR 1545, HL.

It will be unjust to stay proceedings in favour of the natural forum if the claimant, unable to afford the costs of litigation in that other court, will be deprived of the right to trial: *Lubbe v Cape plc* [2000] 1 WLR 1545, HL. **17.92**

For the view that construction is neutral, see *McGowan v Summit at Lloyd's* 2002 SLT 1258 (Inner House). For the view that bringing proceedings in a foreign **17.93** court may breach a *non*-exclusive jurisdiction clause for the English courts, see *Sabah Shipyard (Pakistan) Ltd v Islamic Republic of Pakistan* [2002] EWCA Civ 1643, [2003] 2 Lloyd's Rep 571, CA (relief sought in Pakistan sought to make it impossible to give effect to the agreement at all).

n174: see now also *Donohue v Armco Inc* [2001] UKHL 64, [2002] 1 Lloyd's Rep 425, HL.

n175: for severability, see now also *IFR Ltd v Federal Trade SpA*, 19 September 2001. For invalidity under the Unfair Terms in Consumer Contract Regulations 1999, SI 1999/2083 (enacting Directive 93/13 on Unfair Terms in Consumer Contracts (1993 OJ L95/29) see Case C-240/98 *Océano Grupo Editorial SA v Quintero* [2000] ECR I-4941.

17.94 See also *Donohue v Armco Inc* [2001] UKHL 64, [2002] 1 Lloyd's Rep 425, HL (effect in relation to non-parties). And see also *Union Discount Co Ltd v Zoller* [2001] EWCA Civ 1755, [2002] 1 WLR 1517, CA (damages claim allowed where English jurisdiction clause broken by suing overseas; also to this effect, *Donohue v Armco Inc*, above, at [36] and [48]).

n179: *Donohue v Armco Inc* [2001] UKHL 64, [2002] 1 Lloyd's Rep 425, HL, reverses the decision of the Court of Appeal.

(c) Jurisdiction established by service out of the jurisdiction with the permission of the court

(i) General

17.95 Authorities decided under the former RSC Ord 11 remain pertinent: *The Baltic Flame* [2001] EWCA Civ 418, [2001] 2 Lloyd's Rep 203.

(ii) The paragraphs of Rule 6.20

17.100 Where a claimant in defamation proceedings complains only in respect of reading in England, the tort will be committed in England and England will be the natural forum for it: *Berezovsky v Michaels* [2000] 1 WLR 1004, HL (magazine); and cf *Gutnick v Dow Jones & Co Inc* (2003) 210 CLR 575 (Aust HC) (internet).

17.101 For consistency in interpretation, see *ABCI v Banque Franco-Tunisienne* [2003] EWCA Civ 205, [2003] 2 Lloyd's Rep 146, CA.

17.102 The acts within the jurisdiction must have something to do with the defendant: *Dexter Ltd v Harley*, The Times, 2 April 2001 (on Article 5.3 of the Brussels Convention).

17.103 **n202:** see now also *The Baltic Flame* [2001] EWCA Civ 418, [2001] 2 Lloyd's Rep 203.

(d) Anti-suit injunctions

The general compatibility of the anti-suit injunction with the scheme of the Brussels Convention was referred to the ECJ in *Turner v Grovit* [2001] UKHL 65, [2002] 1 WLR 107, HL. The decision of the European Court in Case C-159/02 *Turner v Grovit*, 27 April 2004, was that the granting of an anti-suit injunction against proceedings before the courts of another member state was inconsistent with the Convention. No exception to this principle was allowed for by the Court. **17.107**

(i) Personal jurisdiction over the respondent

On jurisdiction by submission, by having played a part in the proceedings at an earlier stage, see *Glencore International AG v Exter Shipping Ltd* [2002] EWCA Civ 524, [2002] CLC 1090, CA. **17.108**

(ii) Discretion

But in *Turner v Grovit* [2001] UKHL 65, [2002] 1 WLR 107, HL, it was suggested that an injunction may be sought and ordered only if the claimant has a legal right not to be sued, or has brought proceedings in the English courts which will be protected by the injunction. But in Case C-159/02 *Turner v Grovit*, 27 April 2004, the ECJ repudiated this suggestion as being inconsistent with the scheme of the Brussels Convention. And on vexation and oppression, see *Glencore International AG v Exter Shipping Ltd* [2002] EWCA Civ 524, [2002] CLC 1090, CA. **17.109**

An injunction was not granted in aid of an exclusive jurisdiction clause in *Donohue v Armco Inc* [2001] UKHL 64, [2002] 1 Lloyd's Rep 425, HL (reversing [2000] 1 Lloyd's Rep 427, CA), because there were other parties to the foreign proceedings who were not party to the agreement and whose behaviour could not be stigmatized as being oppressive or vexatious. **17.110**

n219: for anti-suit injunctions to protect a non-exclusive jurisdiction clause (the conduct being oppressive or vexatious and making enforcement of the jurisdiction agreement impossible) see *Sabah Shipyard (Pakistan) Ltd v Islamic Republic of Pakistan* [2002] EWCA Civ 1643, [2003] 2 Lloyd's Rep 571, CA.

n222: see now also *The Ivan Zagubanski* [2002] 1 Lloyd's Rep 106; *OT Africa Line Ltd v Hijazy* [2001] 1 Lloyd's Rep 76, CA. **17.111**

n223: the general compatibility of the anti-suit injunction with the scheme of the Brussels Convention was referred to the ECJ in *Turner v Grovit* [2001] UKHL 65, [2002] 1 WLR 107, HL. The decision of the European Court in Case C-159/02 *Turner v Grovit*, 27 April 2004, was that the granting of an anti-suit injunction against proceedings before the courts of another member state was inconsistent with the Convention. No exception to this principle was allowed for by the Court.

(e) Jurisdiction to obtain interim relief

17.112 For analysis of the jurisdictional and discretionary criteria which govern this issue, see *Motorola Credit Corp v Uzan* [2003] EWCA Civ 752, [2004] 1 WLR 113, CA.

C. Recognition and Enforcement of Foreign Judgments

(1) General

17.116–17.136 For judgments given in member states on or after 1 March 2002, the Brussels Convention is superseded by Council Regulation (EC) 44/2001 ([2001] OJ L12/1) in respect of all contracting states except Denmark (for which the Brussels Convention remains in effect, as it does for judgments given before 1 March 2002). The Lugano Convention is unaffected. Gibraltar is part of the United Kingdom for the purposes of the Regulation. Where the rules of the Regulation diverge from the corresponding provisions of the Brussels Convention this is pointed out, otherwise the substance of the law is unchanged apart from the numbering.

(2) The Brussels and Lugano Conventions

(a) **Recognition under the Conventions**

17.117 Recognition under Council Regulation (EC) 44/2001 is substantially the same as under the Convention; Article 26 of the Convention is reproduced as Article 33 of the Regulation.

n230: now see Article 33.2 of Council Regulation (EC) 44/2001 and CPR 74.10.

(i) Judgments

17.118 Articles 50 and 51 of the Convention are reproduced with minor modifications as Articles 57 and 58 of Council Regulation (EC) 44/2001.

n234: Article 43 of the Convention is reproduced as Article 49 of Council Regulation (EC) 44/2001.

(ii) Civil or commercial matters

17.119 **n239**: Article 42 of the Convention is reproduced as Article 48 of Council Regulation (EC) 44/2001.

(iii) Jurisdictional errors

17.120 **n244**: Article 28 of the Convention is reproduced as Article 35 of Council Regulation (EC) 44/2001.

Article 35 of Council Regulation (EC) 44/2001 does not add a provision for lack of jurisdiction derived from the rules on jurisdiction over employment contracts (as to which see Supplement para 17.50A). For the relationship with Article 27, see *Prudential Insurance Co Ltd v Prudential Insurance Co of America* [2003] EWCA Civ 327, [2003] 1 WLR 2295, CA. **17.121**

(iv) Other grounds of objection

Article 27 of the Convention is reproduced with slight amendment as Article 34 of Council Regulation (EC) 44/2001. **17.122**

n249: Article 27.1 of the Convention is reproduced with slight amendment as Article 34.1 of Council Regulation (EC) 44/2001.

Article 34.1 of Council Regulation (EC) 44/2001 requires the recognition to be *manifestly* contrary to public policy. **17.123**

n250a: Case C-7/98 *Krombach v Bamberski* is now reported at [2000] ECR I-1935. See now also Case C-38/98 *Régie Nationale des Usines Renault SA v Maxicar* [2000] ECR I-2973 (EU competition law not fundamental enough to invoke public policy). For further authority supporting the view that it would be contrary to public policy to recognize a judgment which had been obtained in breach of European Convention on Human Rights, Article 6, see *Krombach v France,* 13 February 2001, ECHR; *Pellegrini v Italy* (2002) 35 EHRR 44, ECHR; *Maronier v Larmer* [2002] EWCA Civ 774, [2003] QB 620, CA.

By contrast with Article 27.2 of the Convention, Article 34.2 of Council Regulation (EC) 44/2001 is inapplicable if the defendant had the opportunity to bring proceedings to challenge the judgment but did not do so. And see also *TSN Kunststoffrecycling GmbH v Jurgens* [2002] EWCA Civ 11, [2002] 1 WLR 2459, CA. **17.124**

Irreconcilability is also a reason to refuse recognition to an interim order: Case C-80/00 *Italian Leather SpA v WECO Polstermöbel GmbH & Co* [2002] ECR I-4995. **17.125**

Article 27.4 of the Convention is not reproduced in Council Regulation (EC) 44/2001. **17.126**

Article 34.4 of Council Regulation (EC) 44/2001 extends Article 27.5 of the Convention to apply also to cases of conflict between two member state judgments, where the first in time will prevail. **17.127**

(v) Bilateral treaty requiring non-recognition

Existing bilateral treaties continue in effect by reason of Article 72 of Council Regulation (EC) 44/2001. **17.128**

(vi) No other grounds for non-recognition

17.129 Articles 28, 29 and 24 of the Convention correspond to Articles 35, 36 and 31 of Council Regulation (EC) 44/2001.

(vii) Judgments under appeal

17.130 Article 30 of the Convention is reproduced as Article 37 of Council Regulation (EC) 44/2001.

(b) Enforcement under the Conventions

(i) Procedure

17.132 Articles 31–49 of the Convention are reproduced, with amendments, as Articles 38–56 of Council Regulation (EC) 44/2001. Enforcement is governed by Civil Jurisdiction and Judgments Order 2001 (SI 2001/3929) Articles 1–5, which substantially reproduce ss 4–8 of the 1982 Act.

n268: Article 53 of Council Regulation (EC) 44/2001 now specifies the documents required; and RSC Ord 71 r 28 is replaced by CPR 74.4.

(ii) First application without notice

17.133 Article 34 of the Convention is reproduced in altered form as Article 41 of Council Regulation (EC) 44/2001, but the court applied to may not investigate the possible bars to recognition. Article 35 of the Convention is reproduced as Article 42 of the Regulation.

n269: RSC Ord 71 rr 46, 47 are replaced by CPR 74.3.

(iii) Appeal against the result of the first application

17.134 The right of appeal is conferred on both sides by Article 43 of Council Regulation (EC) 44/2001.

(iv) Further appeal on a point of law

17.135 The further appeal is provided by Article 44 of Council Regulation (EC) 44/2001.

(v) Other procedural points during enforcement

17.136 Article 39 is reproduced as Article 46 of Council Regulation (EC) 44/2001, though the power to stay the proceedings or grant conditional enforcement is extended to the court hearing the further appeal, reversing the effect of Case C-439/93 *SISRO v Ampersand Software BV* [1995] ECR I-2269 (see Main Work n270).

(3) Recognition and Enforcement at Common Law

(a) Recognition of judgments

(i) International jurisdiction

The Supreme Court of Canada has confirmed that this principle applies equally to judgments from countries outside Canada: *Beals v Saldanha* (2004) 234 DLR (4th) 1. **17.139**

A defendant who issues an application to contest jurisdiction must prosecute it if he is to be held to not have submitted by appearance: *Starlight International Inc v Bruce* [2002] Intl Litigation Procedure 617. **17.140**

(ii) Defences to recognition

n295: *Keele v Findley* was considered to have been wrongly decided in *Ki Won Yoon v Yong Dung Song* (2000) 158 FLR 296 (Aust Fed Ct). But the Supreme Court of Canada has followed the approach in *Keele v Findley*, and has restricted the other grounds of objection to a foreign judgment, in *Beals v Saldanha* (2004) 234 DLR (4th) 1. **17.147**

For the potential impact of European Convention on Human Rights, Article 6, see *Pellegrini v Italy* (2002) 35 EHRR 44, ECHR (duty to deny recognition to decision of Vatican tribunal). The issue was apparently overlooked in *Government of the USA v Montgomery (No 2)* [2003] 1 WLR 1916, CA (under appeal to House of Lords). **17.150**

(b) Action to enforce the judgment

(i) Final judgments

On the finality of default judgments, see *Schnabel v Lui* [2002] NSWSC 15, 1 February 2002, NSW SC. **17.154**

(ii) Money judgments

On penal damages ordered in favour of claimant, see *Schnabel v Lui* [2002] NSWSC 15, 1 February 2002, NSW SC (not enforced); on Protection of Trading Interests Act 1980, s 5, see *Lewis v Eliades* [2003] EWCA Civ 1758, [2004] 1 WLR 692, CA. **17.155**

n316: amended by the Reciprocal Enforcement of Foreign Judgments (Israel)(Amendment) Order 2003, SI 2003/2618. **17.159**

D. Contracts

(3) *Choice of Law*

(b) Contractual obligations

17.165 The Convention applies to the assignment of rights under contracts, which may not have a separate, proprietary, characterization which would remove them from the domain of the Convention: *Raiffeisen Zentralbank Oesterreich AG v Five Star Trading LLC* [2001] EWCA Civ 68, [2001] QB 825.

(c) Concurrent liability

17.166 Concurrent liability was treated as being unaffected by the Rome Convention in *Base Metal Trading Ltd v Shamurin* [2002] CLC 322. But for a fuller analysis, see *Base Metal Trading Ltd v Shamurin* [2003] EWHC 2419 (Comm), [2004] 1 All ER (Comm) 159; and also Briggs, 'Choice of Choice of Law ?' [2003] LMCLQ 12.

(f) The applicable law

(i) Express choice

17.169 See also now *Marubeni Hong Kong & South China Ltd v Mongolian Government* [2002] 2 All ER (Comm) 873 (choice of English jurisdiction means a good arguable case that English law was chosen to govern the contract).

(ii) No express choice

17.170 For the difference between connections to a country and to a law, see *Credit Lyonnais v New Hampshire Insurance Co* [1997] 2 Lloyd's Rep 1, CA.

In a distributorship contract, the characteristic performance is that of the vendor and not the distributor: *Print Concept GmbH v GEW (EC) Ltd* [2001] EWCA Civ 352, [2002] CLC 352; a view accepted by the French Cour de Cassation: *Optelec v Soc Midtronics BV* [2003] Intl Litigation Procedure 57.

On the operation of Article 4.2, see also *Lincoln National Life Insurance Co v Employers' Reinsurance Corp*, 5 February 2002 (Article 4.2 inapplicable where reinsurer had multiple places of business). The presumption in Article 4.2 will not be displaced by Article 4.5, in favour of the law of the country with which the contract is more closely connected, unless there is a clear preponderance of factors pointing to that country: *Samcrete Egypt Engineers and Contractors SAE v Land Rover Exports Ltd* [2001] EWCA Civ 2019, 21 December 2001, CA; *Ennstone Building Products Ltd v Stanger Ltd* [2002] EWCA Civ 916, [2002] 1 WLR 3059, CA; *Iran Continental Shelf Oil Co v IRI International Corp* [2002] EWCA Civ 1024, CA. An even more restrictive view was preferred in Scotland: *Caledonia Subsea Ltd v Microperi Srl* 2002 SLT 1022 (Inner House) and in the Netherlands:

Soc Nouvelle des Papéteries de l'Aa SA v BV Maschinenfabriek BOA, 1992 Nederlandse Jurisprudentie 750 (noted Struycken [1996] LMCLQ 18).

On the correct application of Article 4.2 in cases where a contract is performed by a company through a place of business other than the one through which the contract was made, contrast *Iran Continental Shelf Oil Co v IRI International Corp* [2002] EWCA Civ 1024, CA (sufficient if the parties understood that this was to be the manner of performance) with *Ennstone Building Products Ltd v Stanger Ltd* [2002] EWCA Civ 916, [2002] 1 WLR 3059, CA (necessary for the contract to make it a specific requirement that the performance be done this way).

(v) General overriding of applicable law

The relevant provisions of the Financial Services Act 1986 are superseded by Financial Services and Markets Act 2000, ss 26, 27. **17.175**

n365: see also the Unfair Terms in Consumer Contracts Regulations 1999, SI 1999/2083 (enacting Directive 93/13/EC: [1993] OJ L95/29).

(g) Domain of applicable law

(ii) Validity

On Article 8.2, see *Welex AG v Rosa Maritime Ltd* [2003] EWCA Civ 938, [2003] 2 Lloyd's Rep 509 (not unreasonable to apply the applicable law to the issue of consent). **17.177**

E. Torts

(3) Choice of Law: Defamation (and Pre-1996 Torts)

nn391, 392: *Berezovsky v Forbes Inc* [1999] Intl Litigation Procedure 358, CA, was affirmed (*sub nom Berezovsky v Michaels*): [2000] 1 WLR 1004, HL. **17.182**

(a) English torts

nn391, 394: now affirmed (*sub nom Berezovsky v Michaels)* [2000] 1 WLR 1004, HL. For internet defamation, and the principle that each reading is a separate tort, see *Gutnick v Dow Jones & Co Inc* (2003) 210 CLR 575 (Aust HC). **17.183**

(4) Choice of Law: All Other Torts

(b) General rule

For the operation of s 11(2)(c), see *Morin v Bonhams & Brooks Ltd* [2003] EWCA Civ 1802, 18 December 2003 (rule requires a judicial value judgment about the significance of the elements of the tort). **17.189**

(c) Displacement of the general rule

17.192 For illustration, *Edmunds v Simmonds* [2001] 1 WLR 1003.

(d) Exclusion of certain laws

17.193 Quantification of damages remains governed by the *lex fori*: *Edmunds v Simmonds* [2001] 1 WLR 1003; so too for the issue of deduction of social security benefits from the sum assessed as compensation: *Roerig v Valiant Trawlers Ltd* [2002] EWCA Civ 21, [2002] 1 WLR 2304, CA.

F. Other Obligations

(3) Equitable Obligations

17.199 For discussion, see *Grupo Torras SA v Al-Sabah* [2001] CLC 221, CA; *Kuwait Oil Tanker SAK v Al-Bader* [2000] 2 All ER (Comm) 271, CA. These difficult cases appear to blend the proper law of the relationship, the law of the place of acting, and English law, into a pragmatic choice of law rule, and to that extent they do not clearly support the distinction proposed at the end of the paragraph in the Main Work. But see also *Base Metal Trading Ltd v Shamurin* [2003] EWHC 2419 (Comm), [2004] 1 All ER (Comm) 159, generally consistent with the view in this paragraph of the Main Work.

G. Property

(2) Immoveable Property

(a) Jurisdiction and title to immoveable property

17.202 Article 16.1 of the Conventions is reproduced as Article 22.1 of Council Regulation (EC) 44/2001 (as to which, see Supplement paras 17.31–17.84).

(3) Moveable Property

(a) Tangible moveables

17.205 See also *Air Foyle Ltd v Genstar Capital Ltd* [2002] EWHC 2535, [2003] 2 Lloyd's Rep 753 (title acquired by Dutch judicial sale).

(i) Exceptions

17.206 *Glencore International AG v Metro Trading Inc* [2001] 1 Lloyd's Rep 283 refused to create any further exceptions to the general rule of the *lex situs*; and confirms that the *lex situs* rule applied to original modes of acquisition.

(b) Intangible moveables

Raiffeisen Zentralbank Oesterreich AG v Five Star Trading LLC [2001] EWCA Civ 68, [2001] QB 825 held that the effect of an assignment of rights under an insurance policy fell under the Rome Convention, and did not have a proprietary, choice of law rule. The view analysed in Main Work para 17.210 was disapproved. **17.208**

The *situs* is critical when applying for a third party debt order (formerly a garnishee order), for the order may only be made if the debt is situated in England. Its *situs* is at the debtor's residence: *Soc Eram Shipping Ltd v Compagnie Internationale de Navigation* [2003] UKHL 30, [2004] 1 AC 260, HL.

(ii) Intellectual property

See also *Peer International Corp v Termidor Music Publishers Ltd* [2003] EWCA Civ 1156, [2004] 1 WLR 849, CA (applied *situs* rule to Cuban attempt to expropriate English copyright). **17.212**

(4) Seizure and Confiscation of Property

n453: see now also *Kuwait Airways Corp v Iraqi Airways Co (Nos 4 and 5)* [2002] UKHL 19, [2002] 2 AC 883; *Peer International Corp v Termidor Music Publishers Ltd* [2003] EWCA Civ 1156, CA, [2004] 1 WLR 849. **17.213**

To order garnishment of a debt situated outside England would be to order the extra-territorial confiscation of property, and such an order cannot be properly made: *Soc Eram Shipping Ltd v Compagnie Internationale de Navigation* [2003] UKHL 30, [2004] 1 AC 260, HL.

The *situs* of a debt is at the debtor's residence: *Soc Eram Shipping Ltd v Compagnie Internationale de Navigation* [2003] UKHL 30, [2004] 1 AC 260, which also held that if the debt was outside the jurisdiction it could not be made the subject of a third party debt order (CPR Part 72, superseding garnishment under RSC Ord 49). **17.215**

H. Family Law

(2) Marriage

(d) Previous marriage

Where recognition falls under Chapter III of Council Regulation (EC) 1347/2000 (as to which, see Supplement para 17.234), Family Law Act 1986 does not apply: European Communities (Matrimonial Jurisdiction and Judgments) Regulations 2001, SI 2001/310, reg 9. It is unclear whether this also serves to exclude s 50 of the Act, but if this is the result, it is uncertain what effect this has on capacity to remarry. **17.231**

(3) *Matrimonial Causes*

(a) Jurisdiction of English courts

17.234 Legislation has altered the jurisdiction of English courts. Main Work para 17.234 is to be replaced with the following text:

The jurisdiction of an English court to grant a decree of divorce, separation, or annulment is governed by Council Regulation (EC) 1347/2000 ([2000] OJ L160/19). If the respondent spouse is habitually resident in a member state (other than Denmark) of the EU, or is a national of a member state other than the United Kingdom or Ireland, or is domiciled in the United Kingdom or Ireland, Article 7 provides that jurisdiction may be taken only in accordance with Articles 2–6 of the Regulation. A court therefore has jurisdiction if both spouses are domiciled in England; if England is where the spouses are habitually resident, or is where they were last habitually resident, insofar as one of them still resides there; or is where the respondent is habitually resident; or is where (in the event of a joint application) either of the spouses is habitually resident; or is where the applicant is, and for a year immediately before the application was made, was, habitually resident; or is where the applicant, who is domiciled in England, was habitually resident for six months immediately prior to the application. If none of these applies, the court has no jurisdiction. If they give jurisdiction to the English courts and those of another member state, Article 11 provides for a first-seised rule to meet any problem of *lis alibi pendens.*

If the respondent is not habitually resident in (or domiciled in or a national of) a member state, Article 8 provides that 'residual' jurisdiction to divorce is a matter for national law. In England this will require that either party to the marriage was domiciled in England on the date the proceedings were begun (Domicile and Matrimonial Proceedings Act 1973, s 5(2) as amended by the European Communities (Matrimonial Jurisdiction and Judgments) Regulations 2001, SI 2001/310, reg 3(4)). Jurisdiction to annul is substantially the same. *Lis alibi pendens* in another member state is regulated by Article 11. Subject to that overriding rule, the 1973 Act gives an English court a statutory power to stay proceedings on *forum conveniens* grounds.

(ba) Recognition of judgments in matrimonial causes

17.235A Two statutory schemes govern the recognition of foreign judgments given in matrimonial causes. A decree from a member state of the EU, in proceedings instituted after 1 March 2001, will be recognized under Council Regulation (EC) 1347/2000 (as to which see Supplement para 17.234). In all other cases, recognition is governed by Family Law Act 1986, Part III.

(bb) Council Regulation (EC) 1347/2000

The scheme of the Regulation follows the rules for recognition of judgments in civil and commercial matters under Council Regulation (EC) 44/2001. A divorce, separation or annulment pronounced by a court (including a non-judicial tribunal: Article 1.2) in a member state is recognized (Article 14). Article 15 permits non-recognition if recognition is manifestly contrary to public policy; if the judgment was given in default of appearance and there was no due and timely service, unless the respondent has unequivocally accepted the judgment; if the judgment is irreconcilable with a local judgment in proceedings between the same parties; or if it is irreconcilable with an earlier judgment from a non-member state in proceedings between the same parties and which qualified for recognition. The jurisdiction of the adjudicating court may not be reviewed nor subjected to the test of public policy (Article 17); recognition may not be withheld on the basis that the recognizing court would not itself have granted the decree (Article 18); and the substance of the judgment may not be reviewed (Article 19). It is not said whether the obligation to recognize a decree means that the parties to the former marriage have restored to them their capacity to marry, even if the personal law of one of them would not acknowledge it. **17.235B**

The remainder of this section deals with recognition of decrees falling outside the Council Regulation: principally decrees obtained within the British Islands, and outside the courts and tribunals of member states of the EU.

(d) Foreign decrees and proceedings

(ii) Decrees obtained without proceedings

n546: this requirement was read minimally in *Wicken v Wicken* [1999] Fam 224. **17.239**

(4) Financial Provision and Maintenance

(a) Jurisdiction of English courts

Council Regulation (EC) 1347/2000 (as to which see Supplement para 17.235B) has no application to proceedings in respect of financial provision. **17.240**

(5) Children

(a) Guardianship and custody

A court which is exercising matrimonial jurisdiction under Council Regulation (EC) 1347/2000 (as to which see Supplement para 17.235B) may also have ancillary jurisdiction over a matter of parental responsibility. If the child is the child of both parents and habitually resident in the member state whose courts are seised, Article 3.1 gives that court jurisdiction. If the child is not so habitually resident, **17.243**

Article 3.2 gives the court jurisdiction if the child is habitually resident in a member state, at least one of the spouses has parental responsibility, and the jurisdiction has been accepted by the spouses and is in the best interests of the child. This jurisdiction ceases once the matrimonial proceedings have terminated.

The remainder of the paragraph in the Main Work applies to jurisdiction outside the provisions of the Regulation.

(b) Foreign Orders

17.244 For the purposes of recognition of foreign orders under Council Regulation (EC) 1347/2000 (as to which see Supplement para 17.235B), a judgment relating to parental responsibility will be recognized under Chapter III of the Regulation, subject to the same minimal objections as may be made in the case of a matrimonial decree recognized under Chapter III.

(c) Abduction

17.245 See also *Re H (Child Abduction: Rights of Custody)* [2000] 2 AC 291.

I. Corporations and Insolvency

(1) Corporations

(c) Dissolution and amalgamation

17.250 See also *Wight v Eckhardt Marine* [2004] 1 AC 147, PC.

(d) Domicile of corporations

17.251 **n586**: but for jurisdiction under Council Regulation (EC) 44/2001 (as to which see Supplement paras 17.31–17.84), and alterations to the definition of a company's domicile, see Supplement paras 17.39 and 17.40.

(e) Jurisdiction over corporations

17.252 **n588**: see now also *Sea Assets Ltd v PT Garuda International* [2000] 4 All ER 371.

(iii) Companies with seats in contracting states

17.255 For cases to which Council Regulation (EC) 44/2001 (as to which see Supplement paras 17.31–17.84) applies, Article 22.2 reproduces Article 16.2 of the Convention.

(g) Winding-up by English court

17.258 A solvent company with its seat in a member state bound by Council Regulation

(EC) 44/2001 (as to which see Supplement paras 17.31–17.84) may only be wound up if the court has jurisdiction under that Regulation.

The law on the winding-up of insolvent companies is complicated by Council Regulation (EC) 1346/2000 on Insolvency Proceedings ([2000] OJ L160/1), in force from 31 May 2002: the Regulation will not apply to proceedings which predate its entry into force. It prescribes the jurisdiction of the courts of member states of the EU (excluding Denmark) in relation to the opening of insolvency proceedings; the choice of law for the insolvency proceedings; and the recognition of judgments from other member states ordering the opening, conduct, and closure of such proceedings.

The Regulation applies to collective insolvency proceedings which involve the complete or partial divestment of a debtor and the appointment of a liquidator or administrative receiver, whether the debtor is an individual or a corporate body. It applies to debtors wherever domiciled, but it is restricted to cases in which 'the centre of a debtor's main interests' is located in a member state. 'Main proceedings' may be opened only in the member state in which the centre of a debtor's main interests is situated; 'secondary' or 'territorial' proceedings may be opened in any member state in which the debtor has an 'establishment'; their effect is confined to assets situated in the member state in which the secondary or territorial proceedings are opened. The *lex fori* is generally applicable to insolvency proceedings.

On the jurisdictional criteria established by the Regulation, see *Re Brac Rent-a-Car International Inc (2003)* [2003] EWHC 128 (Ch), [2003] 1 WLR 1421; *Skeversland v Geveran Trading Co Ltd (No 3)* [2003] BCC 209; *Re Daisytek-Isa Ltd*, 16 May 2003; *Re Salvage Association* [2003] EWHC 1028 (Ch).

The law described in the Main Work will continue to apply where the Regulation does not prescribe the jurisdiction of the court.

(h) Foreign winding-up

According to Council Regulation (EC) 1346/2000 (as to which see Supplement para 17.258), an order from a court in a member state opening insolvency proceedings must be recognized, and be given the same effect as it has in the state of origin. Judgments relating to the conduct and closure of insolvency proceedings will be recognized in all other member states, and their enforcement is to take place under Council Regulation (EC) 44/2001 (as to which see Supplement paras 17.31–17.84). The status of a liquidator appointed in the main proceedings will be recognized. **17.259**

The law described in the Main Work will continue to apply where the Regulation does not apply to the foreign winding-up of an insolvent company.

(2) Insolvency

(a) Jurisdiction

17.260–17.263 Council Regulation (EC) 1346/2000 (as to which see Supplement para 17.258) applies to bankruptcy as well as to corporate insolvencies. The summary of its provisions given at Supplement para 17.258 is equally applicable to bankruptcies.

The law described in the Main Work will continue to apply where the Regulation does not apply to the insolvency.

(b) Choice of law

17.261 See also *Jeeves v Official Receiver*, 30 July 2003 (application for public examination under Insolvency Act 1986, s 133 not restricted by considerations of the conflict of laws, and court must accede to application unless persuaded that no useful purpose will be served by making the order). And see also *Re Drax Holdings Ltd* [2003] EWHC 2743 (Ch) (application to summon creditor meeting and to sanction scheme under Companies Act 1985, s 425).

18

JUDICIAL REMEDIES

A. A General Survey

(1) Introduction

For a rigorous analysis of the concept of a judicial remedy, see R Zakrzewski, 'The Classification of Judicial Remedies' [2003] LMCLQ 477. **18.01**

(2) Pre-Trial and Post-Trial Judicial Remedies

n10: see now also *Series 5 Software v Laddie* [1996] 1 All ER 853. **18.04**

(3) Judicial Remedies Available at Trial

(a) General

In the Main Work the references to paras 18.10–18.13 is to be replaced by a reference to paras 18.10–18.15. **18.09**

n29: if rescission is barred, so are damages under s 2(2) of the Misrepresentation Act 1967: *Govt of Zanzibar v British Aerospace (Lancaster House) Ltd* [2000] 1 WLR 2333. **18.12**

(b) Restitutionary remedies to reverse (autonomous) unjust enrichment

18.14 The fiction referred to in item (1) of the list in the Main Work has, however, been invoked in *Foskett v McKeown* [2001] 1 AC 102, HL. A fraudulent trustee had taken money from a trust fund held by him for the claimants, mixed it with his own in bank accounts, and used it to pay premiums on a life insurance policy (on his life). When he later committed suicide, the defendants (his children) were paid out £1 million under the insurance policy. The claimants argued that they were entitled to a share of the £1 million proportionate to the premiums that, in breach of trust, had been paid using the trust money. Their claim succeeded before the House of Lords by a three to two majority. Each of their Lordships in the majority expressly said that they were applying rules of property and that the claim was not one to reverse unjust enrichment. But, with respect, this was to invoke a fiction. See A Burrows, 'Proprietary Restitution: Unmasking Unjust Enrichment' (2001) 117 LQR 412.

18.15 **n43**: see now also A Burrows, *The Law of Restitution* (2nd edn, 2002) 64–75; P Birks, *Unjust Enrichment* (2003) ch 8.

B. Compensation

(1) Compensatory Damages:Breach of Contract

(a) The compensatory aim

(i) Protection of the expectation interest

18.21 **n53**: for an interesting example of punitive damages being awarded for breach of contract by the Supreme Court of Canada, see *Whiten v Pilot Insurance Co* (2002) 209 DLR (4th) 257.

n54: the correct reference for *Attorney-General v Blake* is [2001] 1 AC 268. See also now *Experience Hendrix LLC v PPX Enterprises Inc* [2003] 1 All ER (Comm) 830.

(ii) Difference in value or cost of cure

18.23 **n57**: the ignoring of resales in *Slater v Hoyle and Smith* [1920] 2 KB 11, CA, was doubted in *Bence Graphics Int Ltd v Fasson UK Ltd* [1998] QB 87, CA.

(iii) Loss of a chance

18.28 **n64**: see now also *Sharif v Garrett & Co* [2002] 1 WLR 3118, CA (solicitors' negligence in handling litigation); *John D Wood & Co Ltd v Knatchbull* [2003] 8 EG 131 (action in contract and tort for surveyor's negligence).

18.29 The second sentence should be amended to read: 'In *Chaplin v Hicks*, the uncertainty was treated as if it was over a hypothetical decision of a third party . . .'

(b) Limiting principles

(iv) Contributory negligence

n94: the correct reference to *UCB Bank plc v Hepherd Winstanley & Pugh* is [1999] Lloyd's Rep PN 963, CA. **18.51**

(v) Mental distress

Johnson v Gore Wood & Co [2001] 2 WLR 72, 96–7, HL authoritatively confirms **18.53–** that, subject to the exceptions recognized in *Watts v Morrow* [1991] 1 WLR 1421, **18.55** 1445, CA (most importantly, where the very object of the contract is to provide pleasure, peace of mind, or freedom from distress) mental distress damages cannot be awarded for breach of contract (and *Addis v Gramophone Co Ltd* [1909] AC 488 therefore largely remains good law).

In relation to the facts of *Addis v Gramophone Co Ltd* itself, which concerned a wrongful dismissal, the House of Lords in *Johnson v Unisys Ltd* [2003] 1 AC 518 has held that, whatever the normal position at common law, wrongful dismissal is a special case because of the need to avoid undermining the statutory regime of unfair dismissal. In other words, there is a special reason for denying mental distress damages (and other damages, eg, for psychiatric illness or loss of reputation) for wrongful dismissal. For decisions as to whether there has been a breach of the employment contract, causing psychiatric illness, that is sufficiently distinct from wrongful or unfair dismissal as to fall outside the *Unisys* bar to damages, see, eg, *Gogay v Hertfordshire CC* [2000] IRLR 703, CA, *Eastwood v Magnox Electric plc* [2002] IRLR 447, *McCabe v Cornwall CC* [2003] PIQR P19.

In *Farley v Skinner* [2001] 3 WLR 899, HL the claimant, who was considering buying a home 15 miles from Gatwick Airport, engaged the defendant as his surveyor. He specifically asked the surveyor to investigate whether the property was in fact affected by aircraft noise. The surveyor reported that it was unlikely that the property would suffer greatly from such noise. After moving in, the claimant discovered that the house was substantially affected by airport noise. Aircraft frequently passed directly over, or nearly over, the house. It was a 'confounded nuisance'. The surveyor was held negligent and in breach of contract and the question was what damages the claimant was entitled to. He had decided not to sell and it was found that he had suffered no financial loss (that is, he had paid the market value of the property where that value took into account the aircraft noise). But the House of Lords upheld the first instance judge's award of £10,000 for mental distress. The principal point laid down by the House of Lords was that the main exceptional category set out in *Watts v Morrow* extends not only to where the very object of the contract is peace of mind but also to where *an important object*—albeit not *the very object*—of the contract is peace of mind. Here, although being satisfied as to the aircraft noise was not the very object of the contract, it was an important object of the contract. The House of Lords further decided that the other exceptional situation applied in *Watts v Morrow*, where the breach of contract causes physical inconvenience, discomfort and consequent distress, also applied to this case. Aircraft noise causes physical inconvenience because that phrase should be interpreted in a wide sense to include matter detrimentally affecting sight, hearing, or smell.

(vi) Loss of reputation

18.61 In *Johnson v Unisys Ltd* [2001] 2 WLR 1076, HL it was held that damages for loss of reputation (so-called 'stigma damages') awarded to ex-employees of BCCI in *Malik v Bank of Credit and Commerce International SA* [1998] AC 20, HL could not be awarded where the claim was for wrongful dismissal (rather than for breach of an implied term of trust and confidence owed by an employer to its employees). The statutory regime for unfair dismissal would otherwise be undermined.

(viii) No damages beyond the defendant's minimum contractual obligation

18.68 **n122**: cf *Lion Nathan Ltd v C–C Bottlers Ltd* [1996] 1 WLR 1438, PC.

(c) **Additional issues**

(i) Compensating advantages

18.72 **n126**: see also *Hussey v Eels* [1990] 2 QB 227; *Gardner v Marsh & Parsons* [1997] 1 WLR 489; *Needler Financial Services Ltd v Taber* [2002] 3 All ER 501; *Primavera v Allied Dunbar Assurance plc* [2002] EWCA Civ 1327.

(ii) Damages in a contract for the benefit of a third party

18.77 **n132**: see now *Alfred McAlpine Construction Ltd v Panatown Ltd* [2001] 1 AC 518, HL. For contrasting views of this decision, see B Coote, 'The Performance Interest, *Panatown*, and the Problem of Loss' (2000) 117 LQR 81; A Burrows, 'No Damages for a Third Party's Loss' (2001) Oxford University Commonwealth Law Journal 107.

(2) Compensatory Damages: Torts

(a) **The compensatory aim and limiting principles**

(i) The compensatory aim

18.80 **n134**: the correct reference for *Smith New Court Securities Ltd v Scrimgeour Vickers (Asset Management) Ltd* is [1997] AC 254, HL.

18.81 **n136**: see now *Sharif v Garrett & Co* [2002] 1 WLR 3118, CA; *John D Wood & Co Ltd v Knatchbull* [2003] 8 EG 131.

18.82 **n137**: see now also *Gregg v Scott* [2002] EWCA Civ 1471.

(ii) Limiting principles

n149: see also now *Geest plc v Lansiquot* [2002] 1 WLR 3111, PC. It was there held that the claimant had not been unreasonable (and therefore had not failed in her duty to mitigate) in refusing an operation on her back where the doctor had made plain that surgery could not guarantee a cure and where he was clearly ready to respect her decision if she decided against the operation. The Privy Council also clarified that, contrary to *Selvanayagam v University of West Indies* [1983] 1 WLR 585, the burden of proof in relation to the duty to mitigate is on the defendant not the claimant. **18.87**

n152: the rule in *The Liesbosch* [1933] AC 449, HL—that loss flowing from impecuniosity cannot be compensated—has finally been removed by the House of Lords in *Lagden v O'Connor* [2003] 3 WLR 1571, HL. All of their Lordships agreed on the removal of that rule. The majority (Lords Nicholls, Slynn and Hope) went on to hold that where a claimant, whose car has been tortiously damaged, reasonably wishes to hire a replacement car but, because of lack of funds, has no real choice other than to hire through an accident-hire scheme, he can recover the costs incurred in so doing. This is so even though those costs are higher (and include incidental benefits) than the normal costs of hiring a replacement car. The minority (Lords Scott and Walker) held that *Dimond v Lovell* [2002] 1 AC 384, HL, could not be distinguished and that therefore only the normal hiring costs (the 'spot-rate' of hire) could be recovered.

The denial that contributory negligence can apply to the tort of deceit in *Alliance and Leicester Building Society v Edgestop Ltd* [1993] 1 WLR 1462 was approved in *Standard Chartered Bank v Pakistan National Shipping Co (No 4)* [2002] 3 WLR 1547, HL. It would seem that the suggestion in *Murphy v Culhane* [1977] QB 94, that contributory negligence might reduce damages for intentional trespass to the person, should be regarded as incorrect after the *Standard Chartered Bank* case (see esp at [2002] 3 WLR 1547, [45]). **18.94**

n166: an apparent exception is where there is concurrent liability in contract and the tort of negligence. Mental distress damages are presumably recoverable in the tort action provided they would be recoverable in that situation for breach of contract. See *Perry v Sidney Phillips & Son* [1982] 1 WLR 1297; *Johnson v Gore Wood & Co* [2001] 1 All ER 481, 516 (*per* Lord Cooke). **18.96**

For the logical view that there can be no separate award of aggravated damages over and above a general award for injury to feelings, see *McConnell v Police Authority for Northern Ireland* [1997] IRLR 625, 629; *Gbaja-Biamila v DHL International (UK) Ltd* [2000] ICR 730. **18.97**

(b) Damages for personal injury

(i) Damages for pecuniary loss

18.107 Exercising his powers under s 1(1) of the Damages Act 1996, the Lord Chancellor set a discount rate of 2.5% as from 28 June 2001: see the Damages (Personal Injury) Order 2001, SI 2001/2301. For the Lord Chancellor's reasons for setting that discount rate, see www.lcd.gov.uk/civil/discount.htm. Although, by s 1(2) of the Damages Act 1996, a court may apply a different rate from that set if it is 'more appropriate in the case in question', the Court of Appeal has shown no willingness to depart from the 2.5% rate: see *Warriner v Warriner* [2002] 1 WLR 1703, CA; *Cooke v United Bristol Health Care* [2004] 1 WLR 25, CA.

18.108 **n183**: see now *Actuarial Tables for Use in Personal Injury and Fatal Accidents Cases* (4th edn, 2000).

(ii) Damages for non-pecuniary loss

18.112 The sixth edition of *Guidelines for the Assessment of General Damages in Personal Injury Cases* was published in 2002.

(iii) Compensating advantages

18.114 The second sentence should read: 'The 1997 Act basically lays down . . .'

n194: see now *Clenshaw v Tanner* [2002] EWCA Civ 1848 in which housing benefit (which is not listed in the Social Security (Recovery of Benefits) Act 1997) was deducted from the claimant's loss of earnings.

(v) Provisional damages

18.117 In March 2002 the Lord Chancellor's Department issued a consultation paper proposing that the courts should be given the power to order reviewable periodical payments, irrespective of either party's consent, in respect of damages for future pecuniary loss in personal injury and death cases. These proposals have been implemented, from a day to be appointed, by s 100 of the Courts Act 2003, which inserts new ss 2, 2A and 2B into the Damages Act 1996. The details of when periodical payments will be appropriate are to be laid down in Civil Procedure Rules; and the details of the reviewability of such periodical payments are to be laid down by the Lord Chancellor in delegated legislation.

(c) Damages for death: Fatal Accidents Act 1976

(ii) Loss of dependency

18.128 In *White v ESAB Group (UK)* Ltd [2002] PIQR Q6 Nelson J, in the light of the views of the Law Commission and the Ogden Working Party, would have preferred to calculate the multiplier from the date of trial but held himself precluded from doing so by *Cookson v Knowles* [1979] AC 556 and *Graham v Dodds* [1983] 1 WLR 808.

As to the discount rate, see Supplement para 18.107.

In *H v S* [2002] 3 WLR 1179 the approach in the leading personal injury case on gratuitous services of *Hunt v Severs* [1994] 2 AC 350 (see Main Work para 18.101) was applied to a Fatal Accidents Act claim. Infant children, following the death of their mother, were receiving care from their father, who was not the tortfeasor and had not previously provided them with any care or support. Although under s 4 of the Fatal Accidents Act 1976 the value of such gratuitous services should not be deducted, the damages in respect of the lost services of the decreased mother were to be held on trust for the gratuitous carer (the father). **18.132**

(iii) Bereavement damages

By the Damages for Bereavement (Variation of Sum) Order 2002, SI 2002/644, the Lord Chancellor increased the fixed sum of bereavement damages from £7,500 to £10,000. **18.135**

(d) Damages for negligent valuation

South Australia Asset Management Corp v York Montague Ltd (the *SAAMCO* case) [1997] AC 191, HL has been applied outside the context of negligent valuation. See, for example, as regards solicitors' negligence, *Bristol & West Building Society v Fancy & Jackson* [1997] 4 All ER 582; *Portman Building Society v Bevan Ashford* [2000] Lloyd's Rep PN 354, CA; *Lloyds Bank plc v Crosse & Crosse* [2001] PNLR 34, CA; as regards insurance brokers' negligence, *Aneco Reinsurance Underwriting Ltd v Johnson & Higgins Ltd* [2001] 2 All ER (Comm) 926, HL; and, more generally, *Blue Circle Industries plc v Ministry of Defence* [1999] Ch 289, CA (only certain types of damage are within the scope of liability under the Nuclear Installations Act 1965). In *Kenny & Good Pty Ltd v MGICA (1992) Ltd* [1999] HCA 25, a negligent valuation case, the *SAAMCO* case was considered and distinguished, but without casting doubt on the actual decision, by the High Court of Australia. See generally E Peel, 'SAAMCO Revisited' and R Butler, 'SAAMCO in Practice' in A Burrows and E Peel (eds), *Commercial Remedies* (2003) 55–87. **18.141**

(e) Damages under the Human Rights Act 1998

Section 6(1) of the 1998 Act creates a new statutory 'tort' constituted by a public authority's infringement of a victim's Convention rights. By s 8(1) the court may grant any remedy, within its powers, as it considers 'just and appropriate'. By s 8(3) no damages are to be awarded unless, taking account of any other remedy granted, the court is satisfied that the award is 'necessary to afford just satisfaction' **18.141A** to the claimant. By s 8(4) the court must take into account in deciding whether to award damages, and the amount, the principles applied by the European Court of Human Rights in relation to the award of compensation. For cases on damages under the Human Rights Act 1998, see, eg, *R (Bernard) v Enfield LBC* [2003] HRLR 4; *R (KB) v Mental Health Review Tribunal* [2003] 2 All ER 209; *Anufrijeva v London Borough of Southwark* [2004] 1 All ER 833, CA.

(3) Equitable Compensation

18.143 **n236**: see also S Elliott, 'Remoteness Criteria in Equity' (2002) 65 MLR 588.

18.146 **n242**: cf *Pilmer v The Duke Group Ltd* (2001) 75 ALJR 1067, High Court of Australia.

(4) Equitable (Compensatory) Damages

18.150 Although reversed on liability by the House of Lords [2003] 3 WLR 1603, there was an interesting discussion at first instance of the power to award equitable damages for an anticipated wrong in *Marcic v Thames Water Utilities Ltd (No 2)* [2002] 2 WLR 1000. The claimant owned a property that was regularly subject to flooding. In an action against the defendant sewerage undertaker, the claimant sought damages and a mandatory injunction ordering the defendant to implement a scheme to stop the flooding. Judge Richard Havery QC held that the defendant was liable in tort under the Human Rights Act 1998 but refused a mandatory injunction on the ground that this would require supervision by the court. As regards damages, he held that these should be awarded for both past and future torts. The claimant was therefore entitled to the difference between the value his property would have had if rendered non-susceptible to wrongful flooding minus its actual value. As regards the damages for the future flooding caused by the future torts, these were being awarded in substitution for the mandatory injunction. The judge was satisfied that the defendant would commit the future torts because it did not intend to carry out works necessary to remedy the flooding. He rejected the argument that he should follow the common law and refuse equitable damages for future wrongs; and he also rejected a novel argument that to award damages for future wrongs would be contrary to jurisprudence on the European Convention on Human Rights.

18.151 **n252**: see now also *Campbell v MGN Ltd* [2004] UKHL 22 and *Douglas v Hello! Ltd (No 3)* [2003] 3 All ER 996 in which it was accepted that 'aggravated damages' (see Main Work para 18.97) can be awarded for breach of confidence.

C. Specific Enforcement, Prevention and Restoration

(1) Award of an Agreed Sum

(a) Award of an agreed price

n259: see also now *Ocean Marine Navigation Ltd v Koch Carbon Inc, The Dynamic*, [2003] 2 Lloyd's Rep 693, [23]. **18.161**

(3) Injunctions

(a) Prohibitory injunctions

(ii) Torts

n321: the correct reference for *Coxflexip SA v Stolt Connex Seaway MS Ltd* is now [2001] 1 All ER 952 (note). **18.194**

Dennis v Ministry of Defence [2003] EWHC 793, (2003) 153 NLJ 634 is a rare and extreme case where the court did refuse a declaration (treated as being equivalent to an injunction) in respect of a nuisance because of the strong public interest involved. Buckley J held that the operations of RAF Wittering, where Harrier fighter pilots are trained, did constitute a private nuisance (because of the noise) to the claimant who lived nearby. But the declaration sought was refused because of the strong public interest (that is, the defence of the realm) in the continuation of training at RAF Wittering. Instead, damages of £950,000 (including £50,000 for 'loss of amenity') were awarded. **18.195**

D. Other Relief for Wrongs: Restitution; Punishment; Declaring Rights

(1) Restitution for Wrongs

n372: see now J Edelman, *Gain-Based Damages* (2002) who prefers, as a general label, 'gain-based damages' with a subdivision between 'disgorgement damages' and 'resitutionary damages'. **18.219**

(a) Enrichments gained by a tort

(i) Proprietary torts other than those protecting intellectual property

n382: the reference should be updated to Lord Goff of Chieveley and G Jones, *The Law of Restitution* (6th edn, 2002) 36-003. **18.226**

n385: the references should be updated to A Burrows, *The Law of Restitution* (2nd edn, 2002) 474, 480; Lord Goff of Chieveley and G Jones, *The Law of Restitution* (6th edn, 2002) 36-006.

(c) Enrichments gained by a breach of contract

18.235 See also *Amec Developments Ltd v Jury's Hotel Management (UK) Ltd* (2001) 82 P & CR 22.

n418: a restitutionary interpretation of the *Wrotham Park* case was taken in *Attorney-General v Blake* [2001] 1 AC 268.

18.237 **n419**: the reference should be updated to, cf Lord Goff of Chieveley and G Jones, *The Law of Restitution* (6th edn, 2002) 20-024–20-034a.

18.238 The reference to *Attorney-General v Blake* is now [2001] 1 AC 268, HL. The *Blake* case has been applied in *Esso Petroleum Co Ltd v Niad Ltd* (Ch D, 22 November 2001). But the most important decision on 'restitutionary damages' since the *Blake* case has been *Experience Hendrix LLC v PPX Enterprises Inc* [2003] 1 All ER (Comm) 830. This case followed from a settlement in 1973 of a dispute between the rock star Jimi Hendrix and the defendant record company. By the terms of that contractual settlement, it was agreed that certain master tapes could be used for recording purposes by the defendant but that the rest should be delivered up to Jimi Hendrix. In breach of that contract, the defendant used master tapes that should have been delivered up. The claimant, the estate of Jimi Hendrix, sought damages or an account of profits for that breach of contract. *Attorney-General v Blake* was in part applied and in part distinguished.

The *Blake* case was applied in holding that the claimant was entitled to damages based not on compensating the claimant's loss but on what was a reasonable sum taking into account the gains made by the defendant from its use of the forbidden master tapes. Although the Court of Appeal was not required to assess that reasonable sum, Mance LJ, with whom Peter Gibson LJ and Hooper J agreed, thought that one-third of the defendant's royalties on the retail selling price of records made from the forbidden tapes would probably be an appropriate reasonable sum. Although there are passages where the judges slipped into referring to these damages as 'compensation', the better view is that they are restitutionary (not compensatory) damages concerned to strip some of the defendant's profits. This is in line not only with counsel for the claimant's starting-point that the claimant was not seeking compensation for loss because that was too speculative to assess but also with the acceptance that the claimant would not have agreed to the defendant's use of those master tapes (see esp Peter Gibson LJ at [57]). It is also consistent with the judges' emphasis on the profits made by the defendant in fixing the reasonable sum and with their regarding themselves as applying *Wrotham Park Estates v Parkside Homes* [1974] 1 WLR 798 (see Main Work para 18.235). So, it is submitted that, to the extent that restitutionary not compensatory damages were awarded, *Blake* was being applied.

But the *Blake* case was also distinguished in the sense that an account of profits, stripping the defendant of *all* its gains made from the breach of contract, was not awarded. The Court of Appeal stressed that the facts of this case were not so exceptional as those in *Blake*. In particular, although the defendant knew it was doing something which it had contracted not to do and to which the claimant would not have consented, the defendant was not close to being a fiduciary to the claimant and no issue analogous to national security was involved. The relationship was a straightforward commercial one. The Court of Appeal also referred to *Esso v Niad Petroleum* without disapproval but distinguished that decision—which involved a commercial relationship—on the ground that the contractual obligation broken had been central to the claimant's whole mode of operation and integrity which was not the position on the facts of this case.

(2) *Punishment*

That exemplary damages may be awarded for an equitable wrong now derives some tentative support from *Douglas v Hello! Ltd (No 3)* [2003] 3 All ER 996. While refusing exemplary damages for breach of confidence on the facts—because the defendants' wrongful conduct had not been sufficiently outrageous—Lindsay J said, at [273]: 'I am content to assume, without deciding, that exemplary damages (or equity's equivalent) are available in respect of breach of confidence.' **18.239**

In *Kuddus v Chief Constable of Leicestershire* [2001] 2 WLR 1789 the House of Lords overruled *AB v South West Water Services Ltd* [1983] QB 507 so that there is no longer a requirement that the tort be one for which exemplary damages had been awarded prior to 1964 (the so-called 'cause of action' test). On the facts of the case this meant that, if the other requirements for the award of exemplary damages were satisfied, exemplary damages could be awarded for the tort of misfeasance in public office. **18.240**

(3) *Declaring Rights*

n463: for the suggested use of an interim declaration under CPR 25.1(1)(b) to resolve a bank's dilemma in not wishing to pay money out to a customer suspected of fraud, see *Bank of Scotland v A Ltd* [2001] 1 WLR 751, CA; cf *Amalgamated Metal Trading Ltd v City of London Police Financial Investigation Unit* [2003] 1 WLR 2771. **18.247**

19

CIVIL PROCEDURE

B. Review of the April 1999 Changes

(6) Case Management and the Multi-Track

(a) The range of the courts' new powers

19.32 **n68**: *GKR Karate (UK) Ltd v Yorkshire Post Ltd* is now reported at [2000] 1 WLR 2571, CA. The *GKR* case illustrates the courts' powers to manage an action. The Court of Appeal upheld the first instance judge's decision in a libel action to consider the defence of qualified privilege as a preliminary question. The trial of all the matters raised in the case would be likely to take four to six weeks, but the defence of qualified privilege, which might be decisive, would take only three days. May LJ at [2000] 1 WLR 2571 at 2576–7 commented:

> . . . libel cases generally have historically been notoriously long drawn out and expensive and are especially amenable to the culture of the new procedural code. They need novel and imaginative case management to achieve what has hitherto often not been achieved . . . A fair means of determining [the question of qualified] privilege . . . expeditiously in this case without having to trudge expensively through the mire of [the defence of] justification achieves the overriding objective.

He also noted CPR 32.1 (court's power to control the evidence) and added at 2577:

> . . . the parties no longer have any absolute right to insist on the calling of any evidence they choose provided only that it is admissible and arguably relevant. The court may exclude admissible and relevant evidence or cross-examination which is disproportionately expensive or time-consuming, provided that to do so accords with the overriding objective.

(7) Impact of the April 1999 Rules in Specific Contexts

(c) Expert witnesses

n99: *Daniels v Walker* is now reported at [2000] 1 WLR 1382, CA. **19.48**

C. Commencement of Proceedings

(2) Issue of Process

n142: on late service of particulars of claim see *Totty v Snowden* [2002] 1 WLR 1384, CA. **19.76**

Date of commencement of proceedings

The amended version of the Brussels jurisdictional regime is now contained in Council Regulation (EC) 44/2001 on jurisdiction and the recognition and enforcement of judgments in civil and commercial matters [2001] OJ L12/1. This Regulation took effect on 1 March 2002. Article 30 introduced a new test for determining the date when proceedings begin: **19.79**

> For the purposes of this Section, a court shall be deemed to be seised:
> (1) at the time when the document instituting the proceedings or an equivalent document is lodged with the court, provided that the [claimant] has not subsequently failed to take the steps he was required to take to have service effected on the defendant, or
> (2) if the document has to be served before being lodged with the court, at the time when it is received by the authority responsible for service, provided that the [claimant] has not subsequently failed to take the steps he was required to take to have the document lodged with the court.

It follows that from February 2002, English proceedings begin, for the purpose of the Brussels jurisdictional regime, when the claimant obtains issue of a claim form, that is on the date entered on the claim form by the court (see CPR 7.2(2)), and not when that process is served on the defendant.

(3) Service of Process

(a) Claim form's period of validity

n150: in *Godwin v Swindon BC* [2002] 1 WLR 997, CA the court considered CPR 6.7(1), which presents a table of dates concerning 'deemed service'. Service **19.81**

by first class post is the commonest mode of service and the one applicable to this case. Here service is deemed to have been effected on the second day after the claim form was posted. (It has recently been held that for this purpose CPR 2.8 does not apply; and so Saturdays, Sundays, and Bank Holidays are included in the relevant two day-period when fixing the date of deemed service: *Anderton v Clwyd CC (No 2)* [2002] 1 WLR 3174, CA, at [15], [37]–[45].)

In the *Godwin* case the Court of Appeal held that a claimant who posts a claim form by first class mail must be deemed to have served this claim in accordance with this fiction, and that the court should not take account of the fact that the claim form was delivered by post earlier that the deemed date. Applying this fiction, the court concluded that the action had become time-barred and so could not be recommenced. The Court of Appeal also considered *Vinos v Marks and Spencer plc*, which is now reported at [2001] 3 All ER 784, CA; *Nanglegan v Royal Free Hampstead NHS Trust* [2002] 1 WLR 1043, CA; *Kaur v CTP Coil Ltd* (CA, [2000] CA transcript 1328); and *Elmes v Hygrade Food Products plc* [2001] EWCA Civ 121.

In *Anderton v Clwyd CC (No 2)* [2002] 1 WLR 3174, CA, the court held that CPR 6.9(1) ('the court may dispense with service of a document') can be applied retrospectively, and not just prospectively. But when the applicant has missed the present deadline, this provision will provide relief only in exceptional circumstances (see [58] and [59]), namely where the attempted service was ineffective, perhaps because of the deemed date rule mentioned above, and provided also that there is no dispute that in fact the relevant defendant received notice of the claim form within the prescribed period. On this topic see also *Wilkey v British Broadcasting Corporation* [2003] 1 WLR 1, CA and *Cranfield v Bridgegrove Ltd* [2003] 3 All ER 129, CA.

(b) Modes of service

19.82 **n161**: PD (6) 3.1–3.4 were replaced, as from 31 July 2003. On an earlier version of the rules concerning service by fax, see *Molins plc v GD SpA* [2000] 1 WLR 1741, CA, [19]–[25], where the court held that it is insufficient that a party's letter heading includes a fax number. A party must provide a fax number 'expressly for the purpose of accepting service' if the present rule is to apply; case noted W Kennett (2001) ICLQ 200–2.

(5) Limitation of Actions

(b) Possible reform

19.95 **n189**: the Law Commission's report on this topic is *Limitation of Actions*, (Law Com No 270, 2001). Its recommendations have not yet been enacted.

(c) The main rules

There has been much recent discussion of these special rules. On the fraud category see *Clef Aquitaine SARL v Laporte Materials (Barrow) Ltd* [2000] 3 All ER 493, 504–6, CA *per* Simon Brown, considering *Paragon Finance plc v DB Thakerar & Co* [1999] 1 All ER 400, 418, CA. **19.97**

The deliberate concealment category was considered in *Cave v Robinson Jarvis & Rolf* [2003] 1 AC 368, HL, [2002] UKHL 18 (on which see T Prime, 'Making "Deliberate Concealment" Concealment which is Deliberate . . .' (2002) 21 CJQ 357). The House of Lords held that these statutory provisions deprive a defendant of a limitation defence in two situations (*per* Lord Millett, ibid at [25]):

> (i) where he takes active steps to conceal his own breach of duty after he has become aware of it; or
> (ii) (a) where he is guilty of deliberate wrongdoing and conceals or (b) fails to disclose it in circumstances where it is unlikely to be discovered for some time.

In situation (i) there is no need for the breach of duty to have been deliberate. In situation (ii)(b), which involves dishonest omission, the breach of duty must have been deliberate. Lord Scott noted the forensic advantage to a claimant in being able to rely on limb (ii)(b), as presented above (ibid, at [60]).

The result is that 'deliberate concealment' does not occur where the defendants commits 'negligence if, being unaware of his error or that he has failed to take proper care, there has been nothing for him to disclose' (*per* Lord Millett). Certainly, 'there is no rational justification for depriving a defendant of a limitation defence where neither his original wrongdoing nor his failure to disclose it to the claimant was deliberate' ([27], *per* Lord Millett). The epithet 'deliberate' does not need to be glossed as 'unconscionably', although Lord Scott commented that it would be difficult to imagine a case falling within the 'deliberate concealment' category which does not savour of bad faith (ibid at [65]).

It should also be noted that in *Sheldon v RHM Outhwaite (Underwriting Agencies) Ltd* [1996] 1 AC 102, the House of Lords had held that if the defendant is guilty of deliberate concealment after the cause of action has arisen, the limitation 'clock' is re-set and the period of limitation starts afresh.

Erroneous decisions

The House of Lords decision in the *Cave* case overruled *Brocklesby v Armitage & Guest* [2002] 1 WLR 598 (Morritt LJ, Wilson J). In the latter case, the Court of Appeal had held that deliberate concealment applies even where the defendant commits an intentional act or is guilty of intentional omission in circumstances where the claimant will be unaware of the breach for some time (followed in *Cave v Robinson Jarvis & Rolf* [2002] 1 WLR 581, CA and applied in *Liverpool Roman* **19.97A**

Catholic Archdiocese Trustees Inc v Goldberg [2001] 1 All ER 182, Laddie J and in other cases, cited at L Com No 270 (2001) para 2.86 n165). This meant that there was no need for the defendant to appreciate that his intentional conduct or omission is a breach of duty. The result of these decisions was to postpone commencement of the limitation period until the claimant acquires actual or constructive notice of the breach. When deliberate concealment applies, there is no long-stop limitation period (except in claims concerning product liability under the Consumer Protection Act 1987, Part 1). The reasoning in the *Brocklesby* line of cases was convincingly criticized by the following: Janet O'Sullivan (2000) 16 Professional Negligence, 241–51; C Nasir (2000) New LJ 1526ff; and by the Law Commission in L Com No 270 (2001), paras 2.86ff. Although the Law Commission had recommended legislative reform of 'dishonest' concealment (ibid, paras 3.134–3.137, and 254, cl 26(1) of proposed Bill), the House of Lords decision in the *Cave* case (see above) had rendered this unnecessary.

(d) Main limitation periods

(ii) Actions upon a specialty

19.101 **n205**: for comment on the present law see D Oughton, 'Contract, Specialty or "Sum recoverable by virtue of any enactment": A Limitation Conundrum' (2001) 20 CJQ 150. The Law Commission has recommended that there should be no special rule of limitation applicable to deeds and other 'specialties': *Limitation of Actions* (Law Com No 270, 2001) paras 4.7–4.9.

(ix) Claims in equity

19.108 **n216**: the reference to *Hanbury and Martin Modern Equity*, J Martin (ed) should now be to the 16th edn (2001), 670–5. For comment see A McGee and G Scanlan, 'Fiduciary Duties and Limitation Periods' (2001) 20 CJQ 171. For the Law Commission's report on this topic, see *Limitation of Actions* (Law Com No 270, 2001) paras 4.94 –4.125.

19.110 **n220**: *Cia de Seguros Imperio v Heath (REBX) Ltd* [2001] 1 WLR 112, CA decides that a six-year period of limitation will be applied 'by analogy' to a claim for equitable compensation for breach of fiduciary duty, even if the breach is deliberate. For comment see A McGee and G Scanlan, 'Fiduciary Duties and Limitation Periods' (2001) 20 CJQ 171.

The second sentence of the Main Work should now read:

However, the six-year period does not apply where the agent has trust duties with respect to the relevant property, namely to keep it separate, rather than mixing it with his own property.

(x) Human rights claims

If a person sues a public authority and alleges violation of his protection under the Human Rights Act 1998, s 7(5) of that Act prescribes a period of one year beginning on the date of the act complained of. However, the court or tribunal has a discretion to extend this period if it is 'equitable' so to do. **19.110A**

(xi) Claims for judicial review

CPR 54.5 states that a claim for judicial review must be made 'promptly' but in any case not more than three months after the grounds of complaint first arose (on this rule see the critical dictum in *R (Burkett) v Hammersmith and Fulham LBC* [2002] 1 WLR 1593, HL, at [60], *per* Lord Hope). The parties cannot validly agree to relax this time bar. CPR 54.5 does not override any statutory rule prescribing a different period for bringing such a claim in specific cases. **19.110B**

(7) Counterclaims and Related Part 20 Claims

On the Civil Liability (Contribution) Act 1978 see *Royal Brompton Hospital NHS Trust v Hammond and others (Taylor Woodrow Construction (Holdings) Ltd, Part 20 defendant)* [2002] 1 WLR 1397, HL and *Dubai Aluminium Co Ltd v Salaam* [2002] 3 WLR 1913, HL. In the *Brompton* case at [6], Lord Bingham identified various questions which must be posed when applying the 1978 Act. He also held that 'damage' in the 1978 Act signifies 'loss' or 'harm'. The House of Lords in the *Brompton* case also repudiated the Court of Appeal's expansive interpretation of the 1978 Act in *Friends' Provident Life Office v Hillier Parker May and Rowden* [1997] QB 85, CA, which had involved treating a restitutionary claim for recovery of money as equivalent to a claim for compensation for 'damage'. **19.117**

D. Progress of the Action

(1) Emergent New Approach

n239: however, an important development is *Securum Finance Ltd v Ashton* [2001] Ch 291, CA, noted NH Andrews [2001] CLJ 56–8 (held that the court can strike out an action for serious delay even when the relevant claim has not yet become statute barred. If, following such a striking out, the same matter were relitigated by the same claimant, the new action could also be struck out by the court as an abuse of process). **19.121**

(3) Pre-1999 Case Law Development: Abuse of Process and Delay Flowing from Repeated Procedural Non-Compliance

See Supplement para 19.121 n239 on *Securum Finance Ltd v Ashton* [2001] Ch 291, CA, noted NH Andrews [2001] CLJ 56–8. **19.126**

E. Abuse of Process

(1) Scope of Concept

19.128 n247: abuse of process, an expansive rubric, is also exemplified in the following two important contexts:

(a) illegitimate attempts to relitigate civil matters, on which see Supplement para 19.369 n637, *Johnson v Gore Wood & Co* [2002] 2 AC 1, HL; and
(b) excessive and unjustified delay in the prosecution of actions, on which see Supplement para 19.374 n644, *Securum Finance Ltd v Ashton* [2001] Ch 291, CA, noted NH Andrews [2001] CLJ 56–8 (action can be struck out for want of prosecution even when the relevant claim has not yet become statute barred; new action could be struck out by the court as an abuse of process).

19.130 n250: see now *Turner v Grovit* [2002] 1 WLR 107, HL; the House of Lords held that the English courts can issue an injunction to prevent an English litigant from issuing foreign proceedings in bad faith which are designed to frustrate or obstruct pending English litigation; this decision and *Donohue v Armco Inc* [2002] 1 All ER 749, HL review the principles governing English 'anti-suit' injunctions to prevent foreign proceedings; the *Turner* decision also affirms that *forum non conveniens* doctrine does not apply when the relevant foreign state is party to the Brussels or Lugano jurisdictional regimes (*per* Lord Hobhouse at [25], [34]).

(3) Modes of Protection Against Abuse

(c) Striking out for abuse

19.137 n256: in *Three Rivers DC v Bank of England (No 3)* [2001] 2 All ER 513, HL, Lord Hope (at [13]) adopted counsel's submission that there is no exact dividing line between the grounds that a statement of case discloses no reasonable cause of action and that it is an abuse of the court's process. In the same case it was noted that a statement of case can also be attacked by a defendant on the basis of the summary judgment power in CPR Part 24, on which see Supplement para 19.166.

See also Supplement at para 19.121 n239 above concerning *Securum Finance Ltd v Ashton* [2001] Ch 291, CA, noted NH Andrews [2001] CLJ 56–8.

F. Accelerated and Interim Relief

(1) Classification

19.146 Generally on the matters within section F, see I Goldrein *et al*, *Commercial Litigation: Pre-Emptive Remedies* (4th edn, 2002).

(3) Summary Judgment

(c) Test

n286: *Swain v Hillman*, now reported at [2001] 1 All ER 91, CA, was considered by the House of Lords in *Three Rivers DC v Bank of England (No 3)* [2001] 2 All ER 513, HL. In the *Three Rivers DC* case, the claimant was a creditor of the BCCI bank, which collapsed in 1991 because of internal fraud by its senior employees. The claimant sued the Bank of England, alleging that the bank had committed the tort of misfeasance in public office. This cause of action requires an element of dishonesty. It was estimated that trial in this very complex case would take a year ([153]). **19.166**

The decision in the *Three Rivers* case concerned an application to strike out the claim on the basis that the action was an abuse of process because improperly pleaded, or that it disclosed no reasonable cause of action. The House of Lords noted that these heads of attack overlap ([13], *per* Lord Hope). But the House of Lords also held that the matter could be treated as an application by the defendant for summary judgment against the claimant under CPR Part 24 ([13], [88], [120]).

The House of Lords, by a majority (Lords Steyn, Hope and Hutton with Lords Hobhouse and Millett dissenting), held that the action should not be struck out, nor should summary judgment be awarded in favour of the defendant. The House of Lords thus reversed a first instance and majority Court of Appeal decision to strike out the action.

The speeches contain interesting discussion of the importance of preventing hopeless cases from proceeding to trial, whether under the courts' striking out powers or summary judgment and CPR Part 24: notably Lord Hope at [87] ff and [94] ff, Lord Hobhouse at [153]–[62], Lord Millett at [181] and [182].

There is much to be said in favour of the minority view, adopted by Lords Hobhouse and Millett, that the House of Lords ought not to have disturbed the first instance court's decision, upheld on first appeal. Lord Millett at [180] and [181] described the claim as 'a most implausible one', 'scarcely credible' and 'extravagant'. He concluded, at [182]:

> I do not take the view that the Bank can do no wrong or that public officials are incapable of acting in bad faith . . . It is not unfair to observe that, in the absence of some financial or other incentive, a charge of dishonesty against professional men and public officials is possible but inherently improbable.

Lord Hope, at [100], speaking for the majority, considered that this attitude smacked of prejudging the matter.

Lord Hobhouse, at [160], although also dissenting, made this authoritative comment:

> The difficulty in the application of the criterion used by CPR Pt 24 ['no real prospect of success'] is that it requires an assessment to be made in advance of a full trial . . . Therefore the courts in the present case recognised that they must have regard not only to the evidence presently available to the plaintiffs but also to any realistic prospect that this evidence would have been strengthened between now and the trial.

Lord Hobhouse added (at [161]; similarly, see Lord Millett at [184]):

> The law quite rightly requires that questions of dishonesty be approached more rigorously than other questions of fault. The burden of proof remains the civil burden—the balance of probabilities—but the assessment of the evidence has to take account of the seriousness of the allegations and, if that be the case, any unlikelihood that the person accused of dishonesty would have acted in that way. Dishonesty is not to be inferred from evidence which is equally consistent with mere negligence.

(d) Scope

19.169 Erratum: 'contentions' should read 'contentious'.

The legitimate scope of summary judgment has been twice considered by the Court of Appeal. The first case, *Safeway Stores plc v Tate* [2001] QB 1120, CA, appeared substantially to preclude resort to summary judgment in defamation actions because of the constitutional role of the jury in such litigation. But that case was explained in *Alexander v Arts Council of Wales* [2001] 1 WLR 1840, CA, esp [39], [58]–[61], where it was held that the true decision in the *Safeway Stores* case is that it would be a wrong and indeed ultra vires use of summary judgment under CPR Part 24 for the trial judge to remove from the jury questions of fact in the absence of the high threshold test of anticipated perversity (see below).

In the *Alexander* case the Court of Appeal held that a judge sitting with a jury in a defamation trial, after hearing eight days of evidence, had legitimately dismissed the action, giving summary judgment under CPR Part 24, on the basis that the claimant had no chance of demonstrating malice by the defendant and so no chance of defeating the defence of qualified privilege. It held that the proper test is whether there is no point in leaving the jury to decide the factual issue because a jury could only be acting perversely were it to find against the relevant party on the point ('anticipated perversity' test). It was wrong to read the *Safeway Stores* case as inconsistent with the trial judge acting as a filter in such hopeless cases.

(4) Set-Off

(c) Types of set-off

(i) Independent set-off

19.178 **n311**: these authorities were followed in *Fuller v Happy Shopper Markets Ltd* [2002] 1 WLR 1681, [23].

(iii) Transactional set-off in equity

n314: similarly, *Fuller v Happy Shopper Markets Ltd* [2002] 1 WLR 1681, at [22], where Lightman J employed the touchstone whether denial of the set-off would be 'unconscionable'. For another examination of equitable set-off see *Bim Kemi v Blackburn Chemicals Ltd* (CA, 3 April 2001). **19.181**

In *Muscat v Smith* [2003] 1 WLR 2853, CA, [2003] EWCA Civ 962, the principle of equitable set-off was extended in a novel fashion to take account of money owed to the defendant by the claimant's assignor, in other words by a third party. A1, while landlord of D, had breached its repair covenant. D withheld rent as a result. A1 sold the property, subject to the tenancy, to A2. The price paid by A2 to A1 was adjusted to take account of D's unpaid rent. D now fell into arrears vis-à-vis A2. At first instance, in an action by A2 for unpaid rent, it was held that D could not raise as against A2 an equitable set-off based upon compensation arising from A1's breach of covenant. And so, on the facts, the judge awarded repossession of the property in favour of the landlord, A2. The Court of Appeal (Sedley, Buxton and Ward LJJ) reversed this and held that equitable set-off, to take account of A1's default, should apply in this dispute between A2 and D, even though A1 was a third party to that relationship. This was a legitimate extension of the doctrine of equitable set-off and consistent with the principle that an assignee takes subject to the assignor's disabilities and burdens. Buxton LJ's judgment at [37]–[54] reviews the case law and principles concerning these doctrines, especially equitable set-off.

(6) Interlocutory Injunctions

(c) *American Cyanamid* side-railed

The grant of interim injunctions is now subject to s 12(3)(4) of the Human Rights Act 1998. Section 12(3) states: **19.194**

> No such relief is to be granted so as to restrain publication before trial unless the court is satisfied that the applicant is likely to establish that publication should not be allowed.

Section 12(4) states (both in connection with interim and final injunctions):

> The court must have particular regard to the importance of the Convention right to freedom of expression and, where proceedings relate to material which the respondent claims, or which appears to the court, to be journalistic, literary or artistic material (or to conduct connected with such material), to—
> (a) the extent to which—
> (i) the material has, or is about to, become available to the public; or
> (ii) it is, or would be, in the public interest for the material to be published;
> (b) any relevant privacy code.

In *Douglas v Hello! Ltd* [2001] QB 967, CA, at [150], Keene LJ said that s 12(3) requires the court to look at the merits of the case and not merely apply the *American Cyanamid* test. The respondent had acquired unauthorized photographs of the applicants' wedding which had taken place in private so that the applicant could sell authorized photographs to a magazine. A rival magazine acquired photographs of the event, which had been taken surreptitiously and probably in breach of confidence. On the facts, the court rejected the application for an interim injunction and left the claimant to his remedy in damages.

In *A v B plc* [2003] QB 195, CA (reversing [2001] 1 WLR 2341, Jack J) the court refused to uphold an injunction to prevent a newspaper from publishing salacious details of the applicant's extra-marital sexual activity. It held that the applicant's right to privacy under Article 8 of the European Convention on Human Rights was outweighed by the respondent newspapers' interest in 'freedom of expression' under Article 10 of the European Convention. The court enunciated detailed guidelines for cases, such as this, where a conflict arises between an individual's privacy and freedom of expression, noting also s 12(3) of the Human Rights Act 1998.

The threshold evidential test applicable to the grant of interim injunctions which might inhibit freedom of expression was further examined in *Cream Holdings v Banerjee* [2003] Ch 650, CA (once more considering the Human Rights Act 1998).

Venables v News Group Newspapers Ltd [2001] Fam 430 (which was considered in the *A v B plc* case, see above) involved another and novel balancing of the public interest in freedom of expression and individuals' interest. The applicants were convicted child-killers who feared for their safety and lives once released from imprisonment. The judge recognized the applicants' interest in preserving confidentiality in their whereabouts and identity and granted a final injunction *contra mundum*, restraining the world at large, to preserve this confidentiality.

(7) Freezing Injunctions

(a) **Nature**

19.197 It is established that an application made 'without notice' (formerly known as an 'ex parte' application) imports a duty to make full and frank disclosure to the court (for detailed discussion see S Gee, *Mareva Injunctions and Anton Piller Relief* (4th edn, 1998) ch 8). This duty was considered, in the context of family law applications, in *Re S (A Child) (Family Division: Without Notice Orders)* [2001] 1 WLR 211, 219, 222–3.

19.200 The proposition that freezing relief does not confer proprietary protection upon the applicant was affirmed in *Flightline Ltd v Edwards* [2003] 1 WLR 1200, CA.

(b) Criteria

Neuberger J succinctly restated the criteria for award of freezing relief in *Flightwise Travel Services v Gill* The Times, 5 December 2003. **19.203–19.209**

Erratum: 'element (a) of this test' should read 'element (b) of this test'. **19.206**

(c) The impact of freezing injunctions upon non-parties

n350: cf *C Inc plc v L* (2001) NLJ 535. D acquired loan stock in C and D held this stock on trust for X. C claimed payment in respect of the loan stock and obtained judgment. A freezing injunction was applied to prevent dealings with this loan stock. The judge noted that D, as trustee for X, was entitled to an indemnity for expenses incurred on these assets. This factor made it fair to extend the freezing injunction to that loan stock. **19.210**

n352: in *Bank of China v NBM LLC* [2002] 1 All ER 717, CA, [5], the Court of Appeal (approving [2001] 4 All ER 954, David Steel J in the Commercial Court) authorized the inclusion of the following amendment to a freezing injunction, and recommended that a similar provision should become a standard aspect of freezing injunctions affecting foreign assets and impinging on banks with foreign branches, seats, or subsidiaries operating outside the jurisdiction: **19.211**

> It is further ordered and directed that nothing in this order shall, in respect of assets located outside England or Wales, prevent [the non-party bank] or any of its subsidiaries from complying with:
> 1. What it reasonably believes to be its obligations under the criminal law of the country or state in which those assets are situated; and
> 2. Any orders of the courts of that country or state provided reasonable notice of any application for such an order by [the non-party bank] or any of its subsidiaries (to the extent such notice is permitted by the criminal law of such country or state), is given to the claimant's solicitors.

Steel J at first instance, ibid, also noted (at [15]) that in *Baltic Shipping v Translink Shipping Ltd* [1995] 1 Lloyd's Rep 673, 678–9, Clarke J had commented that a non-party should apply to the local foreign court as soon as possible in case of doubt and that it might also be protected if it has 'the powerful opinion of a lawyer' in support of its position, provided that opinion is 'reasonable'.

(d) Freezing injunctions to support foreign proceedings

n356: *Ryan v Friction Dynamics Ltd* The Times, 14 June 2000, Ch Div, contains an important survey of principles in cases of overlapping foreign and English freezing or similar relief. More recently, *Motorola Credit Corporation v Uzan (No 2)* [2003] EWCA Civ 752 CA, The Times, 19 June 2003, CA examines the jurisdiction to grant worldwide freezing relief in support of another primary jurisdiction. **19.214**

(e) **Freezing injunctions and foreign assets**

19.215 **n357**: see the *Bank of China* case, noted in Supplement para 19.211 n352; see also the authorities cited at Supplement para 19.214.

G. Settlement

n369: the reference to D Foskett, *The Law and Practice of Compromise* should now be to the 5th edn (2002).

(3) Settlement and Evidential Privileges

19.226 **n376**: *Unilever plc v The Proctor & Gamble Co* is now reported at [2000] 1 WLR 2436, CA. Other recent discussions are *Somatra Ltd v Sinclair Roche Temperley* [2000] 1 WLR 2453, CA; *Gnitrow Ltd v Cape Ltd* [2000] 1 WLR 2317, CA; *Murrell v Healy* [2001] 4 All ER 345, CA; *Berg v IML London Ltd* [2002] 1 WLR 3271; *Savings and Investment Bank Ltd v Fincken* [2003] EWCA Civ 1630 (reversing Patten J [2003] 3 All ER 1091; [2003] EWHC 719 Ch); generally on this privilege see Neil Andrews, *English Civil Procedure* (2003) ch 25.

(4) Alternative Dispute Resolution

n380: for details of burgeoning literature and judicial enthusiasm for 'ADR', including use of costs sanctions for failure to pursue such alternative forms of dispute resolution, see Neil Andrews *English Civil Procedure* (2003) 23.12–23.28.

(5) Payments into Court and Offers to Settle

Generally on this hectic and technical topic, see Neil Andrews, *English Civil Procedure* (2003) ch 24 and *Blackstone's Civil Practice 2003* at paras 64.1ff.

19.230 A party must make a payment into court, whenever this is feasible, if the defendant is to take full advantage of this costs rule: *Amber v Stacey* [2001] 1 WLR 1225, CA. The trial judge awarded the claimant judgment for £2,056. Before trial the defendant had made (a) a written offer of settlement of £4,000; (b) later a payment into court of £3,000 (in fact made in two tranches). The trial judge awarded costs in favour of the defendant from the date of (a). The Court of Appeal held that this was an invalid costs order because it treated the written offer of payment as equivalent to a payment into court and this is contrary to CPR 36.3(1). When a payment into court is made but the claimant fails to beat it, CPR 36.20(2) provides that normally the claimant must pay the defendant's costs from the date on which the payment could have been accepted. The judge erred when he ordered the claimant to pay the defendant's costs in full from the date of (a), the written offer (notably at [36]). Simon Brown LJ at [41] fortified this decision by saying:

> Payments into court have advantages. They at least answer all questions as to (a) genuineness, (b) the offeror's ability to pay, (c) whether the offer is open or without prejudice, and (d) the terms on which the dispute can be settled. They are clearly to be encouraged, and written offers, although obviously relevant, should not be treated as precise equivalents.

Nor could this order be justified by reference to the wide discretion which governs generally the award of costs: see CPR 44.3.

The Court of Appeal thought a reasonable costs award in this case should have consisted of these two elements:

(a) from the date of the written offer, the claimant should pay half of the defendant's costs, in exercise of CPR 44.3;
(b) from the date when the payment into court could have been accepted by the defendant, the claimant should pay all the defendant's costs, in exercise of CPR 36.20(2).

Such an offer is revocable until accepted. This is in accordance with the general law of contract. Although CPR 36.5(6) declares that a Part 36 offer must be 'expressed to remain open for acceptance for 21 days from the date that it is made', CPR 36.5(8) explicitly allows such an offer to be withdrawn: *Scammell v Dicker* [2001] 1 WLR 631, CA, esp at [19], contrasting payments into court under Part 36 which can be withdrawn only with the court's permission: CPR 36.6(5). **19.231**

(a) Indemnity costs award against a defendant who suffered judgment in excess of a claimant's Part 36 offer

Petrotrade Inc v Texaco Ltd [2002] 1 WLR 947, CA, contains important guidance on the award of indemnity costs and higher rate interest on costs against a defendant who is held liable for more than the proposal contained in a Part 36 offer made by the claimant. **19.232A**

Although CPR 36.21(1) is confined to judgment awarded at trial, and does not cover summary judgment, the Court of Appeal held that the court nevertheless has a discretion to award indemnity costs and interest on those costs on a basis exceeding base rate in order to support the procedural interest in promoting settlement and to vindicate the claimant's interest in stimulating a speedy and fair conclusion of the action. Latham LJ at [88] attributed this to the wide general costs discretion at CPR 44.3(4)(c), which refers to Part 36 offers.

(b) Indemnity costs under Part 36 not penal

In *Petrotrade Inc v Texaco Ltd* [2002] 1 WLR 947, CA (see Supplement para 19.232A) and *McPhilemy v Times Newspapers Ltd (No 2)* [2002] 1 WLR 934, CA, it was held that an order for indemnity costs against a defendant and in favour of **19.232B** a claimant who has made a Part 36 offer (the defendant eventually having suffered judgment in excess of the claimant's offer) is not a penal award and carries no stigma or implied disapproval of the defendant's conduct.

H. Disclosure

(3) Scope of Documentary Disclosure

Note that a new edition of C Hollander, *Documentary Evidence* (8th edn) is imminent, but was not available at the time this supplement went to press.

(c) Summary of restrictions upon duty to disclose

19.246 n415: the references here and in the next two notes to I Dennis, *The Law of Evidence* should now be to the 2nd edn (2002).

n418: *Unilever plc v The Proctor & Gamble Co* is now reported at [2000] 1 WLR 2436, CA. Other recent discussions are *Somatra Ltd v Sinclair Roche Temperley* [2000] 1 WLR 2453, CA; *Gnitrow Ltd v Cape Ltd* [2000] 1 WLR 2317, CA; *Murrell v Healy* [2001] 4 All ER 345, CA; *Berg v IML London Ltd* [2002] 1 WLR 3271; *Savings and Investment Bank Ltd v Fincken* [2003] EWCA Civ 1630 (reversing Patten J [2003] 3 All ER 1091, [2003] EWHC 719 Ch); generally on this privilege, see Neil Andrews, *English Civil Procedure* (2003) ch 25.

(4) Protection Against Abuse of Disclosure

19.250 n427: in *Douglas v Hello! Ltd* [2003] 1 All ER 1087, [2003] EWHC 55 Ch, Morritt V-C was asked to strike out the action on the ground that one party had deliberately destroyed relevant documents and erased electronic records in anticipation of the present proceedings; the judge reviewed Commonwealth and US discussion of this context, especially Australian case law (the topic is known in some jurisdictions as 'spoliation'); the judge concluded that such a jurisdiction does exist but is confined to the situation where destruction is tantamount to an attempt to pervert the course of justice; he did not find such abuse on the present facts.

(b) Implied undertaking

19.253 n435: the reference to P Matthews and HM Malek, *Disclosure* should now be to the 2nd edn (2000) ch 13. See also SMC Gibbons, 'Subsequent use of documents obtained through disclosure in civil proceedings . . .' (2001) 20 CJQ 303–26.

19.255 n442: the Court of Appeal in *Lilly Icos Ltd v Pfizer Ltd (No 2)* [2002] 1 All ER 842, CA (reversing Laddie J in [2000] 59 BMLR 123) considered the court's discretion under CPR 31.22(2) to make a special order to protect a document even though it has prima facie lost protection of the implied undertaking because, as provided by CPR 31.22(1)(a), it has been 'read to or by the court, or referred to, at a hearing which has been held in public'.

The case concerned extremely sensitive commercial information which had been included in a file and referred to in passing by counsel during the trial. The information concerned the monthly advertising expenditure incurred by a patent holder in promotion of its drug, 'Viagra', used to improve male sexual performance. The material had been included in this documentary form as part of the patent holder's attempt to preserve its patent.

The Court of Appeal held that, exceptionally, this was a case which justified an order under CPR 31.22(2) to re-instate the implied undertaking and protect the information. It emphasized the commercial sensitivity of this data, and noted how little use had been made of it at trial. It formulated the following guidelines (at [25]):

> 1. The court has to start from the principle that very good reasons were required for departing from the normal rule of publicity.
> 2. . . . the court should take into account the role that the document had played or would play in the trial.
> 3. . . . the court had to consider the chilling effect of an order on the interests of third parties [viz the order will carry the sanction of contempt of court if the information is used or publicized by a non-party].
> 4. . . . Simple assertions of confidentiality and of the damage that would be done by publication, even if supported by both parties, should not prevail. The court would require specific reasons why a party would be damaged by the publication of a document.
> 5. It was highly desirable to avoid the holding of trials in private, or partially in private. In the present case, the entire trial was held in public, even though the judge regarded it as justified to retain confidentiality in respect of a significant number of specific documents.
> 6. Patent cases were subject to the same general rules as any other cases, but did present problems and were subject to some particular considerations.

The topic is further examined in *SmithKline Beecham plc v Generics (UK) Ltd* [2003] 4 All ER 1302, CA; [2003] EWCA Civ 1109.

(5) Pre-Action Disclosure

n443: the leading case is *Black v Sumitomo Corporation* [2002] 1 WLR 1562 CA. **19.256**

(6) Disclosure and Non-Parties

(a) Qualifications upon the mere witness rule

(ii) Statutory exceptions

n451: Section 9(2) of the Bankers' Book Evidence Act 1879 (as amended) states: **19.260**

> Expressions in the Act relating to 'bankers' books' include ledgers, day books, cash books, account books and other records used in the ordinary business of the bank, whether those records are in written form or are kept on microfilm, magnetic tape or any other form of mechanical or electronic data retrieval mechanism.

In *Re Howglen Ltd* [2000] 1 All ER 376, 380–2, Pumfrey J held that this definition did not cover taped records of conversations between senior bank officials. He noted that s 9(2) of the 1879 Act has been restrictively interpreted in *R v Dadson* (1983) 77 Cr App R 91, 93–4, CA and *Williams v Williams* [1988] QB 161, 168, CA, *per* Sir John Donaldson MR.

(iii) Equity practice: Norwich Pharmacal

19.261 The leading discussion is now the House of Lords decision *Ashworth Hospital Authority v MGN Ltd* [2002] 1 WLR 2033, HL; the decision is fully examined (see also Supplement para 19.262 n455).

19.262 n455: *Axa Equity & Life Assurance Society plc v National Westminster Bank plc* is now reported at [1998] PNLR 433, CA; [1998] CLC 1177, CA.

Ashworth Hospital Authority v MGN Ltd [2002] 1 WLR 2033, HL is an important examination of this jurisdiction. The claimant hospital sought an order to compel a national newspaper to reveal the identity of a 'mole', one of the hospital's employees. This employee had leaked confidential information concerning Ian Brady, the Moors murderer, who was a patient at the secure hospital. The information consisted of 17 pages of material printed out from the hospital's database. These documents had been received by an intermediary, who was certainly paid by the newspaper, and who probably paid money to the mole. The intermediary faxed the information to a journalist who then used it in a story published by the defendant newspaper.

The House of Lords (at [32]) held that the hospital enjoyed rights of confidentiality in this material and that the 'leak' had involved a breach of contract. It then held that the *Norwich Pharmacal Co v Customs and Excise Commissioners* [1974] AC 133 (jurisdiction to compel a non-party to reveal details of the identity of a principal wrongdoer) is not confined to cases where the principal's wrong is a tort ([1] and [34]).

Finally, the House of Lords considered the protection afforded to journalistic sources contained in s 10 of the Contempt of Court Act 1981. It held that the mole's breach of confidence in the present case violated private interests and posed a significant threat to the proper running of a sensitive part of the National Health Service. The court also emphasized the importance of maintaining patients' confidentiality. An order compelling the newspaper to reveal the source's identity was necessary, proportionate and justified. The *Ashworth* case is fully examined by in Neil Andrews, *English Civil Procedure* (2003) 26.120ff.

n463: *Axa Equity & Life Assurance Society plc v National Westminster Bank plc* is now reported at [1998] PNLR 433, CA, [1998] CLC 1177, CA. 19.264

(b) Non-parties and the CPR (1998)

n464: the scope of this rule was considered in *Re Howglen Ltd* [2000] 1 All ER 376. Pumfrey J emphasized that this rule requires judicial caution, and that it should not be applied in a speculative fashion, so as to 'fish' for documents which 'might' exist. Instead, the documents must be described in detail and the court should be satisfied that such documents do indeed exist. The non-party cannot be placed in the position of exercising the initiative to decide whether documents might fall within the scope of widely defined classes of material. 19.265

In *Frankson v Home Office* [2003] 1 WLR 1952, CA, disclosure against non-parties was held to be justified in the interest of gaining access to relevant evidence, even though this information had been imparted during a criminal investigation and was protected by confidentiality; a weighing of competing public interests was necessary.

(7) Legal Professional Privilege

n466: the reference to P Matthews and HM Malek, *Disclosure* should now be to the 2nd edn (2000) ch 9, sections C, D, and E.

Note that a new edition of C Hollander, *Documentary Evidence* (8th edn) is imminent, but was not available at the time this Supplement went to press.

(b) Legal advice privilege

n471: see now also P Matthews and HM Malek, *Disclosure* (2nd edn, 2000) [9-16]–[9-22]. 19.266

'This head of privilege is to be applied generously.' However, this has been contradicted by recent developments which require careful attention (note that the second of these decisions, see below, for *Three Rivers (No 10)*, was to be considered by the Court of Appeal in late January 2004). 19.269

Legal advice privilege is also recognized in the jurisprudence of the European Union (*A M & S Europe Ltd v Commission of the European Communities* Case 155/79 [1982] ECR 1575, 1610–1613, ECJ, [18], [25]) and under Article 8 of the European Convention on Human Rights (*Silver v UK* (1983) 5 EHRR 347, ECHR, *Campbell v UK* (1992) 15 EHRR 137, ECHR; *Niemietz v Germany* (1992) 16 EHRR 97, ECHR, and *Foxley v UK* (2000) 31 EHRR 637, ECHR; in the *Foxley* case, at [50], the court said that the *Niemietz* case indicated that Article 6(1) is also relevant when domestic law encroches on professional secrecy of consultation with a lawyer, but the point was obiter). 19.270

Lord Hoffmann said in *R (Morgan Grenfell Ltd) v Special Commissioner of Tax* [2003] 1 AC 563, HL, at [7]:

> Legal professional privilege is a fundamental human right long established in the common law. It is a necessary corollary of the right of any person to obtain skilled advice about the law. Such advice cannot be effectively obtained unless the client is able to put all the facts before the adviser without fear that they can be afterwards disclosed and used to his prejudice.

(ba) Legal advice privilege's erosion by *Three Rivers*

19.270A This protracted litigation (trial, scheduled for early 2004, is estimated to take 18 months) has twice provoked radical re-examination of the scope of legal advice privilege. Final appeal in the second of these decisions (see *Three Rivers (No 10)* below) will be heard by the House of Lords in July 2004. For further reading on this topic, see the 'Bibliography on Legal Professional Privilege' below.

(i) Strict delimitation of the lawyer–client relationship

In *Three Rivers DC v Governor and Company of the Bank of England (No 5)* [2003] 3 WLR 667, CA, [2003] EWCA Civ 474 the Court of Appeal held (Longmore LJ giving the court's judgment) that although legal advice privilege applies to communications between the 'client' and the legal adviser, that nexus must be strictly delimited.

It has long been settled law that legal advice privilege will not apply to documents created by an *outsider* for the purpose of facilitating the client's obtaining legal advice (*Three Rivers (No 5)* case at [17]–[18], [27] noting *Wheeler v Le Marchant* (1881) 17 Ch D 675, CA). However, the restrictive aspect of the *Three Rivers (No 5)* case is the decision that legal advice privilege does not arise when *internal* documentation is created and communicated to a legal adviser by an employee or sub-body of employees or officer of the *client* company, *unless* that person or group of persons can be regarded as the 'client' within the company which is interested in obtaining legal advice.

In the present case 'the client' was the Bingham Inquiry Unit which consisted of a few senior employees of the bank: but the court emphasized that 'the client' on these facts was *not* 'any [other] officer however eminent he or she may be' (*Three Rivers (No 5)* case at [31]).

(ii) Background to the Three Rivers (No 5) *application*

Three Rivers (No 5) arose as a pre-trial issue on the following facts. Following the financial collapse of BCCI (a former bank trading in the United Kingdom), the UK Government commissioned Bingham LJ (as he then was) to conduct a private non-statutory inquiry into the circumstances of this debacle. The claim in present litigation, brought by the liquidator and former depositors of BCCI against the Bank of England, alleges misfeasance in public office.

The present application was for a declaration that various categories of document held by the bank are not subject to legal professional privilege. The documents in question were 'generated' by the bank's employees as 'raw material' for possible use in this inquiry. These documents might be described as 'commentary' within the bank on the closure of BCCI. However, some might be regarded as 'best evidence' available to the bank concerning the whole affair.

The bank had created a 'Bingham Inquiry Unit' (BIU), an internal panel of three of its officials, which had responsibility to co-ordinate its submissions to the Inquiry. The BIU at all times closely consulted with its solicitors, Freshfields, on how to prepare its submissions to the inquiry.

The bank did not dispute that the lengthy submission presented to the inquiry should be disclosed in the present action, nor that transcripts of witness statements for the same inquiry should be similarly available.

(iii) Counsel's concession that litigation privilege does not apply to any form of 'inquisitorial' proceedings

The bank's counsel conceded that 'litigation privilege' did not apply to the present facts. They considered that *Re L* [1997] 1 AC 16, a House of Lords decision concerning family proceedings relating to a child's welfare, establishes that 'litigation privilege is essentially a creature of adversarial proceedings and thus cannot exist in the context of non-adversarial proceedings'. The Bingham Inquiry was not 'adversarial'.

However, *Re L* has attracted much discussion: see A Zuckerman (1996) 112 LQR 535; Neil Andrews, *English Civil Procedure* (2003), para 27-33; *Murphy on Evidence* (8th edn, 2003), para 14.11; IH Dennis, *The Law of Evidence* (2nd edn, 2002), 364–6; P Matthews and H Malek, *Disclosure* (2nd edn, 2000), paras 9-32–9-33; C Tapper (ed), *Cross and Tapper on Evidence* (9th edn, 1999), 461.

For present purposes, the main problem with counsel's concession is that the adversarial/inquisitorial distinction is too bald. It is in fact unhelpful in determining the proper limits of 'litigation privilege'. The distinction between an adversarial procedure (concerning a *lis inter partes*, and directly affecting 'legal rights and obligations') and an inquisitorial procedure (not directly involving such a *lis*, and not directly affecting a person's 'legal rights and obligations') is formalistic. This distinction fails to reflect the fact that the latter is often a prelude to adversarial proceedings involving a claim for substantive relief. For trenchant comment on this point, see the dissenting speech of Lord Nicholls in *Re L* [1997] 1 AC 16, 30–3, HL, with which Lord Mustill agreed. See also Neil Andrews, *Principles of Civil*

Procedure (1994), para 12-021, a passage written before *Re L*, but against which that decision's proper scope might be reconsidered.

(iv) Questions of policy and principle articulated by the court in Three Rivers (No 5)

The Court of Appeal in *Three Rivers (No 5)* justified its narrow approach to the scope of legal advice privilege by making the following general points (at [26]):

(1) that a client's need to be candid when consulting a lawyer is 'paramount when litigation either exists or is contemplated';
(2) in this same context, the 'vital public interest is in deterring bad claims or defences and encouraging strong cases';
(3) in the absence of such a prospect of litigation, 'it is by no means clear' that a client's candour might be impeded by denial of legal advice privilege;
(4) there is 'the public interest that the courts, if possible, should come to correct [viz, accurate] judgments on the basis of all relevant material'. And so legal advice privilege should, according to the Court of Appeal, 'be confined to its proper limits'.
(5) The Court of Appeal in the *Three Rivers (No 5)* case added: 'The judges of the nineteenth century thought that [legal advice privilege] should only apply to communications between client and legal advisor. That is the proper compass of the privilege. It is not, in our judgment, open to this court to extend the privilege, even if we thought we should.'
(6) Admittedly, *R (Morgan Grenfell & Co Ltd) v Special Commissioners for Income Tax* [2003] 1 AC 563, HL, shows that legal advice privilege 'is a fundamental human right which can be overridden only by the express words of a statute or by necessary implication'.
(7) However, lawyer/client privilege is unique. Other advisers, such as doctors and priests, do not give advice under a similar protective mantle. 'In these circumstances', the Court of Appeal in the *Three Rivers (No 5)* case suggested, 'it is important that it be confined to its proper limits'.
(8) The Court of Appeal in *Three Rivers (No 5)*, commenting on the *Wheeler v Le Marchant* rule, see (1881) 17 Ch D 675, CA, ('third party' restriction on the scope of legal advice privilege: see above) said at [18]:

> . . . it may, moreover, be a mere matter of chance whether a solicitor, in a legal advice privilege case, gets his information from an employee or an agent or other third party. It may also be problematical, in some cases, to decide whether any given individual is an employee or an agent and undesirable that the presence or absence of privilege should depend upon that answer.

(v) Assessment of the merits of the Three Rivers (No 5) *decision: against the modern trend?*

The central proposition in *Three Rivers (No 5)* is technically supported by *Anderson v Bank of British Columbia* (1876) 2 Ch D 644, CA: namely, creation and communication by a company's employees or officers of documents for non-litigious purposes is not privileged even though it was communicated for the purpose of obtaining legal advice or facilitating the same. But the actual result in the *Anderson* case was rightly doubted by Bingham LJ in 1991, who considered that the facts would now be regarded as supporting a claim to litigation privilege (see *Ventouris v Mountain* [1991] 1 WLR 607, 612 H, CA, *per* Bingham LJ; a point noted by the Court of Appeal in the *Three Rivers (No 5)* case at [10]).

However, despite its disputable nineteenth-century pedigree, the decision in *Three Rivers (No 5)* came as a jolt to many commentators and experienced practitioners. This is because the modern leading decision on the ambit of legal advice privilege, *Balabel v Air India* [1988] Ch 317, CA (on which see *Three Rivers (No 5)* [29]–[30]) had been widely interpreted as giving a broad ambit to the 'continuum' of communications 'necessary' to obtain and to maintain effective legal advice in civil matters. The *Balabel* judgment refers to communications which 'form part of that necessary exchange of information of which the object is the giving of legal advice as and when appropriate' ([1988] Ch 317, 332, CA, *per* Taylor LJ). This decision had been applied in *Nederlandse Reassurantie Groep Holding v Bacon & Woodrow* [1995] 1 All ER 976 by Colman J so as to render privileged commercial advice offered by a City firm of solicitors to a client concerning the tactics and wisdom of a particular set of negotiations. The case is clearly sound.

The *Balabel* case had persuaded Tomlinson J at first instance in *Three Rivers (No 5)* [2002] EWHC 2730 (Comm), [30]–[31] to adopt a relatively broad approach to legal advice privilege, citing also statements by C Passmore, *Privilege* (1998) at 37–8 and Hollander and Adam, *Documentary Evidence* (7th edn, 2000) 126 (now in its 8th edition). The learned judge added: 'that privilege has routinely been claimed and probably never challenged in relation to precisely similar or analogous exercises conducted in relation to statutory inquiries and other non-adversarial proceedings' (ibid, at [34]).

Another reason for regarding the Court of Appeal's ungenerous approach to legal advice privilege as surprising is that the category of legal professional privilege which had been ear-marked as ripe for re-consideration was 'litigation privilege' and not legal advice privilege. This was the result of lengthy dicta of Scott V-C, as he then was, in *Secretary of State for Trade & Industry v Baker* [1998] Ch 356, 362–71. His argument (which is unlikely to be upheld) is that litigation privilege is justified only to the extent that it protects a person from being made to disclose material or information which would enable another to peer into the inner sanctum of confidential legal consultation. Scott V-C's suggested repudiation of litigation privilege is considered by Neil Andrews, *English Civil Procedure* (OUP, 2003) at paras 27.21–27.41. He and several other commentators regard it as ill-founded and instead they prefer the traditional view that litigation privilege is a discrete head of privilege, not parasitic upon or a mere species of legal advice privilege, but rather enjoying its own rationale (see Andrews, op cit, for details).

(vi) Lawyer's confidential 'presentational' advice and assistance to client concerning participation at an 'inquiry' not subject to legal advice privilege

Three Rivers DC v Governor and Company of the Bank of England (No 10) [2003] EWHC 2565 (Comm), Tomlinson J (noted D Sandy [2003] NLJ 1912–13) is the sequel to the Court of Appeal's decision in *Three Rivers (No 5)*, noted above. For those who had assumed that the ambit of legal advice privilege would continue to be sensibly drawn to reflect the realities of complex modern commercial relations and bona fide legal advice and assistance, this is the second bombshell produced by this litigation (for the first, see above). **NB**: On 1 March 2004, the Court of Appeal [2004] 2 WLR 1065, [2004] EWCA Civ 218 affirmed Tomlinson J's decision in *Three Rivers (No 10)*. The House of Lords has granted permission for a final appeal, which will be heard in July 2004.

Tomlinson J confessed at [5] to being in an 'invidious' position because it was necessary for him to interpret *Three Rivers (No 5)*, in which the Court of Appeal had reversed his more generous approach to legal advice privilege. He held that it was a logical implication of the Court of Appeal's decision and discussion in *Three Rivers (No 5)* (on which see above) that legal advice privilege should not apply to communications between a client and lawyer concerning how best the client might present factual material at a non-adversarial inquiry. Such an inquiry does not attract litigation privilege (this follows the concesssion made in the earlier decision, on which see above). Furthermore, such an inquiry does not normally directly declare, modify or enforce a person's legal rights and duties (ibid at [7]).

The learned judge held that a line must be drawn between legal advice concerning the client's legal rights and obligations (this type of advice will be covered by privilege) and a lawyer's advice on how best to present material to an inquiry 'in the way least likely to attract criticism' (ibid, at [8]): the latter form of advice does not fall within the scope of 'legal advice privilege'.

Furthermore, Tomlinson J in *Three Rivers (No 10)* considered that *Three Rivers (No 5)*, CA establishes that legal advice privilege is subject to a 'dominant purpose' test (at [7]). And so, the court must be satisfied that it was the dominant purpose of a communication between lawyer and client that legal advice should be given or obtained concerning the client's rights and obligations.

Tomlinson J's decision in the present case was to be reconsidered by the Court of Appeal in late January 2004.

(vii) Assessment of Tomlinson J's decision in Three Rivers (No 10) *to withhold legal advice privilege from legal consultation concerning client's participation in an inquiry: options available to the Court of Appeal*

Tomlinson J's decision in *Three Rivers (No 10)* is unsatisfactory. Individuals, companies and financial entities who are called upon to assist non-adversarial inquiries will be concerned to discover the scope of their duties (if any) to co-operate with the relevant inquiry. But Tomlinson J has decided that confidential discussion between a client and lawyer as to how to 'present' material at an inquiry is not covered by legal advice privilege.

Need to reinstate a broader ambit of legal advice privilege. The better option is for the Court of Appeal to declare that Tomlinson J's decision misapplies legal advice privilege, and that the true test or approach was correctly stated in the *Balabel* case (see above) as applicable to all bona fide confidential legal consultation between lawyer and client concerning not just the client's rights and obligations but matters falling within the legitimate compass of modern legal consultation, including prudent business advice (as in the *Nederlandse* case, see above); it is consistent with this approach that privilege should attach to legal advice concerning compliance with regulatory inquiries and other inquiries.

An inferior option. This second option is less attractive, but it would at least offer some privileged assistance to those called upon to co-operate with inquiries.

The decision restricts legal advice privilege to such consultation as is concerned with ascertaining a client's legal rights and duties (this is Tomlinson J's unfortunately narrow definition in *Three Rivers (No 10)*). But even this ungenerous test definition, it is submitted, must provide some protection in the present context. Arguably, legal advice privilege must continue to arise if the lawyer is asked to offer confidential advice concerning the following matters:

(1) 'is the client obliged to co-operate with the Inquiry?'
(2) 'if so, what is the extent of the client's obligation to search out, compose or otherwise divulge information or documents which might assist the Inquiry?'
(3) 'are there any grounds of privilege or confidentiality, or perhaps statutory constraints, which justify withholding certain information or documents (in whole or in part)?'
(4) 'what will be the evidential status of information which is divulged to the Inquiry?'
(5) relatedly, 'to what extent, if any, might our co-operation with the Inquiry prejudice us legally in the future, for example, by stimulating or supporting

adversarial litigation; conversely, might such co-operation enable us to convince others that they have no valid or arguable claims against us?'

The matters listed at (1)–(3) were the subject of an inconclusive passage at [8] in Tomlinson J's judgment. It is to be hoped, therefore, that if the Court of Appeal does hear an appeal in the present case its decision will clarify this point. The matters arranged above as (1)–(5) raise practical concerns for lawyers and their clients. But the better option, with respect, is to reinstate a sensible and generous test of legal advice privilege which properly reflects the legitimate ambit of legal consultation in modern commercial and other complex dealings.

(viii) Bibliography on Legal Professional Privilege

Neil Andrews, *English Civil Procedure* (2003) ch 27 (Legal professional privilege) and ch 28 (Inadvertent disclosure of privileged material);
J Auburn, *Legal Professional Privilege: Law and Theory* (2000);
Blackstone's Civil Practice 2003 (2003), paras 48.23–48.29;
Cross and Tapper on Evidence, C Tapper (ed), (9th edn, 1999) 438ff, esp 446;
IH Dennis, *The Law of Evidence* (2nd edn, 2002) ch 10, esp 333–43;
C Hollander, *Documentary Evidence* (8th edn, 2003);
P Matthews and HM Malek, *Disclosure* (2nd edn, 2000) paras 9-05–9-71;
Murphy on Evidence (8th edn, 2003) 14.7ff;
C Passmore, *Privilege* (1998), 37ff, esp 51–2;
Phipson on Evidence (15th edn, 2000) ch 20, esp paras 20-04–20-24; and on the scope of 'litigation' for the purpose of 'litigation privilege', para 20-34.

(c) Distinction between legal advice and litigation privilege

19.271 n474: the reference to P Matthews and HM Malek, *Disclosure* should now be to the 2nd edn (2000) para 9-043.

(d) Litigation privilege and its limits

19.273 n477: the reference to P Matthews and HM Malek, *Disclosure* should now be to the 2nd edn (2000) paras 9-040–9-042.

19.275 *Sumitomo Corporation v Crédit Lyonnais Rouse Ltd* [2002] 1 WLR 479, CA contains an important discussion of litigation privilege. Three points of decision must be noted.

(i) Translation of own client's unprivileged documents does not produce privilege

The court held that no privilege arose in translations of documents which were (a) in a party's control and (b) unprivileged. The process of translation should be regarded as equivalent to that of copying unprivileged documents within the copying party's control.

This conclusion was consistent with the 'copying rule'. It is established that a copy of an original document which is not itself privileged is privileged only if (a) the copy came into existence for the purpose of litigation, and (b) the original document is not and has not at any time been in the control of the party claiming privilege (see *The Palermo* (1883) 9 PD 6 and *Watson v Cammell Laird & Co* [1959] 1 WLR 702, CA).

The Court of Appeal in the *Sumitomo Corporation* case held (at [44]):

> Neither the process of copying nor the process of translation involves the addition of anything or the subtraction of anything from the sense of the original document or the information contained in it. In particular, neither process in itself introduces any element of confidentiality which does not or did not exist in the original document. The fact that, unlike a copy, a translation is not a 'replica' of the original document . . . does not seem to us to be a relevant distinction for present purposes.

(ii) Selection from own client's unprivileged documents does not produce privilege on basis of revealing trend of legal advice

The claimants next contended that the translations were privileged on the basis of *Lyell v Kennedy (No 3)* (1884) 27 Ch D 1, CA. This 1884 case was summarized by Bingham LJ in *Ventouris v Mountain* [1991] 3 All ER 472, 479F as establishing that privilege can arise in (a) the selection or compilation of documents, (b) even from unprivileged sources, if (c) the exercise is carried out by a lawyer for his client predominantly in connection with litigation, or perhaps simply as part of the process of giving legal advice. The Court of Appeal in the *Sumitomo Corporation* case then decided (at [72]):

> *Lyell v Kennedy* is undoubtedly authority for the proposition that where a solicitor has copied or assembled a selection of third party documents the selection will be privileged if its production would 'betray the trend of the advice which he is giving the client' (see *Ventouris v Mountain* at 479 F *per* Bingham LJ); *but in our judgment it is not authority for the proposition that a selection made from own client documents may similarly attract privilege.*

(iii) In absence of privilege, court has discretion not to order disclosure of documents

The Court of Appeal, without giving further guidance, held that the courts have a discretion whether to order production of material controlled by a party and that this discretion extends to the case where an unprivileged selection of documents has been made by a lawyer from his client's material. It cited (at [79]) Bingham LJ's comment in *Ventouris v Mountain* [1991] 3 All ER 472 at 485:

> . . . [Counsel for the defendant in the *Ventouris* case] appeared to assume that there was no choice between a finding of legal professional privilege and an order for immediate disclosure and inspection. In my judgment, that is not so. The process of discovery is not an uncontrollable juggernaut. In *Science Research Council v Nasse* [1980] AC 1028, HL and *Dolling-Baker v Merrett* [1991] 1 WLR 1205, CA, the

court made plain that production and inspection are not automatic once relevance and the absence of entitlement to privilege are established. While the court's ultimate concern must always be to ensure the fair disposal of the cause or matter, it need not be unmindful of other legitimate concerns nor is it powerless to control the terms upon which production and inspection may be ordered.

(h) Statutory exceptions

19.281 **n490**: Add new text:

The courts will declare void secondary legislation which purports to suppress legal advice privilege unless it is plain that the relevant parent statute explicitly authorizes, or necessarily requires, such abrogation (*General Mediterranean Holdings SA v Patel* [1999] 3 All ER 673, declaring CPR 48.7(3) to be ultra vires; noted NH Andrews [2000] CLJ 47–50).

In *R (Morgan Grenfell Ltd) v Special Commissioner of Tax* [2002] 2 WLR 1299, HL (considering Taxes Management Act 1970, s 20 as substituted by Finance Act 1976 and amended by Finance Act 2000) the House of Lords held that the Taxes Management Act 1970 (as amended) did not expressly qualify or abrogate legal advice privilege, which is a fundamental right, and that the Revenue lacked power, therefore, to issue notices to taxpayers requiring them to disclose privileged discussion with lawyers relating to their business affairs. Similarly, see the Privy Council's decision in *B v Auckland District Law Society* [2003] 3 WLR 859, PC; [2003] UKPC 38.

(i) Nefarious purposes

19.282 Section 328 of the Proceeds of Crime Act 2002 has been held in *P v P (Ancillary Relief: Proceeds of Crime)* [2003] 3 WLR 1350, Butler-Sloss P, to require a lawyer to disclose to the National Criminal Intelligence Service details of a known or suspected acquisition or retention (etc) of criminal property; this includes untaxed income or other untaxed assets; but the lawyer can tell the client that such a staurtory disclosure has occurred.

(k) Waiver of privilege

n499: note that a new edition of C Hollander, *Documentary Evidence* (8th edn) is imminent, but was not available at the time this Supplement went to press). See also P Matthews and HM Malek, *Disclosure* (2nd edn, 2000), ch 10. The Court of Appeal in *Al Fayed (Mohamed) v Commissioner of Police for the Metropolis* (CA, 29 May, 2002), [16], has summarized the principles governing equitable relief against inadvertent disclosure of privileged material. This decision is examined fully in Neil Andrews, *English Civil Procedure* (2003), at para 28.24ff.

I. Trial

(3) Hearsay Evidence in Civil Proceedings

n508: for comment see SE Salako, 'The Hearsay Rule and the Civil Evidence Act 1995: Where are we now?' (2000) 19 CJQ 371. **19.293**

Relaxation of the hearsay rule in civil proceedings (as described in the preceding paragraphs in the Main Work) is part of a more general trend to allow 'free evaluation' of evidence, unfettered by technical and anachronistic rules which enjoyed their heyday in the era of jury trial in civil matters. As the Law Commission noted:

> . . . recent development in the law and practice of civil litigation point to a new approach, where the main emphasis is upon ensuring that, so far as possible and subject to considerations of reliability and weight, all relevant evidence is capable of being adduced.

(The Hearsay Rule in Civil Proceedings (Law Com No 216, 1993, Cm 2321), para 1.5.)

It is consistent with this trend that the 'best evidence' rule, namely the requirement that a party should adduce an original of a document on which he intends to rely, has been declared no longer applicable in civil cases.

This rule's demise was adumbrated in earlier cases; for example, in *Ventouris v Mountain (No 2)* [1992] 1 WLR 887, Balcombe LJ said (at 899): 'The modern tendency in civil proceedings is to admit all relevant evidence, and the judge should be trusted to give only proper weight to evidence which is not the best evidence.'

The best evidence rule has been declared inapplicable in civil matters by the Court of Appeal in *Springsteen v Masquerade Music Ltd* [2001] Entertainment & Media LR 654, CA.The action concerned infringement of copyright in musical recordings. The claimant's title to the copyright had to be traced through various hands. One link in this chain of title was disputed. The Court of Appeal upheld the trial judge's decision to admit secondary evidence of assignments of copyright. After a copious review of the best evidence rule, Jonathan Parker LJ, giving the court's judgment, said (at [85]):

> . . . the time has now come when it can be said with confidence that the best evidence rule, long on its deathbed, has finally expired. In every case where a party seeks to adduce secondary evidence of the contents of a document, it is a matter for the court to decide, in the light of all the circumstances of the case, what (if any) weight to attach to that evidence.

He continued:

> Where the party seeking to adduce the secondary evidence could readily produce the document, it may be expected that (absent some special circumstances) the court will decline to admit the secondary evidence on the ground that it is worthless. At the other extreme, where the party seeking to adduce the secondary evidence genuinely cannot produce the document, it may be expected that (absent some special circumstances) the court will admit the secondary evidence and attach such weight to it as it considers appropriate . . .

He concluded:

> In cases falling between these two extremes, it is for the court to make a judgment as to whether in all the circumstances any weight should be attached to the secondary evidence. Thus, the 'admissibility' of secondary evidence of the contents of documents is . . . entirely dependent upon whether or not any weight is to be attached to that evidence. And whether or not any weight is to be attached to such evidence is a matter for the court to decide . . .

(a) Standard of proof

19.296A The Court of Appeal in *Springsteen v Masquerade Music Ltd* [2001] Entertainment & Media LR 654, CA, at [89], followed Lord Nicholls's seminal comments in *Re H (Minors) (Sexual Abuse: Standard of Proof)* [1996] AC 563, 586, HL:

> The balance of probability standard means that a court is satisfied an event occurred if the court considers that, on the evidence, the occurrence of the event was more likely than not. When assessing the probabilities the court will have in mind as a factor, to whatever extent is appropriate in the particular case, that the more serious the allegation the less likely it is that the event occurred and, hence, the stronger should be the evidence before the court concludes that the allegation is established on the balance of probabilities.

Lord Nicholls continued:

> Fraud is usually less likely than negligence. Deliberate physical injury is usually less likely than accidental physical injury . . . Built into the preponderance of probability standard is a generous degree of flexibility in respect of the seriousness of the allegation.

Lord Hoffmann in *Secretary of State for the Home Department v Rehman* [2003] 1 AC 153, HL (also citing Lord Nicholls in *Re H* (above)), said (at [55]):

> It would need more cogent evidence to satisfy one that the creature seen walking in Regent's Park was more likely than not to have been a lioness than to be satisfied to the same standard of probability that it was an Alsatian. On this basis, cogent evidence is generally required to satisfy a civil tribunal that a person has been fraudulent or behaved in some other reprehensible manner. But the question is always whether the tribunal thinks it more probable than not.

The different standards of proof in criminal and civil litigation are discussed in *Cross and Tapper on Evidence* (9th edn, 1999) 140–3.

(4) Other Features of Trial

(c) Recording of proceedings

The first sentence of the Main Work para 19.299 should read: **19.299**

An oral judgment, and generally oral evidence, will be recorded by the court at any hearing in the High Court or county court.

(5) Court Management at Trial

n534: *GKR Karate (UK) Ltd v Yorkshire Post Ltd* is also reported at [2000] 1 WLR 2571, CA. In *GKR Karate (UK) Ltd v Yorkshire Post Ltd* [2000] 1 WLR 2571, the Court of Appeal upheld the first instance judge's decision to consider the defence of qualified privilege as a preliminary question in a libel action, with postponement of the factually broader defence of justification. In reaching this decision the trial judge noted that the trial would be likely to take four to six weeks, but the question of qualified privilege, which might be decisive, would take only three days. On appeal from this procedural decision May LJ, noting CPR 32.1 (court's power to control the evidence), said (at 2577): **19.306**

> . . . the parties no longer have any absolute right to insist on the calling of any evidence they choose provided only that it is admissible and arguably relevant. The court may exclude admissible and relevant evidence or cross-examination which is disproportionately expensive or time-consuming, provided that to do so accords with the overriding objective.

(6) Witnesses

(a) Witnesses of fact

n545: a witness's direct testimony cannot be used by party X when it is contradictory of X's case or defence on the basis that X will straight away invite the court to disregard that testimony as untrue: *McPhilemy v Times Newspapers Ltd (No 2)* [2000] 1 WLR 1732, 1736–40, CA. **19.311**

Lords Hope, Clyde and, especially, Hutton in *Darker v Chief Constable of the West Midlands Police* [2001] 1 AC 435 surveyed this doctrine's expansion; another important discussion is found in *L (A Child) v Reading BC* [2001] 1 WLR 1575, 1590–4, CA.

In *Darker v Chief Constable of the West Midlands Police* the House of Lords distinguished the false presentation of evidence in court, whether deliberately or not (if deliberate the crime of perjury arises), and out-of-court steps taken to produce false evidence, such as fabrication of evidence and conduct aimed at setting up an accused. The latter is conduct aimed at distorting the system of justice, criminal or civil, and does not attract witness immunity.

Similarly, in *L (A Child) v Reading BC* [2001] 1 WLR 1575, 1593 Otton LJ refused to apply witness immunity to protect police officers against an allegation (presented under the causes of action of negligence, conspiracy and misfeasance in public office) that they had pressurized a child into making a false allegation of sexual abuse, that they had passed on false evidence, and that their conduct was such as to frustrate and pervert justice rather than to promote it.

More generally, Lord Hope in *Arthur JS Hall & Co v Simons* [2002] 1 AC 615, HL said that in the light of Article 6(1) of the European Convention on Human Rights and the Human Rights Act 1998, Sch 1, *any immunity* from civil suit can be justified nowadays only if designed to pursue a legitimate aim and proportionate to the achievement of that aim. His Lordship was speaking in the immediate context of the former 'advocates' immunity' from civil liability for court-room negligence (this immunity was abolished in the *Hall & Co* case).

(b) Expert witnesses

19.312 n547: here there have been extensive developments (see also Supplement n550 below).

New literature: P Matthews and H Malek, *Disclosure* (2nd edn, 2000) paras 15.25ff; J Day and Louise Le Cat, *Expert Evidence under the CPR* (2001); for comparative observations see JA Jolowicz, *On Civil Procedure* (2000) ch 12 ('The Expert, the Witness and the Judge in Civil Litigation: French and English Law'). See also the *Code of Guidance on Expert Evidence: A Guide for Experts and Those Instructing Them for the Purpose of Court Proceedings* (December, 2001) (drafted by a working group chaired by Sir Louis Blom-Cooper QC).

n 550: *Daniels v Walker* is now reported at [2000] 1 WLR 1382, CA.

(i) Single joint experts

In *Daniels v Walker* [2000] 1 WLR 1382 the Court of Appeal reviewed the power contained in the CPR (1998) to appoint a single joint expert. Lord Woolf MR said:

> (1) . . . in a case where there is a modest amount involved, it would be disproportionate to obtain a second report in any circumstances. At most what should be allowed is merely to put a question to the expert who has already prepared a report.
> (2) In a substantial case . . . the correct approach is to regard the instruction of an expert jointly by the parties as *the first step* in obtaining expert evidence . . . If, having obtained a joint expert's report, a party, for reasons which are not fanciful, wishes to obtain further information before making a decision . . . they should, subject to the discretion of the court, be permitted to obtain that evidence.
> (3) It is only as a last resort that you accept that it is necessary for *oral evidence* to be given by the experts before the court. The expense of cross-examination of expert witnesses at the hearing, even in a substantial case, can be very expensive.

In a later decision, *Peet v Mid-Kent Healthcare Trust* [2002] 1 WLR 210, CA, at [28], Lord Woolf CJ changed the emphasis and affirmed the primacy of single joint experts. He said: 'The starting point is: unless there is reason for not having a single expert, there should be only a single expert.'

Lord Woolf admitted that there might be circumstances in the individual case which justify 'more evidence than that from a single expert on a particular topic'. The court has a discretion to allow a party-appointed expert to be used to amplify the evidence, and a discretion to allow this expert to be called at trial. He also said that 'in the normal way . . . there should be no need for that report to be amplified or tested by cross-examination'. But the court has a discretion to allow this.

His Lordship emphasized that discretion in the context of single joint experts is governed by the 'Overriding Objective' in CPR Part 1. This discretion applies to the following issues: whether to use such an expert; whether to allow further clarification of his report by written answers beyond the 'once only' scope of CPR 35.6(2); whether to supplement his report by appointing party-nominated experts; whether to allow the latter expert to give evidence at trial; and whether to allow a single joint expert to appear at and be cross-examined at trial. This discretion is emphasised at [14] of the *Peet* case.

(ii) Pre-action protocol and selection of experts

In *Carlson v Townsend* [2001] 3 All ER 663, CA, the claimant sued in respect of a back injury. In accordance with paras 3.14 and 3.16 of the 'Pre-Action Protocol for Personal Injury Claims' (PPPIC), the claimant gave the defendant a list of three experts, X, Y, Z, and the defendant objected to Z only. The claimant then obtained a report from X, but the defendant contended that this had become a single joint expert's report.

The court held that it was not a single joint expert's report. Although para 3.16 of the PPPIC refers to a 'mutually acceptable expert', this does not render the expert appointed by one party a jointly instructed expert ([18], [19], [22] *per* Simon Brown LJ, [36] *per* Brooke LJ). Accordingly, the claimant retained legal professional privilege ('litigation privilege') in the report, which had not been waived in advance on the facts of the case ([19] *per* Simon Brown LJ).

(iii) Meetings between rival parties' experts

The court has power to order a meeting between rival parties' experts: CPR 35.12. The Court of Appeal in *Hubbard v Lambeth, Southwark and Lewisham AHA* The Times, 8 October 2001, has tried to assuage litigants unhappy with the prospect of experts, under pressure from fellow experts in a relevant profession, and without legal representation at such a meeting (as the court put it) 'selling a party down the river'. The court said that such a meeting is not contrary to the guarantee in

Article 6(1) of the European Convention on Human Rights of a fair trial and process. In the case itself, the sting was taken out of this challenge when the defendants undertook to tape the experts' meeting. The court noted that any misunderstanding or impropriety would appear on the recording of the meeting.

See also the *Stanton* case immediately below.

(iv) Experts' immunity from negligence liability to client

(See also discussion of witness immunity in Supplement para 19.311 n45.)

In *Stanton v Callaghan* [2000] 1 QB 75, CA it was held that an expert is immune from liability in negligence when agreeing to a joint expert's statement in terms which the client contends were culpable and caused harm to his interests. The Court of Appeal was unanimous that it was in the public interest that rival parties' experts participating in discussions for a joint statement in a civil action should feel free to resile from their earlier positions. The decision ante-dates the CPR but is *a fortiori* justified when considered in the light of the 'Overriding Objective' in CPR Part 1. Party-appointed experts must feel free to adopt a co-operative attitude when discussing rival theories. Nothing could be more inimical to this than the prospect of a contract or tort claim by a disgruntled client. Chadwick LJ summarized the law as follows:

> (i) an expert witness who gives evidence at a trial is immune from suit in respect of anything which he says in court, and that immunity will extend to the contents of the report which he adopts as, or incorporates in, his evidence;
> (ii) where an expert witness gives evidence at a trial the immunity which he would enjoy in respect of that evidence is not to be circumvented by a suit based on the report itself;
> (iii) the immunity does not extend to protect an expert who has been retained to advise as to the merits of a party's claim in litigation from a suit by the party by whom he has been retained in respect of that advice, notwithstanding that it was in contemplation at the time when the advice was given that the expert would be a witness at the trial if that litigation were to proceed. (Considering also *Palmer v Durnford Ford* [1992] QB 483 Simon Tuckey J and Holland J in *Landall v Dennis Faulkner & Alsop* [1994] 5 Med LR 268.)

In *Arthur JS Hall & Co v Simons* [2002] 1 AC 615, HL, Lord Hoffmann said that the *Stanton* decision fell squarely within traditional witness immunity. The alleged cause of action was a statement of the evidence which the expert wished to give to the court. The witness's only duty in that context is to tell the truth.

In *Raiss v Palmano* [2001] PNLR 540, in the first action, R's counterclaim against X was withdrawn when R's expert, P, was discredited in the witness box by X's counsel. It turned out that P had falsely said that he was a member of a particular expert panel and had negligently misled R into supposing that P was expert in the special field (valuation of properties in the Covent Garden area, London). In the second action, R sued P for breach of contract and in tort for the loss of the counterclaim. It was held that P had a defence based upon expert witness immunity and that the claim should be struck out.

Eady J held that witness immunity applied to P's statements to R, although preparatory to production of an expert's opinion to be tendered as evidence (citing the test in *Palmer v Durnford Ford* [1992] 2 QB 683) and—assuming this for the purpose only of decision—even if dishonest (citing the observations in *Darker v Chief Constable of West Midlands Police* [2001] 1 AC 435, HL). The decision, with respect, appears unconvincing. It is submitted that misleading statements made by a potential expert which lead the client to hire that expert, or stick with him, should not be subject to witness immunity. The integrity of the expert witness system requires the law to provide a client with a cause of action against fraudulent and, at least in plain and obvious cases, other culpable misstatements which lead the client to hire or to decline to sack an expert.

(v) Expert: lack of perceived objectivity or independence

In *Liverpool RC Archdiocese Trustees Inc v Goldberg (No 3) (Practice Note)* [2001] 1 WLR 2357 the defendant, a barrister in a professional negligence case, wished to use as an expert a friend, who was also a barrister in his chambers. The trial judge held that the party and expert's close relationship would lead a reasonable observer to think that this expert's views might be coloured by this tie of friendship and working proximity. The expert's opinion was not, therefore, sufficiently objective. However, in *Admiral Management Services Ltd v Para-Protect Europe Ltd* [2002] 1 WLR 2722 at [33] Stanley Burnton J considered that the *Liverpool RC* decision could not be easily reconciled with the Court of Appeal's decision to allow an employee to give expert evidence on behalf of an employer in *Field v Leeds CC* [2000] 1 EGLR 54 CA (this CA decision had been cited to Evans-Lombe J in the *Liverpool RC* case but he did not discuss it in his judgment).

(7) Sequence of Trial

n557: *Prudential Assurance Co v McBains Cooper* is now reported at [2000] 1 WLR 2000, CA and is considered in *Liverpool RC Archdiocese Trustees Inc v Goldberg (No 3) (Practice Note)* [2001] 1 WLR 2357, at [2]–[5]. **19.315**

(i) Judgment: power to amend pleaded case before judgment completed

The court has a discretion to reopen a case and allow amendment of pleadings before perfecting a judgment: *Stewart v Engel* [2000] 1 WLR 2268, CA. In the case itself the Court of Appeal, reversing the judge's exercise of this discretion, held that the facts revealed no satisfactory reason for allowing amendment at this very late stage.

(ii) Judgment: court's delay in giving judgment

This topic is reviewed in *Cobham v Frett* [2001] 1 WLR 1775, PC.

(iii) Judgment: duty to give reasons

This duty was extensively considered by the Court of Appeal in *English v Emery Reimbold & Strick Ltd* [2002] 1 WLR 2409, CA. Earlier, in *North Range Shipping Ltd v Seatrans Shipping Corporation* [2002] 1 WLR 2397, CA, it was held that the Commercial Court should give reasons if it refuses to grant permission, under Arbitration Act 1996, s 69, for an arbitration award to be taken on appeal to the High Court. In both decisions, Article 6(1) of the European Convention on Human Rights was held to require such reasons, which can be brief. This discussion is consistent with the recognition of a general judicial duty to give reasoned decisions at common law in *Flannery v Halifax Estate Agencies Ltd* [2000] 1 WLR 377, CA. Generally on this topic see Neil Andrews, *English Civil Procedure* (2003) paras 5.39–5.68.

J. Costs

(3) Other Features

(c) **Machinery**

19.327 **n577**: reference should now be to PD (44) 13.2(2): 'any other hearing which has lasted not more than one day'.

(4) Conditional Fee Agreements

19.329 **n582**: *Awwad v Geraghty & Co* is now reported at [2001] QB 570, CA, and was noted by A Walters (2000) 116 LQR 371–7.

Generally on this dynamic and technical field, see Neil Andrews, *English Civil Procedure* (2003) ch 35, and *Cook on Costs 2004*; see also Andrews, ibid, ch 35 n5 for a large bibliography; notable discussion includes: A Cannon, 'Designing Cost Policies to Provide Sufficient Access to Lower Courts' (2002) 21 CJQ 198, at 226-30; M Zander, 'Where are We Heading with the Funding of Civil Litigation?' (2003) 22 CJQ 23–40; also by M Zander, 'Will the Revolution in the Funding of Civil Litigation in England Eventually Lead to Contingency Fees?' (2003) 52 DePaul LR 259 (for the website address of the De Paul LR article, see (2003) 22 CJQ 23, 25 n5); 'The Ethics of Conditional Fee Arrangements' (Society for Advanced Legal Studies, 2001); and for discussion of this topic from the perspective of US law, Thomas D Rowe, 'Shift Happens: Pressure on Foreign Attorney-Fee Paradigms from Class Actions' (2003) 13 Duke J Comp & Int'l L 125.

(i) Challenges to the level of the success fee

The fact that the success fee can be recovered from the defeated opponent has caused defendants' insurers to challenge the level of these uplifts. The House of Lords in *Callery v Gray (Nos 1 and 2)* [2002] 1 WLR 2000, HL (upholding *Callery v Gray* [2001] 1 WLR 2112, [103], CA, *per* Lord Woolf CJ) held that 20% of normal fees is an appropriate uplift in modest and straightforward traffic accident cases. But the Court of Appeal in *Halloran v Delaney* [2003] 1 WLR 28, decided that 5% of normal fees is the appropriate uplift in a straightforward and simple traffic case which settles without commencement of formal proceedings. The *Halloran* case's guideline was declared to take effect from the date of the *Callery* litigation.

(ii) Recovery of the 'after-the-event' insurance premium

Section 29 of the Access to Justice Act 1999 (effective 1 April 2000) allows a successful party to recover from the opponent any insurance premium which he has paid to protect himself against the risk of paying his opponent's costs in the event of defeat in the relevant litigation. This topic is discussed in these cases: *Callery v Gray (Nos 1 and 2)* [2002] 1 WLR 2000, HL (considering *Callery v Gray (No 2)* [2001] 1 WLR 2142, CA, concerning the nature and reasonableness of insurance cover taken out by, or on behalf of, a claimant in respect of conditional fee litigation); *Sarwar* v *Alam* [2002] 1 WLR 125, CA (relationship between 'before-the-event' and 'after-the-event' legal expenses insurance cover); and *Hollins v Russell* [2003] 1 WLR 2487, CA; [2003] EWCA Civ 718 and *Re Claims Direct Test Cases* [2003] 4 All ER 508, CA; [2003] EWCA Civ 136.

(iii) The indemnity principle

The so-called indemnity principle of costs renders a losing party liable for the other party's costs only if the latter would be liable under an enforceable obligation to pay those same costs to his lawyer whether he wins or not (see Neil Andrews, *English Civil Procedure* (2003) paras 36.13–36.17). However, this principle has been explicitly disapplied in the context of conditional fee agreements. And so the losing party is liable to pay the victorious party's fee, success fee, and insurance premium, even though the victorious party would not be liable to pay these sums if he had lost the case. CPR 43.2(3) now states:

> Where advocacy or litigation services are provided to a client under a conditional fee agreement, costs are recoverable under Parts 44 to 48 notwithstanding that the client is liable to pay his legal representative's fees and expenses only to the extent that sums are recovered in respect of the litigation, whether by way of costs or otherwise.

(iv) Formalities

Statutory changes on 2 June 2003 loosen slightly the formalities of conditional fee agreements: see the Conditional Fee Agreements (Miscellaneous Amendments) Regulations 2003 (SI 2003/1240), reg 2 (inserting new reg 3A(3)–(6) into the Conditional Fee Agreements Regulations 2000).

First, before concluding the agreement, the 'legal representative' must 'inform the client as to the circumstances in which the client may be liable to pay the legal representative's fees and expenses, and provide such further information, advice or other information as to those circumstances as the client may reasonably require' (ibid, reg 3A(6)).

Now it suffices that a conditional fee agreement 'specifies the particular proceedings or parts of them to which it relates' (new reg 3A(4), the Conditional Fee Agreements Regulations 2000); '[specifies] the circumstances in which the legal representative's fees and expenses, or part of them, are payable' (ibid); and 'if it provides for a success fee' the agreement must 'briefly specify the reasons for setting the percentage increase at the level stated in the agreement' and state that the lawyer is permitted to disclose those reasons if ordered by the court so to do' (ibid).

Before these amendments were made in June 2003, the Court of Appeal in *Hollins v Russell* [2003] 1 WLR 2487, CA; [2003] EWCA Civ 718 (also reported as *Sharratt v London Central Bus Co Ltd; 'The Accident Group Test Cases'* [2003] 4 All ER 590 CA), decided a set of 'test' cases and held that trifling or modest failures to satisfy these formalities should not invalidate the agreement. Brooke LJ, giving the court's judgment at [226], said that 'judges must be . . . astute to prevent satellite litigation about costs from being protracted by allegations about breaches of the CFA regulations where the breaches do not matter'.

(v) Forensic assistance by accountants: contingency fee agreement declared valid

The Court of Appeal in *R (Factortame Ltd) v Secretary of State for the Environment, Transport and the Regions (No 8)* [2002] 3 WLR 1104, CA, [54], [57], [87], [90]–[91], *per* Lord Phillips MR, has upheld a US-style contingency fee arrangement in favour of a firm of accountants. The accountants agreed to assist Spanish trawlermen to calculate their claims for loss caused by the defendant Secretary of State's unlawful refusal to grant them fishing licences. In return, the accountants would be paid 8% of any final settlement moneys 'received' by the claimant trawlermen. The accountant's fee agreement was declared to be consistent with public policy.

(vi) No success fees for experts

In the *R (Factortame Ltd)* case, [2002] 3 WLR 1104, CA, at [73], the Court of Appeal held that:

> . . . the threat to [an expert's] objectivity posed by a contingency fee agreement may carry greater dangers to the administration of justice than would the interest of an advocate or solicitor acting under a similar agreement. Accordingly, we consider that it will be in a very rare case indeed that the court will be prepared to consent to an expert being instructed under [such an agreement].

This is consistent with the recommendation in the 'Code of Guidance on Expert Evidence: A Guide for Experts and those Instructing Them for the Purpose of Court Proceedings' (December, 2001), para 1.9.

(5) Security for Costs

The new rules, CPR 25.12–25.15, took effect on 2 May 2000; for the position in arbitration see the Arbitration Act 1996, s 38(3) and *K/S A/S Bani v Korea Shipbuilding and Engineering Corp* [1987] 2 Lloyd's Rep 445, CA; generally on the provision of security for costs see MJ Cook, *Cook on Costs: 2000* (2000) ch 13. **19.335**

After the first sentence of Main Work para 19.335 the existing text is to be deleted and replaced with the following:

The grant of security for costs is discretionary in all cases. Thus CPR 25.13(1) states: 'The court may make an order for security for costs . . . if (a) it is satisfied, having regard to all the circumstances of the case, that it is just to make such an order.'

CPR 25.13(2) specifies the following seven grounds for the grant of security for costs (it preserves the capacity to grant security under any 'enactment' other than the CPR):

> (a) the claimant is an individual who is ordinarily resident out of the jurisdiction and is not a person against whom a claim can be enforced under the Brussels Conventions or the Lugano Convention (as defined by section 1(1), Civil Jurisdiction and Judgments Act 1982, as amended by section 2(2)(3), Civil Jurisdiction and Judgments Act 1991);
> (b) the claimant is a company or other incorporated body which is ordinarily resident out of the jurisdiction and is not a body against whom a claim can be enforced under the Brussels Conventions or the Lugano Convention;
> (c) the claimant is a company or other body (whether incorporated inside or outside Great Britain) and there is reason to believe that it will be unable to pay the defendant's costs if ordered to so;
> (d) the claimant has changed his address since the claim was commenced with a view to evading the consequence of the litigation;
> (e) the claimant failed to give his address in the claim form, or gave an incorrect address in that form;
> (f) the claimant is acting as a nominal claimant, other than as a representative claimant under [CPR] Part 19, and there is reason to believe that he will be unable to pay the defendant's costs if ordered to do so;
> (g) the claimant has taken steps in relation to his assets that would make it difficult to enforce an order for costs against him.

(i) Claimant resident outside England and outside the territories of the Brussels and Lugano Conventions

The new 'foreign residence' rule was analysed by the Court of Appeal in *Nasser v United Bank of Kuwait* [2002] 1 WLR 1868, CA. Mance LJ noted that the foreign residence ground must be reconciled with the prohibition against discrimination contained in Article 14 of the European Convention on Human Rights, which is now incorporated as part of Sch 1 to the Human Rights Act 1998. Article 14 prohibits discrimination in the enjoyment of Convention rights, including those in Article 6(1), which ensures fairness in matters of civil proceedings. The prohibition in Article 14 against discrimination covers 'any ground such as sex, race, colour, language, religion, political or other opinion, national or social origin, association with a national minority, property, birth or other status'.

Most non-UK residents are likely to be non-UK citizens. Therefore, the foreign residence ground in CPR 25.13 (see above) has the potential to infringe Article 14. It then becomes necessary to consider whether this element of prima facie unlawful discrimination can be justified by regard to what is legitimate and objectively justified (para 56 especially).

Mance LJ concluded that the distinction drawn between residents in member states party to the Brussels and Lugano Conventions and those not so resident can be declared to be reasonable and objectively justifiable because the system of mutual recognition and enforcement under those two Conventions is superior to the general position in other parts of the world.

For this reason the *rule* itself in CPR 25.13(2)(a) and (b) cannot be declared incompatible with Article 14 of the European Convention or Sch 1 to the Human Rights Act 1998 (incorporating Article 14). But the *exercise* of the discretion whether to award security against a person resident in a non-Brussels/Lugano Convention state must be conducted in a way which is not discriminatory.

Mance LJ held that the English court cannot 'start with any inflexible presumption that any person not resident in a Brussels or Lugano state should provide security for costs'. Instead the discretion should be based on 'objectively justified grounds relating to obstacles to or the burden of enforcement in the context of the particular foreign claimant or country concerned'. The English court should consider whether the foreign jurisdiction would present difficulties such as expense, incurring of irrecoverable costs, and delay. The English court 'may and should, however, take notice of obvious realities without formal evidence'.

Mance LJ added that there will be a spectrum of situations, ranging from jurisdictions which are very user-friendly to those in which enforcement of an English costs order is plainly impossible. Security can be adjusted to reflect these differences.

In the present case the claimant was resident in the USA. Although the US courts would recognize and enforce the English security for costs order, Mance LJ was persuaded that this process would be more burdensome and expensive than in a Brussels/Lugano Convention state. He ruled that security for costs of £5,000 should be awarded.

(ii) Limited companies

Security can be ordered against a claimant which 'is a company or other body (whether incorporated inside or outside Great Britain) and there is reason to believe that it will be unable to pay the defendant's costs if ordered to do so' (CPR 25.13(2)(c)). The new rule applies whether the company is resident in England or elsewhere or whether it is incorporated in Great Britain or elsewhere. The gist of the rule is that the defendant should enjoy protection against the risk that the claimant company might default upon an eventual costs order against it. Even so, security is not available as of right in this context. The court has a discretion whether to award it.

(iii) Factors relevant to the discretion to order security for costs

The approach should be flexible and ample scope should be given to the first instance court's band of discretionary decision-making. The courts have enunciated relevant factors which the judge should consider when exercising his discretion to award security for costs:

(1) the action is a sham or is made in good faith;
(2) the claimant has a reasonably good prospect of success in the case;
(3) there is an admission by the defendant in the statement of case or elsewhere that the money is due (or the claim is otherwise sound);
(4) there is a substantial payment into court or offer to settle;
(5) the application is being used by the defendant to stifle an honest and sound claim;
(6) the claimant's lack of funds has been caused by, or aggravated by, the defendant's failure to pay;
(7) the application for security for costs has been made late.

On these factors see *Sir Lindsay Parkinson v Triplan Ltd* [1973] QB 609 at 626–7, CA *per* Lord Denning MR, which is the classic statement, to be read in conjunction with *Keary Developments Ltd v Tarmac Construction Ltd* [1995] 3 All ER 534, 539–42, CA, enunciating various guidelines.

In *Olatawura v Abiloye* [2002] 4 All ER 4 All ER 903, CA, the court recognized a power to make an order for a security payment by an individual claimant resident outside the jurisdiction, and having modest financial means; this power subsists independently of the general regime concerning security for costs contained in CPR Part 25, section II.

In *De Beer v Kanaar & Co* [2002] 3 All ER 1020, CA (noted W Kennett [2002] 51 ICLQ 468-70), it was held that CPR 25.13(2)(a) does not preclude the court from ordering security for costs against a claimant who happens to have substantial assets in a Convention state (within the Brussels or Lugano regimes) but who is not ordinarily resident within any such Convention state; on the facts the claimant was ordinarily resident within the USA, but his assets included property situated in Holland and Switzerland; this decision also prevents a claimant from escaping liability to provide security for costs by placing assets temporarily in a Convention state; the court, at [37]–[50], considered at length the important discussion in *Nasser v United Bank of Kuwait* [2002] 1 WLR 1868, CA (on the latter case see above in this section (para 19.335)).

(6) Wasted Costs Orders

19.336 **n591**: these provisions were surveyed in *Medcalf v Weatherill* [2003] 1 AC 120, HL, [2002] UKHL 27, HL and earlier in *Brown v Bennett (No 2)* [2002] 1 WLR 713 where Neuberger J at [187] clarifies numerous points.

19.338 **n594**: *Re Merc Property* is now reported at [1999] 2 BCLC 256, The Times, 19 May 1999.

19.339 **n595**: *Re G (Minors)* is now reported at [2000] Fam 104.

The courts might also need to reconsider this aspect of the *Ridehalgh* case in the light of *Arthur JS Hall & Co v Simons* [2002] 1 AC 615, HL, overturning the advocates' civil immunity for negligence (a long-standing principle affirmed in *Rondel v Worsley* [1969] 1 AC 191, HL and *Saif Ali v Sydney Smith Mitchell & Co* [1980] AC 198, HL).

K. Appeals

n606: reference to *Tanfern Ltd v Cameron-MacDonald* should now be: [2000] 1 WLR 1311, 1314–21, CA.

(1) Controls

(a) The need for permission

19.349 It is now necessary in nearly all situations to obtain permission to appeal 'from a decision of a judge in a county court or the High Court', whether the proposed venue of the appeal is the Court of Appeal or a lower court.

For discussion of the system for obtaining transcripts of judgment (or exceptionally evidence) at public expense, and other aspects of the process of obtaining permission to appeal, see *Hyams v Plender* [2001] 2 All ER 179, CA.

n607: in *Colley v Council for Licensed Conveyancers* [2002] 1 WLR 160, CA it was held that the general requirement to obtain permission to appeal does not apply to various statutory rights of appeal, whether appeals are to the county court or High Court

n610: the *Tanfern* case is now reported at [2000] 1 WLR 1311, CA; see here at 1319. **19.351**

n611: the *Tanfern* case is now reported at [2000] 1 WLR 1311, CA; see here at 1320. **19.352**

(c) Matters of evidence

Designers Guild Ltd v Russell Williams (Textiles) Ltd [2001] 1 All ER 700, 707, HL, *per* Lord Hoffmann contains an attractive discussion of reasons why an appellate court should not interfere with a mixed law/fact question. It was held that the Court of Appeal had erred when reopening the question of whether a defendant's copying of a claimant's original design had been 'substantial' and so a breach of copyright. **19.354**

(d) Power to allow appeals

n615: the note should now read: **19.355**

The *Tanfern* case is now reported at [2000] 1 WLR 1311, CA; see here at 1317 on consideration on appeal of discretionary decisions. For examination of the grounds upon which a discretionary decision can be reversed on appeal, see *Adamson v Halifax plc* [2003] 1 WLR 60, CA.

(g) Routes of appeal

n618: the note should now read: **19.358**

See now *Tanfern Ltd v Cameron-MacDonald* [2000] 1 WLR 1311, 1315, CA.

(2) Other Features

(a) Records of all judgments

n620: see now *Tanfern Ltd v Cameron-MacDonald* [2000] 1 WLR 1311, 1317–18, CA. **19.359**

L. Res Judicata and the Principle of Finality

(2) Cause of Action and Issue Estoppels

(c) Issue estoppel

19.368 In *Friend v Civil Aviation Authority* [2001] 4 All ER 385, at [42], CA Chadwick LJ said (issue estoppel was held not to apply on the facts of the case):

> . . . the doctrine of issue estoppel is a useful tool . . . But it is a tool which must be used with caution. It is essential that, before a claimant is prevented from bringing his claim before the court on the ground of issue estoppel, the court must be satisfied after careful examination of all the circumstances that the issue on which he has to succeed in the claim which he seeks to bring is indeed the same issue as that which has been considered and decided in earlier proceedings.

(d) The rule in *Henderson v Henderson*

19.369 **n637**: the leading modern examination of the doctrine is now *Johnson v Gore Wood & Co* [2002] 2 AC 1, HL. Accordingly, the material in this note has now been superseded. In *Friend v Civil Aviation Authority* [2001] 4 All ER 385, esp at [20] and [21], CA (see also Supplement para 19.368) Simon Brown LJ said that 'the recent decision of the House of Lords in *Johnson v Gore Wood & Co* cautions against too ready an application of the *Henderson v Henderson* principle to stifle legitimate claims on abuse of process grounds'. For comment, see G Watt, 'The Danger and Deceit of the Rule in *Henderson v Henderson*: A new approach to successive civil actions arising from the same factual matter' (2000) 19 CJQ 287–314 and KR Handley, 'A Closer Look at *Henderson v Henderson*' (2002) 118 LQR 397, contending that the rule should be regarded not as a separate institution but as an ancillary aspect of cause of action and issue estoppels; also demonstrating that the eponymous case concerned cause of action estoppel; also discussing recent decisions, notably, at 403, 405, *Gairy* v *Attorney-General of Grenada* [2002] 1 AC 167, PC, and *Barakot v Epiette Ltd* [1998] 1 BCLC 283, CA; finally, suggesting that some cases cannot survive the House of Lords decision in *Johnson* v *Gore Wood & Co* [2002] 2 AC 1, HL, namely *Talbot v Berkshire CC* [1994] QB 290, CA and *Sanctuary Association v Baker (No 2)* (1998) 31 HLR 746, CA.

(h) Other qualifications

19.374 The text should now read:

When the court strikes out an action for want of prosecution, this does not produce res judicata. However, the Court of Appeal has now held that it can strike out any new action in the same matter as an abuse of process.

n644: this should now read:

Securum Finance Ltd v Ashton [2001] Ch 291, CA, noted NH Andrews [2001] CLJ 56–8 (action can be struck out for want of prosecution even when the relevant claim has not yet become statute barred; new action could be struck out by the court as an abuse of process); this reflects other robust abuse of process decisions, notably *Grovit v Doctor* [1997] 1 WLR 640, HL and *Arbuthnot Latham Bank Ltd v Trafalgar Holdings Ltd* [1998] 1 WLR 1426, CA, on which see Main Work paras 19.122–19.125, in which the courts declared that they could bar a second action. For the absence of res judicata in the context of striking out for want of prosecution, *James Lazenby & Co v McNicholas Construction Co* [1995] 1 WLR 615, 630; for earlier and related authorities in this connection, see Neil Andrews, *Principles of Civil Procedure* (1994) 13-034 nn 70–1.

(3) *Other Aspects of Finality*

(e) Single cause of action: the rule against successive actions: merger by judgment

In a fatal accident action brought by dependants, the Court of Appeal held that an abortive first claim, in which the writ was issued but not served, did not bar a second action brought within the limitation period: *Cachia v Faluyi* [2001] 1 WLR 1966, at [18]–[20], construing s 2(3) of the Fatal Accidents Act 1976 in the light of the Human Rights Act 1998 and jurisprudence of 'access to court' under Article 6(1) of the European Convention on Human Rights. **19.381**

M. Enforcement

n661: on 25 March 2002 new rules were introduced and appear as Parts 70–73 of the CPR. The matters covered are: general rules about enforcement (new Part 70); orders to obtain information from debtors (known as oral examinations under the earlier rules) (new Part 71); third party debt orders (known as garnishee orders under the earlier rules) (new Part 72), charging orders (stop orders and stop notices) (new Part 73).

The new structure is as follows.

Money judgments are enforceable by any of the following methods:

(1) a writ of fieri facias or warrant of execution (see RSC Ord 46 and 47 and CCR Ord 26);
(2) a third party debt order (see CPR Part 72);
(3) a charging order, stop order or stop notice (see CPR Part 73);
(4) in a county court, an attachment of earnings order (see CCR Ord 27);

(5) appointment of a receiver (see RSC Ord 30 and 51, which apply both in the High Court and county court).

Non-money judgments are enforced by:

(6) an order of committal (see RSC Ord 45, r 5 and CCR Ord 29, r 1); or
(7) a writ of sequestration, in the High Court only (see RSC Ord 45, r 5).

Further change in this field is expected: see the 'White Paper', 'Effective Enforcement' (Cmnd 5744, Lord Chancellor's Department, 2003).

(2) Seizure of Goods

19.384 **n663**: this note should now read:

RSC Ord 46 and 47; CCR Ord 26, in Schs 1, 2, CPR 50 (all these rules unaffected by April 1999 changes); J Kruse, *Dealing with Distraint* (6th edn, 1996); J Kruse, 'Legal Problems in the Process of Impounding of Distrained Goods by Private Bailiffs' (1998) 17 CJQ 41, 'Further Aspects of Impounding Distrained Goods Considered' (1999) 18 CJQ 58, 'The Nature of Legal Custody—the implications and effect of impounded distrained goods in "custodia legis" '(2000) 19 CJQ 267.

(3) Garnishee and Attachment of Earnings Orders

19.390 **n673**: new rules, introduced on 25 March 2002, prescribe 'third party debt orders' (known as garnishee orders under the earlier rules) (new CPR Part 72).

For both general discussion of the jurisdiction to issue garnishee orders (now third party debt orders), and more specifically of the English courts' power to issue such orders in respect of foreign debts, see *Société Eram Shipping Co Ltd v Cie Internationale de Navigation* [2003] 3 WLR 21; [2003] UKHL 30, 12 June 2003, House of Lords and *Kuwait Oil Tanker Co SAK v Qabazard* [2003] 3 WLR 14, [2003] UKHL 31.

(4) Charging Orders

19.396 **n676**: on 25 March 2002 new rules were introduced which govern charging orders, stop orders and stop notices: see new CPR Part 73.

(6) *Injunctions and Orders*

(b) Contempt of court

n695: *Newman v Modern Bookbinders Ltd* is now reported at [2000] 1 WLR 2559, CA. **19.403**

n698: this topic was fully reviewed in *Attorney-General v Punch* [2003] 1 AC 1046, HL; see also *Jockey Club v Buffham* [2003] 2 WLR 178. **19.404**

(ii) Committal for contempt

n707: add to note: **19.409**

In *Harris v Harris* [2002] Fam 253, CA the court discussed a judge's discretion concerning terms of imprisonment for civil contempt. Once part of such a sentence has been served, the court can only release the contemnor or maintain the sentence in full. The court cannot attach strings to the decision to release him, placing the unserved term in suspense. Here the applicant had purged his contempt and it was held that he should be released straight away.

BIBLIOGRAPHY

Chapter 7: Succession

Theobald on Wills (16th edn, 2001): the editors are JG Ross Martin, S Bridge, and M Oldham

Hanbury & Martin, *Modern Equity* (16th edn, 2001)

Hawkins and Ryder is now *Hawkins on the Construction of Wills* (5th edn, 2000)

Parry & Clark, *The Law of Succession* (11th edn, 2002)

Williams, Mortimer, and Sunnocks, *Executors, Administrators and Probate* (18th edn, 2000)

Chapter 11: Carriage of Goods by Sea

The reference to Boyd, SC *et al* (ed), *Scrutton on Charterparties and Bills of Lading* (1996) is to the 20th edn of that year

Add:

Treitel, Sir G and Reynolds, FMB, *Carver on Bills of Lading* (2001)

Chapter 19: Civil Procedure

Hollander, C and Adam, T, *Documentary Evidence* (8th edn, 2003)

See also:

Code of Conduct of the Bar of England and Wales (7th edn, 2000)

Law Society of England and Wales, *The Guide to the Professional Conduct of Solicitors* (8th edn, 1999)

Neil Andrews, *English Civil Procedure* (2003)

M Andenas, N Andrews, and R Nazzini (eds), *The Future of Transnational Civil Litigation: English Responses to the ALI-UNIDROIT Draft Principles and Rules of Transnational Civil Procedure* (2004)

Cook on Costs (2004)

Stephen Gee, *Commercial Injunctions* (5th edn, 2004) (formerly *Mareva Injunctions and Anton Piller Relief* (4th edn, 1998))

AAS Zuckerman, *Civil Procedure* (2003)

INDEX